STUDY GUIDE

Security Essentials

Dr. Adam Beatty

Publisher
The Goodheart-Willcox Company, Inc.
Tinley Park, IL
www.g-w.com

Introduction

This *Study Guide* is designed to complement and help you review the terminology and concepts presented in *Security Essentials* by Linda K. Lavender. When used correctly, it can also help prepare you to sit for the CompTIA Security+ Certification Exam. The Study Guide is divided into two sections: Chapter Review and CompTIA Security+ Reference.

The first half of this guide functions much like a workbook and provides opportunities to review important terminology and concepts presented in the *Security Essentials* textbook. Each chapter begins with an introduction that outlines the importance of the activities, and each practice set is grouped according to related terms or concepts. These activities consist of completion and matching activities to help you recall and reinforce important terminology.

The second half of this guide does not offer an opportunity to apply concepts, but it does serve as a reference to help you study for the CompTIA Security+ Exam. Each Security+ objective is presented individually with a description of the objective. Following the description is some type of example to help you remember the important points related to the topic. Examples consist of illustrations, tables, lists, and text-based scenarios. Additionally, a list of related concepts is presented to help you make connections between the Security+ objectives. The final element on each objective page is the full language of the objective. It is recommended that you use the CompTIA Reference Guide as a study source or checklist throughout your preparation for the certification exam, as it can help you isolate individual objectives with which you have struggled mastering.

When used as a supplement to the *Security Essentials* textbook, this *Study Guide* will help you successfully complete a course in IT security and increase your chances of passing the CompTIA Security+ Certification Exam.

Contents

Introduction iii

CHAPTER REVIEW

Chapter 1 Introduction to Information Security 1

Chapter 2 Threats, Attacks, and Vulnerabilities 5

Chapter 3 Security Evaluation 17

Chapter 4 Managing User Security 27

Chapter 5 Physical Security 33

Chapter 6 Device Security 39

Chapter 7 Application Development and Security 43

Chapter 8 Mobile Devices and Embedded Systems 51

Chapter 9 Introduction to Cryptography 57

Chapter 10 Public Key Infrastructure 63

Chapter 11 Command-Line Interface Management 69

Chapter 12 Secure Network Design 77

Chapter 13 Secure Network Administration 85

Chapter 14 Wireless Network Security 91

Chapter 15 Cloud Computing 97

Chapter 16 Governance, Risk, and Compliance 103

Chapter 17 Incident Response and Digital Forensics 111

Chapter 18 Business Continuity and Disaster Recovery 115

Chapter 19 Employment and Soft Skills 119

COMPTIA SECURITY+ REFERENCE GUIDE

Instructions for Using the CompTIA Security+ Reference Guide 123

ATV-1.1A Phishing 124

ATV-1.1B Smishing 125

ATV-1.1C Vishing 126

ATV-1.1D Spam 127

ATV-1.1E Spam over Internet Messaging (SPIM) 128

ATV-1.1F Spear Phishing 129

ATV-1.1G Dumpster Diving 130

ATV-1.1H Shoulder Surfing 131

ATV-1.1I Pharming 132

ATV-1.1J Tailgating 133

ATV-1.1K Eliciting information 134

ATV-1.1L Whaling 135

ATV-1.1M Prepending 136

ATV-1.1N Identity Fraud 137

ATV-1.1O Invoice Scams 138

ATV-1.1P Credential Harvesting 139

ATV-1.1Q Reconnaissance 140

ATV-1.1R Hoax 142

ATV-1.1S Impersonation 143

ATV-1.1T Watering Hole Attack 144

ATV-1.1U Typo Squatting 145

ATV-1.1V Influence Campaigns 146

ATV-1.1W Principles (Reasons for Effectiveness) 147

ATV-1.2A Malware 148

ATV-1.2B Password Attacks............. 152

ATV-1.2C Physical Attacks............... 153

ATV-1.2D Adversarial Artificial Intelligence (AI)........................... 154

ATV-1.2E Supply Chain Attacks............155

ATV-1.2F Cloud-Based vs. On-Premises Attacks.................... 156

ATV-1.2G Cryptographic Attacks.......... 157

ATV-1.3A Privilege Escalation............ 158

ATV-1.3B Cross-Site Scripting (XSS).........159

ATV-1.3C Injections..................... 160

ATV-1.3D Pointer/Object Dereference 161

ATV-1.3E Directory Traversal.............. 162

ATV-1.3F Buffer Overflow 163

ATV-1.3G Race Conditions 164

ATV-1.3H Error Handling 165

ATV-1.3I Improper Input Handling 166

ATV-1.3J Replay Attacks................. 167

ATV-1.3K Integer Overflow 168

ATV-1.3L Request Forgeries 169

ATV-1.3M Application Programming Interface (API) Attacks 171

ATV-1.3N Resource Exhaustion 172

ATV-1.3O Memory Leak 173

ATV-1.3P Secure Sockets Layer (SSL) Stripping......................174

ATV-1.3Q Driver Manipulation............175

ATV-1.3R Pass the Hash 176

ATV-1.4A Wireless...................... 177

ATV-1.4B Man in the Middle 178

ATV-1.4C Man in the Browser.............179

ATV-1.4D Layer 2 Attacks................ 180

ATV-1.4E Domain Name System (DNS) 181

ATV-1.4F Distributed Denial of Service (DDoS)............................ 182

ATV-1.4G Malicious Code or Script Execution 183

ATV-1.5A Actors and Threats 186

ATV-1.5B Attributes of Actors............. 187

ATV-1.5C Vectors 188

ATV-1.5D Threat Intelligence Sources 189

ATV-1.5E Research Sources 191

ATV-1.6A Cloud-Based vs. On-Premises Vulnerabilities...........................192

ATV-1.6B Zero-Day.....................193

ATV-1.6C Weak Configurations 194

ATV-1.6D Third-Party Risks.............. 195

ATV-1.6E Improper or Weak Patch Management........................... 196

ATV-1.6F Legacy Platforms 197

ATV-1.6G Impacts 198

ATV-1.7A Threat Hunting................. 199

ATV-1.7B Vulnerability Scans 200

ATV-1.7C Syslog/Security Information Event Management (SIEM)............... 201

ATV-1.7D Security Orchestration, Automation, and Response (SOAR)........ 202

ATV-1.8A Penetration Testing 203

ATV-1.8B Passive and Active Reconnaissance........................ 204

ATV-1.8C Exercise Types................. 205

AD-2.1A Configuration Management 206

AD-2.1B Data Sovereignty 208

AD-2.1C Data Protection................. 209

AD-2.1D Hardware Security Module (HSM) 210

AD-2.1E Geographical Considerations.......211

AD-2.1F Cloud Access Security Broker (CASB) 212

AD-2.1G Response and Recovery Controls. 213

AD-2.1H Secure Sockets Layer (SSL)/ Transport Layer Security (TLS) Inspection. 214

AD-2.1I Hashing 215

AD-2.1J API Considerations 216

AD-2.1K Site Resiliency. 217

AD-2.1L Deception and Disruption. 218

AD-2.2A Cloud Models .219

AD-2.2B Cloud Service Providers 220

AD-2.2C Managed Service Provider (MSP)/ Managed Security Service Provider (MSSP). 221

AD-2.2D On-Premises vs. Off-Premises 222

AD-2.2E Fog Computing. 223

AD-2.2F Edge Computing. 224

AD-2.2G Thin Client. 225

AD-2.2H Containers 226

AD-2.2I Micro-Services/API 227

AD-2.2J Infrastructure as Code. 228

AD-2.2K Serverless Architecture 229

AD-2.2L Services Integration 230

AD-2.2M Resource Policies 231

AD-2.2N Transit Gateway. 232

AD-2.2O Virtualization. 233

AD-2.3A Environment. 234

AD-2.3B Provisioning and Deprovisioning . . 235

AD-2.3C Integrity Measurement 236

AD-2.3D Secure Coding Techniques 237

AD-2.3E Open Web Application Security Project (OWASP) 238

AD-2.3F Software Diversity. 239

AD-2.3G Automation/Scripting 240

AD-2.3H Elasticity 241

AD-2.3I Scalability 242

AD-2.3J Version Control 243

AD-2.4A Authentication Methods 244

AD-2.4B Biometrics. 245

AD-2.4C Multifactor Authentication (MFA) Factors and Attributes. 246

AD-2.4D Authentication, Authorization, and Accounting (AAA) 247

AD-2.4E Cloud vs. On-Premises Requirements 248

AD-2.5A Redundancy .249

AD-2.5B Replication 250

AD-2.5C On-Premises vs. Cloud 251

AD-2.5D Backup Types 252

AD-2.5E Non-Persistence 253

AD-2.5F High Availability. 254

AD-2.5G Restoration Order 255

AD-2.5H Diversity 256

AD-2.6A Embedded Systems. 257

AD-2.6B Supervisory Control and Data Acquisition (SCADA)/Industrial Control System (ICS). 258

AD-2.6C Internet of Things (IoT) 259

AD-2.6D Specialized 260

AD-2.6E Voice over IP (VoIP) 261

AD-2.6F Heating, Ventilation, Air-Conditioning (HVAC) 262

AD-2.6G Drones/AVs 263

AD-2.6H Multifunction Printer (MFP) 264

AD-2.6I Real-Time Operating System (RTOS) 265

AD-2.6J Surveillance Systems. 266

AD-2.6K System on a Chip (SoC) 267

AD-2.6L Communication
Considerations 268

AD-2.6M Constraints. 269

AD-2.7A Bollards/Barricades. 270

AD-2.7B Mantraps 271

AD-2.7C Badges 272

AD-2.7D Alarms 273

AD-2.7E Signage. 274

AD-2.7F Cameras 275

AD-2.7G Closed-Circuit Television (CCTV) 276

AD-2.7H Industrial Camouflage. 277

AD-2.7I Personnel 278

AD-2.7J Locks 279

AD-2.7K USB Data Blocker 280

AD-2.7L Lighting 281

AD-2.7M Fencing. 282

AD-2.7N Fire Suppression 283

AD-2.7O Sensors 284

AD-2.7P Drones/UAV 285

AD-2.7Q Visitor Logs. 286

AD-2.7R Faraday Cages. 287

AD-2.7S Air Gap 288

AD-2.7T Demilitarized Zone (DMZ) 289

AD-2.7U Protected Cable Distribution 290

AD-2.7V Secure Areas. 291

AD-2.7W Secure Data Destruction. 292

AD-2.8A Digital Signatures 293

AD-2.8B Key Length 294

AD-2.8C Key Stretching 295

AD-2.8D Salting. 296

AD-2.8E Hashing 297

AD-2.8F Key Exchange 298

AD-2.8G Elliptical-Curve Cryptography
(ECC). 299

AD-2.8H Perfect Forward Secrecy (PFS) 300

AD-2.8I Quantum. 301

AD-2.8J Post-Quantum. 302

AD-2.8K Ephemeral. 303

AD-2.8L Modes of Operation 304

AD-2.8M Blockchain 305

AD-2.8N Cipher Suites 306

AD-2.8O Symmetric vs. Asymmetric. 307

AD-2.9P Lightweight Cryptography 308

AD-2.8Q Steganography 309

AD-2.8R Homomorphic Encryption 310

AD-2.8S Common Use Cases 311

AD-2.8T Limitations .312

IMP-3.1A Protocols .313

IMP-3.1B Use Cases .314

IMP-3.2A Endpoint Protection 315

IMP-3.2B Boot Integrity. 316

IMP-3.2C Database .317

IMP-3.2D Application Security. 318

IMP-3.2E Hardening 320

IMP-3.2F Self-Encrypting Drive (SED)/Full
Disk Encryption (FDE). 321

IMP-3.2G Hardware Root of Trust 322

IMP-3.2H Trusted Platform Module
(TPM). 323

IMP-3.2I Sandboxing. 324

IMP-3.3A Load Balancing 325

IMP-3.3B Network Segmentation 326

IMP-3.3C Virtual Private Network (VPN) 329

IMP-3.3D DNS. 330

IMP-3.3E Network Access Control (NAC).....331

IMP-3.3F Out-of-Band Management....... 332

IMP-3.3G Port Security................... 333

IMP-3.3H Network Appliances 334

IMP-3.3I Access Control List (ACL)......... 336

IMP-3.3J Route Security................. 337

IMP-3.3K Quality of Service (QoS) 338

IMP-3.3L Implications of IPv6............. 339

IMP-3.3M Port Spanning/Port Mirroring 340

IMP-3.3N Monitoring Services 341

IMP-3.3O File Integrity Monitors.......... 342

IMP-3.4A Cryptographic Protocols 343

IMP-3.4B Authentication Protocols........ 344

IMP-3.4C Methods...................... 345

IMP-3.4D Installation Considerations...... 346

IMP-3.5A Connection Methods and Receivers 348

IMP-3.5B Mobile Device Management (MDM) 350

IMP-3.5C Mobile Devices 352

IMP-3.5D Enforcement and Monitoring.... 353

IMP-3.5E Deployment Models 355

IMP-3.6A Cloud Security Controls 356

IMP-3.6B Solutions 358

IMP-3.6C Cloud Native Controls vs. Third-Party Solutions 359

IMP-3.7A Identity 360

IMP-3.7B Account Types................. 361

IMP-3.7C Account Policies 362

IMP-3.8A Authentication Management.... 363

IMP-3.8B Authentication................ 364

IMP-3.8C Access Control Schemes 366

IMP-3.9A Public Key Infrastructure (PKI).... 367

IMP-3.9B Types of Certificates 369

IMP-3.9C Certificate Formats 370

IMP-3.9D Concepts 371

OIR-4.1A Network Reconnaissance and Discovery 372

OIR-4.1B File Manipulation 378

OIR-4.1C Shell and Script Environments 379

OIR-4.1D Packet Capture and Replay 381

OIR-4.1E Forensics...................... 383

OIR-4.1F Exploitation Frameworks 384

OIR-4.1G Password Crackers 385

OIR-4.1H Data Sanitization 386

OIR-4.2A Incident Response Plans 387

OIR-4.2B Incident Response Process....... 388

OIR-4.2C Exercises...................... 389

OIR-4.2D Attack Frameworks............. 390

OIR-4.2E Stakeholder Management....... 392

OIR-4.2F Communication Plan............ 393

OIR-4.2G Disaster Recovery Plan.......... 394

OIR-4.2H Business Continuity Plan........ 395

OIR-4.2I Continuity of Operation Planning (COOP) 396

OIR-4.2J Incident Response Team 397

OIR-4.2K Retention Policies 398

OIR-4.3A Vulnerability Scan Output....... 399

OIR-4.3B SIEM Dashboards 400

OIR-4.3C Log Files...................... 401

OIR-4.3D syslog/rsyslog/syslog-ng........ 402

OIR-4.3E journalctl 404

OIR-4.3F nxlog......................... 405

OIR-4.3G Retention 406

OIR-4.3H Bandwidth Monitors 407

OIR-4.3I Metadata...................... 408

OIR-4.3J Netflow/sflow 410

OIR-4.3K Protocol Analyzer Output........411

OIR-4.4A Reconfigure Endpoint Security Solutions...............................412

OIR-4.4B Configuration Changes..........413

OIR-4.4C Isolation.....................414

OIR-4.4D Containment 415

OIR-4.4E Segmentation..................416

OIR-4.4F Secure Orchestration, Automation, and Response (SOAR).........417

OIR-4.5A Documentation/Evidence 418

OIR-4.5B Acquisition....................419

OIR-4.5C On-Premises vs. Cloud 420

OIR-4.5D Integrity 421

OIR-4.5E Preservation 422

OIR-4.5F E-Discovery 423

OIR-4.5G Data Recovery 424

OIR-4.5H Nonrepudiation............... 425

OIR-4.5I Strategic Intelligence/ Counterintelligence...................... 426

GRC-5.1A Category 427

GRC-5.1B Control Type 428

GRC-5.2A Regulations, Standards, and Legislation............................. 429

GRC-5.2B Key Frameworks 430

GRC-5.2C Benchmarks/Secure Configuration Guides.................... 431

GRC-5.3A Personnel 432

GRC-5.3B Diversity of Training Techniques............................. 434

GRC-5.3C Third-Party Risk Management 435

GRC-5.3D Data........................ 436

GRC-5.3E Credential Policies 437

GRC-5.3F Organizational Policies 438

GRC-5.4A Risk Types.................... 439

GRC-5.4B Risk Management Strategies 440

GRC-5.4C Risk Analysis................. 441

GRC-5.4D Disasters..................... 443

GRC-5.4E Business Impact Analysis 444

GRC-5.5A Organizational Consequences of Privacy Breaches 445

GRC-5.5B Notifications of Breaches 446

GRC-5.5C Data Types 447

GRC-5.5D Privacy Enhancing Techniques............................. 448

GRC-5.5E Roles and Responsibilities 449

GRC-5.5F Information Life Cycle 450

GRC-5.5G Impact Assessment 451

GRC-5.5H Terms of Agreement 452

GRC-5.5I Privacy Notice 453

CHAPTER 1

Introduction to Information Security

Introduction

Computers are complex, yet vulnerable, devices. Something as simple as clicking on the wrong URL can open a malicious file capable of slowing or locking up a computer, causing disruptions in services, or stealing data. Moreover, computing devices are used by wide-ranging technology, such as smartphones, wearable technology, automation devices, and data centers. Therefore, the protection of computers—and more importantly, the data on them—is an important responsibility in all organizations.

The basic skills required to obtain a CompTIA Security+ Certification are rooted in comprehending the theories and philosophies of security assessment, incident prevention, and response to various attacks, threats, and vulnerabilities. Additionally, you will be expected to understand not only the implementation of physical and digital security controls but also the architecture and design of computer networks. In this chapter, you will demonstrate your comprehension of information security and assurance, the top frameworks adopted by organizations, commonly referenced security domains, and regulatory compliance.

The practice sets in this chapter will help enhance your knowledge of the theories and philosophies presented in the corresponding textbook chapter. As such, complete each of the following activities to the best of your ability. Make note of the questions or terms you find to be the most difficult so you may revisit those concepts at a later date.

Practice 1.1

For each of the following statements, choose the term that best completes the sentence. Be advised, each term will only be used once.

information assurance	risk
information security	risk management
Internet of Things	

1. The _____ refers to the connection of nontraditional computing devices—such as washing machines, clothes dryers, refrigerators, stoves, wearable devices, and light bulbs—to the Internet.

_____

2. _____ is the processing and implementation of controls to detect vulnerabilities in the use, storage, and transmission of data.

_____

3. A(n) _____ is a situation or circumstance that could cause issues for an organization including its data.

_____

4. The process of _____ evaluates an organization's assets and implements the proper actions needed to avoid or lessen the potential loss of an asset prone to a vulnerability.

_____

5. _____ is the procedures implemented to avoid or prevent data integrity from being compromised or lost.

_____

Practice 1.2

For each of the following, match the term to its correct description. Be advised, each term will only be used once.

A. ARP poisoning
B. attack surface
C. auditing
D. CIA triad
E. defense in depth
F. diversity in cryptographic systems
G. LAN
H. nonrepudiation

I. pretexting
J. security domain
K. security posture
L. technical controls
M. vendor diversity
N. WAN
O. Wi-Fi

1. _____ Assurance that an individual or group of people cannot deny the validity of something

2. _____ Practice of purchasing equipment from different vendors to avoid vulnerabilities exclusive to a single given vendor

3. _____ Relates to the technology used to automate security functions, event scheduling in system logs, and firewall implementation

4. _____ Describes how data is encrypted to provide confidentiality, along with the various form of cryptography, such as MD5, AES, SHA-1, and SHA-2

5. _____ Locations where an attacker can gain entry to a system and generate security risks

6. _____ Actions, philosophies, and strategies for ensuring the security of an organization's software, hardware, network, and data

7. _____ Uses radio waves to transmit data instead of using copper-core or fiber-optic cable and employs multiple forms of security to protect data

8. _____ Network that spans to only one small geographical location and is typically segregated to a single building

9. _____ Regular, ongoing review of an organization's employees use certain resources

10. _____ Form of attack in which an attacker spoofs a LAN-approved approved address to obtain data regarding traffic

11. _____ Network that spans multiple geographical locations and is often segmented to increase security and avoid threats and vulnerabilities

12. _____ Consists of the three main underlying core security principles of data protection

13. _____ Using a lie or scam to obtain private information

14. _____ Comprised list of individuals and the devices they utilize during their work, along with other forms of systems that must comply with an organization's security policy to avoid, threats, attacks, and vulnerabilities

15. _____ Theory that refers to the utilization of diverse controls and vendors to implement redundant levels and methods of protection in case of failure

Practice 1.3

For each of the following federal and international laws, match the term to its correct description. Be advised, each term will only be used once.

A. Computer Fraud and Abuse Act (CFAA)

B. Electronic Communication Privacy Act (ECPA)

C. Gramm-Leach-Bliley Act (GLBA)

D. Sarbanes-Oxley Act

E. Health Insurance Portability and Accountability Act (HIPAA)

F. EU General Data Protection Regulation (GDPR)

1. _____ Act designed to diminish computer fraud

2. _____ Defines the voluntary attempt of unauthorized access of devices from organizations, including governmental, banking and financial, and various forms of communication

3. _____ Approved in April 2016 and provides regulations on data protection and privacy for people in the European Union and European economic area

4. _____ Protects wire and electronic transmissions of data, including e-mail, telephone, and other forms of data, but primarily protects communication by oral or digital data transmissions

5. _____ Requires financial businesses to protect their customers' data and mandates all businesses must develop, implement, and maintain comprehensive information-security programs that present administrative, technical, and the physical safeguards appropriate for their organization

6. _____ Ensures the protection of electronic medical records and a patient's health information along with personal information regarding the patient's identity

Practice 1.4

For each of the following frameworks and standards, match the term to its correct description. Be advised, each term will only be used once.

A. Center for Internet Security (CIS)

B. International Organization for Standardization (ISO)

C. NIST Cybersecurity Framework (CSF)

D. Payment Card Industry Data Security Standard (PCI DSS)

E. Service Organization Control (SOC II)

F. Statement on Standards for Attestation Engagements (SSAE)

1. _____ Type of report designed to be used by organizations that have their customers' data in the cloud and only to be used for organizational purposes

2. _____ Form of auditing that governs ways in which organizations report compliance with laws and regulations

3. _____ Framework that outlines the responsibilities of protecting customers' and clients' credit card or personal data; used by all organizations that process credit card transactions

4. _____ Nonprofit organization that creates standards to support innovation and provide solutions to global changes

5. _____ Assists organizations in managing cybersecurity risks

6. _____ Nonprofit organization that maintains the best practices of simplifying the protection of data

Practice 1.5

For each of the following information assurance methods and implementations, match the term to its correct description. Be advised, each term will only be used once.

A. authentication

B. availability

C. compliance

D. confidentiality

E. nonrepudiation process

1. _____ Employed when the condition of being private or secret is needed and users have access only to the data they need for their roles in an organization

2. _____ Systematic process that tracks the origins and altercations of data and the data's user

3. _____ Validation method that verifies a user's identity; commonly implemented in the form of a username and password

4. _____ Allows data to be accessed and used when appropriately needed by a user

5. _____ Adherence of laws to ensure the security of data storage and its accessibility

Practice 1.6

For each of the following, match the term to its correct description. Be advised, each term will only be used once.

A. framework

B. industry standard

C. information security plan

D. integrity

E. pen register

F. secure-configuration guide

G. vendor-specific guide

1. _____ Documentation that advises polices and processes of how information is managed in an organization

2. _____ Set of rules that certain organizations will adopt to adhere to their needs

3. _____ Procedures that describe an organization's network and how their data will be protected

4. _____ Device that captures and stores the phone numbers, e-mail data, or IP addresses used in network communication

5. _____ Guides generated by a third party regarding certain models of hardware

6. _____ Refers to the data remaining in an unaltered and unimpaired state

7. _____ Documentation that provides assistance to security professionals for securing devices and preventing unauthorized access

CHAPTER 2 — Threats, Attacks, and Vulnerabilities

Introduction

No device is immune to security incidents. Threats, and those responsible for them, come in many forms and pose a significant risk to the security of an enterprise environment. This risk is largely due to the variety of motivations behind, perpetrators of, and methods for attacking electronic devices and networks.

The CompTIA Security+ Certification Exam requires the ability to differentiate and respond to various threats, vulnerabilities, and attacks. In this chapter, you will demonstrate your knowledge of types of malware and physical attacks, social engineering attacks, and threat-intelligence sources.

The practice sets in this chapter will help enhance your knowledge of the theories and philosophies presented in the corresponding textbook chapter. As such, complete each of the following activities to the best of your ability. Make note of the questions or terms you find to be the most difficult so you may revisit those concepts at a later date.

Practice 2.1

For each of the following social engineering attacks, choose the term that best fits each form of attack. Be advised, each term will only be used once.

phishing

smishing

spear phishing

vishing

whaling

1. _____ occurs when a particular recipient, often someone from the lower ranks of an organization, is chosen as a target of an attack.

2. The use of telephone communications to obtain information from a victim is _____.

3. _____ is a form of social engineering in which an attacker attempts to obtain personal information from a user through fake e-mails.

4. _____ is a type of attack in which individuals of a high administrative role in a business or those with a high net worth are targeted.

5. An attack in which a user is tricked into downloading malware or providing confidential information in forms such as a text message or social media site is called _____.

Practice 2.2

For each of the following, choose the term that best fits each statement. Be advised, each term will only be used once.

A. identity fraud
B. impersonation
C. influence campaigns

D. invoice scams
E. spam
F. spam over Internet messaging (SPIM)

1. _____ Social engineering technique in which an attacker claims to be a trustworthy individual from an organization in an effort to obtain personal information from a victim

2. _____ Social engineering attack that occurs when a hacker uses stolen personal information either to obtain additional data or access a victim's secure account

3. _____ Occurs when attackers spread false information in order to influence a vast amount of victims' way of thinking

4. _____ Messages received over the Internet that contain links to malicious websites or viruses

5. _____ Use of fraudulent invoices sent to organizations with the goal of obtaining money

6. _____ Nuisance e-mails, typically sent in bulk, that often contain phishing messages

Practice 2.3

For each of the following attack techniques and vulnerability searches, choose the term that best fits each form of attack and vulnerability practice. Be advised, each term will only be used once.

credential harvesting
dumpster diving
eliciting information
hoax
legacy platform
pharming
prepending

reconnaissance
shoulder surfing
third-party risk
watering hole
weak configurations
zero-day

1. ____ is a tactic that enables attackers to appear to have credible representation to support the information they are seeking from the victim, such as posing as a repair technician and asking a bank about ATM software.

2. A(n) ____ is a falsehood that a person believes is genuine, such as a pop-up alert that claims a computer is infected with malware.

3. An attack in which a threat actor establishes a legitimate-looking website used to steal personal information is a(n) ____ attack.

4. ____ is commonly considered the first phase in a social engineering attack and is the practice of obtaining information from or about the victim.

5. Attackers that use ____ add characters to the beginning of a text or phrase, such as including a username on Twitter to entice a user to click on a link.

   _____

6. A(n) ____ attack is implemented when an attacker targets a specific group, organization, or IP address range on a network to obtain information about their victims.

   _____

7. ____ is a social engineering tactic in which a threat actor views a person's keystrokes while standing behind them or pretending to look away in an effort to monitor login credentials.

   _____

8. An attacker searching through a bin of trash in hopes of obtaining valuable information about a victim is practicing ____.

   _____

9. A threat actor who employs ____ would likely use phishing e-mails to obtain usernames and passwords for targeted systems.

   _____

10. A(n) ____ refers to inadequate security controls in a device, system, or network.

   _____

11. ____ is a flaw that exists in a program and is unknown to the developers of the software until the flaw is exploited by hackers.

   _____

12. A(n) ____ is a vulnerability that is normally assumed by an organization when the organization hires an outside vendor to provide services for the organization.

   _____

13. A(n) ____ is an operating or embedded system that is no longer supported and does not receive important updates, rendering the device, data, and connected resources vulnerable to cyberattacks.

   _____

Practice 2.4

For each of the following, match the attack type to its correct description. Be advised, each term will be used more than once.

A. adversarial artificial intelligence (AI)

B. malware

C. physical attack

1. _____ A hacker installs malicious software on a device with the intent of accessing personal information for monetary or personal gain

2. _____ Use of tainted training data to compromise cryptographic algorithms.

3. _____ Theft of removable storage device in order to steal data or input malware

4. _____ Exploiting machine-learning algorithms to cause systems to behave in a way that benefits the attacker

5. _____ Installing a skimmer on a POS device to steal credit card data

6. _____ Sending an e-mail with a link to a website that installs a Trojan on a device

7. _____ Developing software that records keystrokes of a user and sends them to the software creator

8. _____ Installing a malicious USB cable so keystrokes can be inputted from a rogue device

9. _____ Use of algorithms to create automated e-mail responses and reveal sensitive information

10. _____ Cutting a network cable so a workstation is no longer able to access data, services, or resources

Practice 2.5

For each of the following threat actor attempts, match each vector to the best-fitting description. Be advised, each term will only be used once.

A. cloud

B. direct access

C. e-mail

D. removable media

E. social media

F. supply chain

G. wireless

1. _____ Method of using radio waves in an attempt to gain access to an organization's network

2. _____ Attack vector that cannot be accessed physically or directly but is accessible over an Internet connection from a remote site

3. _____ Attack vector in which an attacker has physical access to a targeted system or network

4. _____ Often utilized through social engineering attacks and entices targets to click on malicious links or download files in messages

5. _____ Vector that provides useful personal information about a target that is used by an attacker to launch an attack

6. _____ Attack vector utilized by a threat actor who attempted to exploit vulnerabilities that exist within systems used by suppliers, trade vendors, or collaborators of an organization

7. _____ Method of infecting flash drives, SIM cards, or optical discs with malicious software that will be installed unknowingly by network users

Practice 2.6

For each of the following types of threat intelligence sources, match the term to its correct description. Be advised, each term will only be used once.

A. Automated Indicator Sharing (AIS)

B. closed threat intelligence sources

C. dark web

D. information sharing centers (ISCs)

E. open-source intelligence (OSINT)

F. threat maps

1. _____ Resource that is not easily attainable by an average user but provides threat intelligence and allows security professionals to monitor activity for valuable information about attackers or victims

2. _____ Provides a visual representation of cyber threats occurring across the world

3. _____ Resource operated by the Department of Homeland Security that provides free information about cyber threat indicators between the federal government and private-sector participants

4. _____ Intelligence source that employs specialized tools and information regarding threats but requires an account to use

5. _____ Industry-specific consortium of business owners and IT professionals working together to collect, analyze, and distribute information about security threats in a timely manner

6. _____ Collects information from public sources as well as governmental sites and shares findings regarding data and threats

Practice 2.7

For each of the following potentially unwanted programs (PUP), match the term to its correct description. Be advised, each term will only be used once.

A. logic bomb

B. ransomware/cryptomalware

C. rootkit

D. time bomb

E. worm

1. _____ Malicious software that executes after a condition the malicious software is seeking for execution is met

2. _____ Form of malware that encrypts data on a device so a user is not able to access it unless a fee is paid for the data to be decrypted

3. _____ Malware that infects a device before an operating system loads, which makes the malware much more difficult to detect and remove

4. _____ Form of malware that is able to spread among multiple devices on a network

5. _____ Malicious software that will not execute until a certain date or time

Practice 2.8

For each of the following, choose the term that best fits each form of malware attack. Be advised, each term will only be used once.

backdoor

keylogger

malware attack

remote access Trojan (RAT)

Trojan

1. A _____ is a form of malware that provides an embedded backdoor to obtain administrative control of a victim's computer.

2. A _____ is software that is installed on a machine or a hardware device connected to a machine that tracks a victim's keystrokes.

3. An attack in which an attacker installs malicious software onto a victim's device for the attacker's ill gain is known as a _____.

4. A _____ is commonly a result from a victim installing a form of Trojan onto their device and allows the attacker to obtain access to the victim's device.

5. Although the software appears to be harmless, a _____ provides a form of access or obtainment of information of a victim's device.

Practice 2.9

For each of the following threats and threat actors, match the term to its correct description. Be advised, each term will only be used once.

A. advanced persistent threat

B. criminal syndicate

C. cyberattack

D. cybercrime

E. cybersecurity

F. hacktivist

G. script kiddie

H. state actor

I. threat actors

J. threats/attributes

1. _____ Attackers who perform attacks due to personal beliefs and agendas

2. _____ Stealth attack in which unauthorized access to a system is obtained but remains undetected for extended periods of time and is typically approved via government support

3. _____ Type of hacker who is typically supported financially via a political entity

4. _____ Attempt to steal or destroy data from a system

5. _____ Anything that could contribute harm to an enterprise

6. _____ Individual, nation state, or an organization that is responsible for an incident that causes an effect on the security of an entity

7. _____ Process of protecting organizations from malicious acts amongst individuals and systems including the Internet

8. _____ Termed for an individual who is not an experienced hacker but rather uses a resource they were given or obtained to perform an attack

9. _____ Any ill gained activity that is committed through a digital device or the Internet

10. _____ Groups of criminals, nationally and internationally, who engage in illegal activity for financial gain

Practice 2.10

For each of the following hacking terms, choose the term that best fits each form of hacking. Be advised, each term will only be used once.

black-hat hacker	hacking attack
gray-hat hacker	white-hat hacker

1. A _____ commits hacks for ill gain.

2. A _____ is an attempt to access a system and steal data.

3. A hacker who does not hack for ill gain but has not obtained permission to perform the hacks is known as a _____ and is often participating in a bug-bounty program to find flaws in software and systems before the flaws can be exploited.

4. A _____ perform hacks legally via pen testing for organizations that wish to discover vulnerabilities on their systems and networks.

Practice 2.11

For each of the following viruses, choose the term that best fits each form of virus. Be advised, each term will only be used once.

armored virus	polymorphic virus
fileless virus	virus
macro virus	

1. A(n) ____ is code that is written in the same language as legitimate software applications but programmed to perform malicious processes to a system.

2. A(n) ____ uses a system's software, files, and applications to launch malware, often via PowerShell scripts.

3. Malicious software code intended to disrupt a system and its data is referred to as a(n) ____.

4. A(n) ____ is designed in such a way that an analyst is not able to read the virus's source code to understand how the virus will perform or how to prevent the virus.

5. A(n) ____ is designed to change its characteristics to avoid detection from antivirus programs.

Practice 2.12

For each of the following terms, choose the term that best fits each physical or mechanical attack method. Be advised, each term will only be used once.

artificial intelligence

card cloning

machine learning (ML)

skimmer

system integration

USB data blocker

1. ____ is the act of stealing credit card information through a(n) ____ and copying the information to a bogus card during a point of sale (PoS) transaction.

   _____

   _____

2. Through ____, computers are able to interpret algorithms and improve its functionality based on how a device is used.

   _____

3. A(n) ____ prohibits the transfer of data between devices that are connected through a USB port.

   _____

4. Using ____ means that a third party is responsible for the security and functionality of a device.

   _____

5. ____ is the use of algorithms used in devices to learn about its uses and the environment it is surrounded by to perform better operations.

   _____

Practice 2.13

For each of the following attacks and attack methods, match the term to its correct description. Be advised, each term will only be used once.

A. command and control (C&C) attack

B. denial of service (DoS) attack

C. distributed denial of service (DDoS) attack

D. doxing

E. spyware

F. watering hole attack

G. whale phishing

H. zero-day vulnerability

1. _____ Malware attack that redirects the victim's machine to signal the attacker's server for instruction, after which the attacker's server sends commands to the victim's machine to give the attacker full access

2. _____ Form of attack in which a range of IP address or a certain group of an organization is targeted

3. _____ Phishing attack that targets members of an organization who have a high net worth

4. _____ Form of attack in which many hosts attack a victim to prohibit a victim's ability to use their system(s)

5. _____ Software that spies on a user's device activity

6. _____ Flaws that have not been discovered by developers or security professionals and are exploited by hackers

7. _____ Attack in which an attacker obtains personal information regarding their victim and shares the information to others

8. _____ Cyberattack that prevents users from accessing a resource

◼ Practice 2.14

For each of the following vulnerability and risk terms, choose the term that best fits each form of potential internal and external vulnerabilities and risks. Be advised, each term will only be used once.

cloud storage

insider

malicious USB cable

Shadow IT

supply chain vulnerabilities

vendor management

vendor support

vulnerability

1. ____ are vulnerabilities stemming from malicious activities of businesses, individuals, and activities that provide products and services to an organization.

   _____

2. Through ____, vulnerabilities may emerge from sources such as attacks from Internet resources.

   _____

3. ____ are third-party services that offer resources such as help-desk support for their services. However, if an issue arises and they are not available, or are not in business any longer, an organization may risk a loss to productivity.

   _____

4. A(n) ____ is any flaw that could cause an organization harm.

   _____

5. ____ is the implementation of management services through a third party and requires a bidding process.

   _____

6. When a(n) ____ is plugged into a computer, it is able to inject the computer with keystrokes to download malware.

   _____

7. A(n) ____ is anyone who is a member of an organization that could pose as an internal threat.

   _____

8. ____ is when members of an organization use technologies that are not approved by the organization's IT staff.

   _____

Practice 2.15

For each of the following terms, choose the term that best fits each description. Be advised, each term will only be used once.

heuristic methodology	open port
hybrid warfare	open services
indicators of compromise (IoC)	payload
nondisclosure agreement (NDA)	

1. ____ are the services that are allowed to operate on a device.

2. A(n) ____ that is not being used augments the possibility of an attack or malicious activity on a device.

3. ____ refers to military strategies that combine conventional, political, and cyberwarfare to publicize false information.

4. A(n) ____ is a legal contract between two parties that ensures that confidential information among either parties will not be shared.

5. The ____ of malware code dictates its malicious actions.

6. ____ provide evidence of a cyberattack.

7. ____ is an attempt to discover previous undetected threats or risks, in software.

CHAPTER 3 — Security Evaluation

Introduction

Vulnerabilities exist in a variety of places within an enterprise environment and are not often obvious in their location. It is not possible to predict where they will appear, and networks are not secure while they exist. Security evaluation must be conducted in order to discover and respond to vulnerabilities before they can be exploited.

In order to obtain a CompTIA Security+ Certification, you will need to prove competencies with threat hunting, penetration testing, reconnaissance, obtaining and evaluating log files. In this chapter, you will demonstrate your knowledge of vulnerability scanning, passive and active reconnaissance, exercise types for augmenting security, and log files.

The practice sets in this chapter will help enhance your knowledge of the theories and philosophies presented in the corresponding textbook chapter. As such, complete each of the following activities to the best of your ability. Make note of the questions or terms you find to be the most difficult so you may revisit those concepts at a later date.

Practice 3.1

For each of the following, match the threat hunting term to the statement that best describes it. Be advised, each term will only be used once.

A. advisories and bulletins

B. intelligence fusion

C. maneuvers

D. threat hunting

E. threat intelligence feeds

1. _____ Method for obtaining cyber threat intelligence by searching and navigating a network for potential threats on its system; instead of waiting for a threat to be detected, cybersecurity professionals can move through the network searching for evidence of cybersecurity threats

2. _____ Cybersecurity practice in which professionals proactively look for threats and vulnerabilities that are not currently detected on their network

3. _____ Combination of multiple valid resources that generate a comprehensive threat profile

4. _____ Provides real-time data regarding cybersecurity threats and risks through resources such as security information and event management system (SIEM) tools

5. _____ Source of cybersecurity threat intelligence that comes from organizations such as government agencies and cybersecurity companies

Practice 3.2

For each of the following, match the vulnerability scanning term to the statement that best describes it. Be advised, each term will only be used once.

A. application scanning

B. common vulnerabilities and exposures (CVE)

C. common vulnerability scoring systems (CVSS)

D. configuration review

E. credentialed scan

F. false negative

G. false positives

H. intrusive test

I. log reviews

J. network vulnerability scanner

K. noncredentialed scan

L. non-intrusive test

M. web application scanner

1. _____ List of known cybersecurity threats identified by the United States Department of Homeland Security

2. _____ Software application that identifies poor configurations, outdated software patches, and other miscellaneous vulnerabilities

3. _____ By using a username and password registered to a device, this method requires credentials of an account registered to the device being scanned

4. _____ Occurs when a scan has registered a vulnerability, but a vulnerability is not present

5. _____ Occurs when a vulnerability is present, but the scanner is incapable of finding any vulnerabilities

6. _____ Displays real-time data and provides insight about vulnerabilities that exist within a given application

7. _____ Vulnerability scanner that focuses on potential vulnerable network activities

8. _____ Assessment and analysis of vulnerability scan logs

9. _____ Occurs when a preformed scan tries to exploit vulnerabilities and may cause harm to a system

10. _____ Tool that searched for vulnerabilities, such as scripting attacks, out-of-date versioning, and unsecure configurations in web-based resources and applications

11. _____ Places vulnerabilities in numeric order based on the severity of the threat it may produce

12. _____ Scan that does not require credentials, such as the username and password, to access a system

13. _____ Scan performed without causing harm to a system and involves searching resources such as the registry in an operating system, open ports on a network, missing software patches, and other various vulnerabilities

Practice 3.3

For each of the following penetration testing techniques, methods, and practices, choose the term that best completes the sentence. Be advised, each term will only be used once.

black-box	persistence
bug-bounty	pivoting
cleanup	privilege escalation
gray-box	rules of engagement
lateral movement	white-box

1. ____ occurs when an attacker exploits a previously unknown vulnerability to obtain administrative access to systems or networks.

   _____

2. ____ occurs when an attacker is able to compromise a networked device and then compromise other devices in search of obtaining higher-level privileges within the system and networks.

   _____

3. A ____ pen tester is one who has been given permission from and information about an organization and its systems prior to conducting a pen test.

   _____

4. ____ is a document given to individual(s) conducting a penetration test and defines how and when the test will be conducted.

   _____

5. A ____ penetration test is one in which the tester is given *some* information about an organization's system before conducting the test.

   _____

6. After gaining initial entry to a system, ____ enables a pen tester, or hacker, to use a system and collect more information about systems and their networks.

   _____

7. The ____ phase takes place after a penetration test and requires scripts, tools, and created accounts be removed from a system and its network.

   _____

8. ____ programs are often utilized to prevent zero-day attacks and other similar vulnerabilities.

   _____

9. ____ is when a pen tester discovers a successful exploit and attempts to maintain a connection by placing tools such as keyloggers to obtain network username and passwords.

   _____

10. A ____ pen tester does not have *any* information from the organization regarding their system before or while conducting the penetration test.

   _____

Practice 3.4

For each of the following forms of reconnaissance, choose the term that best completes the sentence. Be advised, each term will only be used once.

footprinting	war driving
passive reconnaissance	war flying

1. _____ is a pre-attack technique that gathers information about a system and is generally the first step a hacker takes when implementing an attack.

   _____

2. _____ is the act of moving area to area, typically in a vehicle, searching for wireless networks and mapping the location of the networks found.

   _____

3. _____ is the discovery and gathering of data without the target being aware it is happening.

   _____

4. _____ is the practice of detecting wireless networks using devices such as drones to search for open access points.

   _____

Practice 3.5

For each of the following, match each exercise type to the statement that best describes it. Please be advised, the terms will only be used once.

A. blue team

B. purple team

C. red team

D. white team

1. _____ Offensive cybersecurity professionals who attempt to break into systems and stimulate attacks against a network

2. _____ Team that sets the rules of engagement and overseas the exercises being performed but does not conduct any penetration testing or defending

3. _____ Combination of offensive and defensive cybersecurity teams to enhance each team's combined effectiveness

4. _____ Defensive cybersecurity team that is responsible for the security defenses of the network and responds to network threats

Practice 3.6

For each of the following log files, protocols, and practices, choose the term that best completes the sentence. Be advised, each term will only be used once.

application	security
authentication	Session Initiation Protocol (SIP)
Domain Name Service (DNS)	syslog
dump	syslog-ng
journalctl	system
network	VoIP and call manager
NXlog	web
rsylog	

1. A(n) ____ log allows administrators to view successful and unsuccessful logins and authentications.

_____

2. ____ logs are created on a web server each time a user visits a website.

_____

3. Although it is not a traditional log file, a(n) ____ file is generated when a system crashes, and the information about the crash is compiled into a file.

_____

4. The ____ is a protocol that sends system and event log information to a particular server.

_____

5. ____ is a log-management tool that supports multiple platforms such as Android and Windows.

_____

6. Events generates from the operating systems and its components are recorded in the ____ log.

_____

7. ____ logs store data related to Voice over Internet Protocol sessions and provide detailed call information such as diagnostics and the amount of data transmitted during a call.

_____

8. A portable version of rsyslog, called ____, is available on multiple operating systems.

_____

9. ____ logs contain information regarding the process of managing of voice-based data.

_____

10. In Linux distros, ____ queries and displays system journal contents.

_____

11. ____ logs are events that are recorded after modifications are applied to an application.

_____

12. The open-source software utility ____ enables Unix and Linux to forward messages.

_____

13. ____ logs record events related to auditing established configurations.

_____

14. ____ logs are generated and stored on servers that provide the service that enables users to type the name of a web address of the domain instead of the domain's IP address.

_____

15. A(n) ____ log is generated by certain network services such as network address translation (NAT), routers, firewalls, or virtual private networks (VPNs).

_____

Practice 3.7

For each of the following SIEM terms, choose the term that best completes the sentence. Be advised, each term will only be used once.

Security Information and Event Management (SIEM)	SIEM log
SIEM correlation	WORM device
SIEM dashboard	

1. A ____ is a tool used to summarize data and transform it into simple security monitoring information.

_____

2. ____ are the software products that support organizations with real-time security by collecting and compiling the log data generated from network results and reports.

_____

3. ____ are records of events that have been reviewed or analyzed.

_____

4. A ____ searches through aggregated data and reports common characteristics.

_____

5. A ____ is a storage device that allows data to be saved but cannot be changed.

_____

Practice 3.8

For each of the following scanning and integration technologies, choose the term that best completes the sentence. Be advised, each term will only be used once.

configuration-compliance scanner

orchestration

security automation

Security Orchestration, Automation, and Response (SOAR)

vulnerability scan

1. ____ uses an array of software tools that collect data from multiple resources and generates an automatic response without human intervention.

   _____

2. A(n) ____ searches for vulnerabilities through specific frameworks.

   _____

3. ____ uses the integration from various technologies to work together.

   _____

4. ____ is the handling and processing of security tasks automatically.

   _____

5. A(n) ____ is an assessment of possible vulnerabilities or bleak security configurations.

   _____

Practice 3.9

For each of the following forms of active reconnaissance, choose the term that best completes the sentence. Be advised, each term will only be used once.

active reconnaissance

banner grabbing

port scanner

port scanning

SMTP querying

1. ____ results in e-mail account information being obtained.

   _____

2. ____ occurs when information requests about computers or networking services originate from a remote system.

   _____

3. ____ is the gathering of data and information about a system through tools and utilities.

   _____

4. ____ determines the status of communication ports on a system and uses a(n) ____ to probe network devices or hosts for open ports.

   _____

Practice 3.10

For each of the following, match each penetration testing method to the statement that best describes it. Please be advised, the terms will only be used once.

A. escalation of privilege
B. ethical hacking
C. initial exploitation

D. penetration exercise
E. penetration testing
F. penetration testing authorization

1. _____ Form of penetration testing used to identify possible vulnerabilities or attack vectors of a system

2. _____ Test for examining the security defenses of an organization

3. _____ Performed by white-hat hackers after gaining permission by an organization

4. _____ Stage of a pen test that occurs after a penetration tester has conducted research of the organization and their system(s)

5. _____ Permission given by an organization to another party to hack a system to determine how vulnerable the system is to unauthorized access or penetration

6. _____ Penetration test used to determine how easily a hacker can move from a normal user to a root or administrator privileges while accessing a system

Practice 3.11

For each of the following SIEM features, choose the term that best completes the sentence. Be advised, each term will only be used once.

automated alerts and triggers	packet capture
data input	sentiment analysis
event deduplication	time synchronization
log aggregation	user behavior analysis (UBA)
log collection	

1. A(n) ____ occurs when a data packet is intercepted as it crosses a certain network point.

   _____

2. A(n) ____ is the attempt to predict possible outcomes using logged data from sources such as social media and e-mails to determine the attitudes and demeanors of users.

   _____

3. A(n) ____ merges identical events into a single event to reduce overhead.

   _____

4. ____ monitors the behaviors of a system and compares it to the system's baseline behaviors.

   _____

5. ____ is a process that ensures all devices on a network agree on the correct time.

   _____

6. ____ are created to notify administrators if specific events take place on a system.

   _____

7. A(n) ____ is the assembly of logs from various resources in a network environment.

   _____

8. ____ refers to methods used in syslog to record and collect data within logs.

   _____

Practice 3.12

For each of the following log files and management, choose the term that best completes the sentence. Be advised, each term will only be used once.

log analysis	PowerShell
log file	predicative analysis
log management	syslog

1. _____ establishes policies for the collection, review, and analysis of log data.

_____

2. _____ logs allow administrators to see which providers are accessed.

_____

3. _____ is the creation, transmission, analysis, archival, and disposal of log data.

_____

4. _____ is the examination of data and the predictions of a cyberattack based from the examined data.

_____

5. The _____ is the standard event logging protocol.

_____

6. A _____ is a record of events that generate during sever and computing operations.

_____

CHAPTER 4

Managing User Security

Introduction

Organizational security is impossible without user security. End-users represent a number of vulnerabilities, many of which cannot be mitigated or addressed by any type of physical or digital control. Users of an organization's network typically do not have extensive knowledge of digital security; as such, they often do not fully understand how their actions and decisions can easily put data at risk. It is the responsibility of an IT security team to develop, enforce, and monitor restrictions that help lessen or eliminate vulnerabilities created by users.

To adhere to the passing requirements of the CompTIA Security+ Certification Exam, you must be able to differentiate among various types of authentication, access controls, management controls, single sign-on procedures, and file system permissions. Additionally, you will be required to prove your grasp of global position systems and the services they provide to cybersecurity professionals. In this chapter, you will demonstrate your knowledge of digital and data protection via GPS, permissions and policies, and methods to diminish user-generated vulnerabilities.

The practice sets in this chapter will help enhance your knowledge of the theories and philosophies presented in the corresponding textbook chapter. As such, complete each of the following activities to the best of your ability. Make note of the questions or terms you find to be the most difficult so you may revisit those concepts at a later date.

Practice 4.1

For each of the following cybersecurity authentication methods and structures, choose the term that best completes the statement. Be advised, each term will only be used once.

attestation	federation identity management (FIM)
authentication, authorization, and accounting (AAA)	multifactor authentication (MFA)
biometrics	standard naming conventions
directory	token key

1. ____ is an authentication factor of *what you are* and includes authentication technology such as fingerprint scanning, retinal scanning, facial recognition, and voice recognition.

   _____

2. Organizational best practices include ____, which are rules that determine how account names are generated and recognized.

   _____

3. ____ provides confirmation of authentication for remote users and verifies trusts via a certificate authority (CA).

   _____

4. The authentication factor of *something you have* employs hardware devices such as a(n) ____, which often resembles the shape and size of USB and key fob devices.

   _____

5. In order to utilize more than one layer of security, organizations employ ____ to require users to provide multiple methods of authentication, such as "what you know" and "what you are."

   _____

6. A(n) ____ is a hierarchal folder structure for storing files on a computer or server.

_____

7. ____ is an agreement between organizations to allow subscribers to use one set of credentials to access all networks that are associated with the organizations.

_____

8. The ____ framework defines the policies for granting users access.

_____

◥ Practice 4.2

For each of the following terms, match the term to its correct description. Be advised, each term will only be used once.

A. access policies
B. account audits
C. account types
D. attributes
E. directory services
F. disablement
G. geofencing

H. geolocation
I. password complexity
J. password history
K. password lockout
L. password reuse
M. time of day restriction
N. tokens

1. _____ Software systems that generate, store, organize, and determine access to information and resources

2. _____ Uses global positioning technology to create a virtual boundary and is capable of disabling devices and its features in a certain geographical area

3. _____ Policy enforcement that suspends an account's access to a network but does not delete the account; often utilized when an account does not meet the requirements established in an organization's policies

4. _____ Measurements and rules by an organization to grant authorized users access to a network while also prohibiting unauthorized users from accessing the network

5. _____ Control that establishes the amount of unique password a user must generate before an old password may be used again

6. _____ Only allows users to access a network during certain days of the week and certain hours during those days

7. _____ Part of an organization's security plan that provides an examination and evaluation of an account

8. _____ Act of identifying the geographical location of a device

9. _____ Individual's characteristics used to provide authorization

10. _____ Piece of software that provides authentication from accessible sources such as a smartphone app

11. _____ Dictates the level of access a user will have to a system; often titled user, power user, or administrator

12. _____ Control that establishes the amount of days a user may use a new password before a user may change

13. _____ Refers to the degree of difficulty a user must use when generating their password

14. _____ Policy used to prevent access from an account after a certain amount of failed login attempts

▮▮▮ Practice 4.3

For each of the following, match each authentication and authorization method, permission, control, or practice to its correct description. Be advised, each term will only be used once.

A. ABAC
B. DAC
C. file system permissions
D. identity provider (IdP)
E. Kerberos
F. least privilege
G. MAC
H. OAuth
I. offboarding
J. onboarding
K. OpenID
L. privilege access management (PAM)
M. RADIUS
N. role-based access control (RBAC)
O. rule-based access control
P. SAML
Q. TACACS+

1. _____ Strategies and technologies used to maintain control of privileged accounts

2. _____ Determines which users have access to certain files

3. _____ Occurs when an individual is new to an organization and is advised of their user account and responsibilities to the organization, its system, and network

4. _____ Cisco proprietary protocol and authentication service that allows a user's credentials to be forwarded to a central server to obtain access to systems and resources

5. _____ Standard authentication protocol on Microsoft servers when utilizing its Active Directory

6. _____ Practice of assigning rights to a role rather than to each individual user manually

7. _____ Access control method of strict level access to resources based on criteria set by a network administrator

8. _____ Control strategy in which a user's access is determined by the set of rules an administrator establishes

9. _____ Open-standard protocol used instead of TCP/IP to enable functionality with any server or vendor and utilizes User Datagram Protocol (UDP)

10. _____ Open standard that allows the exchange of authentication authorization information to provide Single Sign-On options over the Internet with merged systems

11. _____ Open-standard authentication protocol that supports single sign-on (SSO) and eliminates the need for a user to share a password with a third-party entity

12. _____ Open-standard authentication protocol that supports single sign-on (SSO) but does not provide authentication as it utilizes a third party to access an authentication server

13. _____ Allows employees of an organization to have only the specific privileges needed to perform their jobs

14. _____ Access control that grants a user with more rights to data than the individual's assigned access level; commonly utilized when another user generates forms of data and needs individuals to access the forms of data that is out of their jurisdiction

15. _____ Access control system that uses the characteristics of the user and compares it to the characteristics there are assigned to the data of the organization

16. _____ Practice of gathering all of a user's login credentials, ID badges, and company property when an employee is leaving the organization

17. _____ Identity database that allows assertions regarding identity to be made to other Service Providers (SPs); typically used in SAML

Practice 4.4

For each of the following account directory and login methods, choose the term that best completes the statement. Be advised, each term will only be used once.

account expiration	Lightweight Directory Access Protocol (LDAP) and LDAP with SSL (LDAPS)
account maintenance	recertification
Active Directory (AD)	single sign-on (SSO)
credential management	usage and audit review

1. ____ consists of the routine review of user accounts, their permissions, and usage patterns in comparison to an organization's operational and security needs.

2. The user account authentication service that allows a user to insert their username and password once to access a set of services is called ____.

3. ____ is the process of reviewing account uses, frequency, and the decision whether the account should stay in the same state, be modified, or deleted.

4. ____ are the directories, typically from domains, that allow user on one platform to access resources from another platform such as Windows to Macintosh.

5. The process of disabling an account after a certain date has passed is known as ____.

6. A(n) ____ is a directory of services for a Windows network that manages user accounts.

7. ____ is the process of renewing a user account, the account's group membership, and its permissions.

8. ____ takes the proper actions to manage a user's login name and password.

Practice 4.5

For each of the following, match the biometric device or its method description. Be advised, each term will only be used once.

A. behavioral biometrics

B. biometric authentication

C. fingerprint scanner

D. gait analysis

E. iris scanner

F. retinal scanner

G. vein scanner

H. voice recognition

1. _____ Confirms a person's identity by measuring unique characteristics of a person's retina

2. _____ Uses infrared light to scan an individual's blood vessels to confirm their identity

3. _____ Uses software for authentication via an individual's vocal characteristics

4. _____ Measures certain parts of the human anatomy to verify a person's identity and allow access to resources

5. _____ Confirms a person's identity by measuring unique characteristics of a person's iris

6. _____ Studies and identifies patterns of a user's activities, such as the speed with which they normally type

7. _____ Identity confirmation based upon an individual's walking and movements

8. _____ Identity confirmation based upon an individual's unique skin layers

Practice 4.6

For each of the following authentication and logon methods, choose the term that best completes the statement. Be advised, each term will only be used once.

common access card (CAC)	secondary logon
Federated Identity Management (FIM)	Shibboleth

1. A ____ refers to a situation in which a user is already logged on to a system but must provide additional credentials to access resources such as administrative rights.

_____

2. A smart card that contains a microchip that is inserted into a reader to obtain access to an area or device is called a ____.

_____

3. ____ is the agreement amongst multiple originations to allow subscribers of one resource to use the same credentials to access all resources amongst the agreeing groups.

_____

4. ____ provides an SSO method for websites to make authentication decisions on an individual level.

_____

Practice 4.7

For each of the following account control and permission characteristics, choose the term that best completes the statement. Be advised, each term will only be used once.

---

attribute-based access control (ABAC)

explicit permissions

group-based access control

implicit permissions

inherited permissions

location-based policy

time-of-day restriction

user account control (UAC)

---

1. A(n) _____ enables the ability to revoke a user's access based on their location.

2. _____ are default user permissions based on child and parent objects when the account is created.

3. _____ is a Microsoft technology that controls the settings and permissions users have on their Microsoft device.

4. _____ are permissions obtained through another object.

5. A(n) _____ determines when a user can or cannot log into their account.

6. The control characteristics assigned to a user that compare the user's characteristics to the data they are assigned to is called _____.

7. _____ grant users the permission to access certain folders, files, and network drives.

8. _____ is the practice of placing users into assigned roles where the members are provided the same set of permissions and network access.

Practice 4.8

For each of the following, match the term to its appropriate description. Be advised, each term will only be used once.

A. crossover error rate (CER)

B. efficacy rate

C. false rejection rate (FRR)

D. GPS tagging

E. New Technology File System (NTFS) permissions

1. _____ Geographical information about data

2. _____ Measurement in which false acceptance rates and false rejection rates are equal

3. _____ Rate of biometric authentication accuracy

4. _____ Enables users in an Active Directory (AD) to share files and folders across a network

5. _____ Likelihood of biometric authentication that incorrectly denies a user to an area or resource

CHAPTER 5 / Physical Security

Introduction

Many threats to computers and networks do not originate from an Internet connection. A number of risks are posed just by physical access to devices. Imagine a scenario in which a company has strong digital controls on their workstations but few, if any, physical controls to prevent access to the workstations. It is entirely plausible that a threat actor can enter the organization's premises, access a workstation, and perform malicious actions. With only physical access, attackers can cut network cables, steal hardware, or insert USB-based hacking tools, such as keyloggers or logic bombs, into a machine. Therefore, it is equally important that access to devices is as secure as the devices themselves.

To adhere to the passing requirements of the CompTIA Security+ Certification Exam, you should be able to differentiate, summarize, and explain the theories and philosophies of physical security. In this chapter, you will demonstrated your understanding of physical security control types, authentication measures, and physical controls to limit access to an organization and its devices.

The practice sets in this chapter will help enhance your knowledge of the theories and philosophies presented in the corresponding textbook chapter. As such, complete each of the following activities to the best of your ability. Make note of the questions or terms you find to be the most difficult so you may revisit those concepts at a later date.

Practice 5.1

For each of the following, match each security control term to its correct description. Be advised, each term will only be used once.

A. administrative
B. compensating
C. corrective
D. defective

E. deterrent
F. physical
G. preventive
H. technical

1. _____ Isolates and limits the damage that is caused by an incident

2. _____ Prevents incidents from occurring

3. _____ Identifies incidents that are in progress and categorizes them by specific characteristics

4. _____ Develops and enforces policies, procedures, and processes to control human interactions with a device or network

5. _____ Provides other actions if a typical control is not able to be used

6. _____ Attempts to prevent attacks from occurring by utilizing security tools of discouragement such as lights, cameras, or alarms

7. _____ Uses technology that automates device management for obtainment and use of confidential data

8. _____ Uses noticeable controls to protect physical assets of the organization

Practice 5.2

For each of the following physical security authentication methods, controls, and vulnerabilities, choose the term that best completes each sentence. Be advised, each term will only be used once.

alarm	mantrap
badge	smart card
closed-circuit television (CCTV)	smart card authentication
HMAC-based one-time password (HTOP)	tailgating
lighting	token
lock	

1. ____ utilizes digital certificates to authenticate a user's identity, to encrypt their data transmissions, and allow for digital signatures for connections such as an organization's wireless network.

2. Many organizations use and require their users to have a(n) ____ as a method to authenticate personal identity and role of the organization.

3. A(n) ____ is a control system that is able to confine an individual between two sets of doors that can interlock.

4. ____ occurs when an individual closely following behind authorized personnel to gain entry into a building or secure area of a building, such as a server room.

5. A(n) ____ relies on two forms of data; a seed, which is a secret key that is only known by the token and a counter, which is stored in the token and authentication server.

6. A(n) ____ can be either hardware-based or software-based and provides access to resources.

7. A(n) ____ is a small hardware device that contains an embedded chip with stored information to provide authentication for users to access physical locations of an organization.

8. One of the strongest preventive measures that provides a deterrent to attackers due to high visibility for physical forms of security is ____.

9. The preventive measure that provides a trigger or warning when unwanted activity or access is taking place in an organization is called a(n) ____.

10. ____ is a system that utilizes video cameras to monitor centralized locations of an organization.

11. Using a(n) ____ on doors and equipment in an organization diminishes the possibility of entry or stolen equipment unless the person has approved access.

Practice 5.3

For each of the following, match each control and protocol to its correct description. Be advised, each term will only be used once.

A. 802.1X

B. air gap

C. bollards/barricade

D. Faraday cage

E. fire suppression

F. industrial camouflage

G. personnel

H. protected distribution system

I. signage

J. Simple Network Protocol, version 3 (SNMPv3)

K. visitor log

1. _____ Recorded data that makes it easier to determine, pinpoint, and verify the potential source of a threat

2. _____ Form of obstruction to passage, often made of concrete, that has a cylinder shape and is usually placed on the property of an organization permanently

3. _____ Concept that is employed in the design of an organization's campus and campus to make it an unappealing option for attackers

4. _____ Helps enforce the security of an organization and increases awareness for members of the organization to report suspicious activity

5. _____ Network designed to be located in a secure area and isolated from other networks and the Internet to augment its security

6. _____ Often consists of inside members of the organization that serve as physical controls for the organization

7. _____ Wireless authentication protocol that offers authorized users the required open ports over an organization's wireless network

8. _____ Physical control that consists of five classes (A, B, C, D, and K)

9. _____ Method of securing computer networking or communication cabling with physical safeguards to prevent access or damage from unauthorized users

10. _____ Blocks external electromagnetic singles from reaching protected equipment inside

11. _____ Recommended for organizations to control and monitor the temperatures of the areas in their buildings; enables authentication and encryption during usage

Practice 5.4

For each of the following data destruction methods, choose the term that best completes each sentence. Be advised, each term will only be used once.

data purging	disk sanitization
degaussing	pulping

1. ____ is the act of permanently removing content from a disk.

2. When organizations use ____ methods to destroy paper-based data, they place the paper in a tank of water with chemicals that remove ink from the paper.

3. ____ is a method that removes data from disks without physically destroying the disk.

4. ____ distorts and removes the magnetic fields on a disk in such a way that data is not able to be retrieved.

Practice 5.5

For each of the following data and network control and security methods, choose the term that best completes each sentence. Be advised, each term will only be used once.

data center	hot and cold aisles
electromagnetic interference (EMI) shielding	Jersey walls
electromagnetic radiation (EMR)	physical control

1. A(n) ____ is a room that is equipped to handle vast amounts of power, cabling, and various network equipment.

2. Many organizations use ____ as a method to control temperature within a server room.

3. A(n) ____ is any barrier, component, or individual that prohibits an unauthorized individual from accessing a data center or network components.

4. ____ occurs from devices such as printers, computers, microwaves, and monitors.

5. ____ are tee-shaped blocks of concrete that prevent vehicles from accessing certain portions of an organization's campus and helps diminish the possibility of mass theft of devices and networking equipment.

6. ____ provides a barrier around wires to block interference from electrical signals from the wires.

Name _____

Practice 5.6

For each of the following facility control and security methods, choose the term that best completes each sentence. Be advised, each term will only be used once.

object detection

personal identity verification (PIV)

screen filters

secure token

turnstile

1. A ____ is a device that stores the information needed to authenticate an individual's identity.

   _____

2. A ____ is a device with bars that will block an entryway to where only one person may enter at a time.

   _____

3. ____ are standard-issue smart cards for governmental employees.

   _____

4. ____ refers to technologies that are able to identify programmed objects.

   _____

5. ____ are placed on screens to eliminate the possibility of shoulder surfing.

   _____

Notes

CHAPTER 6 Device Security

Hardening is a security method that relies on tools, techniques, and actions to reduce IT vulnerabilities in an enterprise environment. Hardening user devices is an important step in security in an organization's systems against attacks. Techniques should be applied to harden all devices, including workstations, servers, applications, operating systems, databases, and all networked devices.

To adhere to the passing requirements of the CompTIA Security+ Certification Exam, you should be able to differentiate the theories and philosophies of host hardening, device application, and device security. In this chapter, you will demonstrate your understanding of endpoint protection, patch management, hardening of systems and data, and data loss prevention.

The practice sets in this chapter will help enhance your knowledge of the theories and philosophies presented in the corresponding textbook chapter. As such, complete each of the following activities to the best of your ability. Make note of the questions or terms you find to be the most difficult so you may revisit those concepts at a later date.

Practice 6.1

For each of the following hardening methods, choose the term that best completes each sentence. Be advised, each term will only be used once.

application	hardening
client	host
database	network
endpoint	operating system
endpoint protection	server

1. The fundamental difference between hardening a client and a host is that a(n) ____ is capable of making requests to a server and should be protected accordingly.

   _____

2. A(n) ____ may be perceived as difficult to harden, as these devices, such as computers, printers, and mobile devices, maintain accessibility over the network, doing so with their own IP address on a network.

   _____

3. Hardening ____ devices is an important practice, as these devices function as physical attributes on an organization's network, and securing these devices augments the potential of malicious activity and threats.

   _____

4. ____ is the security practice of utilizing tools and resources to diminish information technology vulnerabilities in an enterprise environment

   _____

5. ____ hardening consists of using firewalls and closing ports that are not needed for organizational or user productivity in an effort to secure data transmissions.

   _____

6. ____ hardening, and denying all unauthorized access, is an important component of a network, as these devices provide the access to an organization's servers and data.

_____

7. A(n) ____ is used to store, modify, and retrieve data for an organization; as such, it is important that hardening is utilized to ensure the data is safe, protected, and not susceptible to data exposure.

_____

8. ____ hardening involves protecting programs from potential exploits.

_____

9. ____ hardening involves modifying default settings and other features with vulnerabilities that could cause potential exploits.

_____

10. ____ is the practice of securing user endpoint devices to prevent malicious activity or attacks.

_____

▰ Practice 6.2

For each of the following, match each patch management, security strategy, and application and system hardening term to its correct description. Be advised, each term will be used only once.

A. blacklisting

B. boot integrity

C. data loss prevention (DLP)

D. disk encryption

E. hardware root of trust

F. patch management

G. Trusted Platform Module (TPM)

H. whitelisting

1. _____ Chip located in a device's hardware to run authentication checks on the hardware, software, and firmware of the device

2. _____ Process that assures a computer is booting from a secure drive with only authorized programs running

3. _____ Process of deploying updates to networked devices; can be either centralized, where an administrator completes the updates after searching for patches from vendors, or via an automated management service that provides installed updates when new patches from vendors are discovered

4. _____ Process of listing approved applications that are allowed on a device

5. _____ Security strategy that detects potential data breaches to ensure the proper data transmissions from outside of the organization remain valid and confidential

6. _____ Process of listing unapproved applications that are not allowed on a device

7. _____ Hardware feature used by Measured Boot to protect from rootkits and other forms of malware during a device's booting process that serves as a starting point for the chain of trust

8. _____ Process of converting data on a disk into unreadable characters by applying a security key; can be performed by FDE or SEDs

█████ Practice 6.3

For each of the following system and hardware security methods, choose the term that best completes each sentence. Be advised, each term will only be used once.

firewall	secure boot
firmware	self-encrypting drive (SED)
full-device encryption (FDE)	tokenization
measured boot	Unified Extensible Firmware Interface (UEFI)
patch	Windows Registry

1. A ____ is an update that is created and provided via a vendor to correct errors or flaws within the software's operation.

   _____

2. A ____ is able to encrypt data on storage drives automatically.

   _____

3. Read-only software on a hardware device to provide instructions as to how it interacts with other forms of hardware is called ____.

   _____

4. The ____ is the configuration tool that contains information, settings, options, and values for all Windows OS installation processes.

   _____

5. ____ is a boot attestation process that protects devices from rootkits as the device is booting into its operating system.

   _____

6. To ensure that only trusted programs will emerge during the booting process, ____ should be employed.

   _____

7. ____ refers to the act of converting data on a hard disk into unreadable characters by applying a security key.

   _____

8. ____ protects data by replacing the data with random bits of data.

   _____

9. Boot-specific firmware that can be accessed to adjust boot options when booting a Windows computer is called ____.

   _____

10. A ____ is a network security tool that protects against unwanted data transmissions.

   _____

Practice 6.4

For each of the following endpoint and data protection methods, choose the term that best completes each sentence. Be advised, each term will only be used once.

blocked port	host intrusion-detection system (HIDS)
closed port	host intrusion-prevention system (HIPS)
disabled service	Open Systems Interconnect (OSI) model
endpoint detection and response (EDR)	salting

1. ____ are the tools that are utilized to monitor devices in order to identify any potential attacks on endpoint devices.

2. The ____ is a seven-layer conceptual example of how data transmits across a network.

3. A security-monitoring program that examines activity from an endpoint device and provides notifications of potential threats to administrators is called a(n) ____.

4. A service that is not permitted to run on a host is called a(n) ____.

5. A(n) ____ security tool that halts traffic if malicious activity is suspected.

6. A(n) ____ is not actively being listened to by a device and is inaccessible to a host.

7. ____ is often performed on a password to increase security by adding insignificant data to create a different hash value.

8. A port that is shut down so no form of traffic can transmit to or from a host is referred to as a(n) ____.

CHAPTER 7 / Application Development and Security

Application development is the process of designing, programming, testing, and quality controlling applications. Security applications and the code that enables them to run is an important step in securing computing devices and networks. Without secure application development, attackers can exploit vulnerabilities in code to alter functionality or implant backdoors or malware on a system

To adhere to the passing requirements of the CompTIA Security+ Certification Exam, you should be able to summarize application security and development, utilize the tools for applications, and know common application attacks. In this chapter, you will demonstrate your understanding of application vulnerabilities, secure coding techniques, and software development life cycles.

The practice sets in this chapter will help enhance your knowledge of the theories and philosophies presented in the corresponding textbook chapter. As such, complete each of the following activities to the best of your ability. Make note of the questions or terms you find to be the most difficult so you may revisit those concepts at a later date.

Practice 7.1

For each of the following waterfall model development life cycle phases, choose the term that best completes each sentence. Be advised, each term will only be used once.

coding	gathering and analyzing requirements
deployment	maintenance
design	testing

1. ____ is the process of turning plans into a blueprint for how the application will be generated and providing an outline for programmers to stay on target.

   _____

2. During the ____ stage, developers are assuring the application is working properly.

   _____

3. ____ is the last stage of the waterfall development model and consists of programmers providing updates and patches for the program.

   _____

4. The first step in the waterfall development method is ____, which helps determine why the application is needed and how it will solve problems or enhance productivity.

   _____

5. Once the program has been tested thoroughly, the ____ stage begins, and the program is released to end-users.

   _____

6. ____ is the process of generating code via computer programming by referencing the blueprint generated at an earlier stage of the development cycle.

   _____

Practice 7.2

For each of the following application practices, choose the term that best completes each sentence. Be advised, each term will only be used once.

code signature	input validation
code signing	sandboxing
dynamic code analysis	secure cookies
fuzzing	static code analysis
Hypertext Transfer Protocol (HTTP) header	

1. ____ is a program configuration where input fields reject characters that do not match its function.

2. A(n) ____ is a block of data that utilizes information used during its transmission.

3. ____ are temporary Internet files set with a secure flag or attribute.

4. ____ is an automated testing tactic that attempts to find errors or bugs in implementation code that could be faulty to avoid malicious attacks.

5. Prior to executing program code, ____ is performed to analyze the code for vulnerabilities or errors, such as unsafe libraries or input validation.

6. ____ is the action of adding a signature to the application.

7. ____ is conducted after the program is running and bugs or errors in the program's code are sought.

8. ____ is the process of running software in an isolated environment so any uncovered errors are not spread or replicated to other devices.

9. A(n) ____ is included in code to verify authenticity and integrity.

10. ____ is the process of modifying or restructuring existing code without changing external behavior.

Name _____

Practice 7.3

For each of the following application attacks, match the term to its correct description. Be advised, each term will only be used once.

A. application programming interface (API) attacks
B. buffer overflow
C. cross-site scripting (XSS)
D. directory traversal
E. driver manipulation
F. error handling
G. integer overflow
H. memory leak

I. pointer/object dereference
J. privilege escalation
K. race conditions
L. request forgeries
M. resource exhaustion
N. secure sockets layer (SSL) stripping
O. shimming

1. _____ Occurs when attackers insert client-side scripts into pages of a trusted website

2. _____ Software vulnerability that occurs when two simultaneous lines of executable code attempt to access a shared resource

3. _____ Exploitation of coding errors, or other design flaws, that allows users to obtain elevated access that would otherwise be restricted

4. _____ Attack that occurs when a hacker impersonates and forges a malicious session with a server

5. _____ Form of attack that takes place when a threat actor accesses and modifies device drivers in an operating system to obtain access and control of a device

6. _____ Vulnerability that occurs when a value has not been obtained from the correct area, such as a variable in memory

7. _____ Occurs when there is more of a buffer than physical memory can handle and the remaining data spills into an adjacent area of memory

8. _____ Vulnerability that is exposed when allocated memory is not available for a program, even when the program is completed

9. _____ Attack in which hackers are able to obtain access beyond the web server's root directory and execute commands

10. _____ Attack that occurs when required computer resources are prevented from executing

11. _____ Practice of using a library of compiled code and driver shim to force an application to run on a program for which it was not intended

12. _____ Occurs when measures are taken to ensure that an application is capable of responding or recovering from an error

13. _____ Condition in which an arithmetic operation results in a number that is larger than the space for which memory has been allocated

14. _____ Set of tools and programs that enables interactions between applications and components and provides communications between a client and server

15. _____ Attack in which a threat actor removes the encryption protection from an HTTPS transmission without the user's knowledge

Practice 7.4

For each of the following social engineering, network design, attack, and application development techniques, match the term to its correct description. Be advised, each term will only be used once.

A. automation/scripting

B. domain hijacking

C. elasticity

D. environment

E. integrity measurement

F. Open Web Application Security Project (OWASP)

G. provisioning and deprovisioning

H. scalability

I. typo squatting

J. version control

K. web application firewall (WAF)

1. _____ Forms of attack that occurs when a connection between a domain name and web server is changed via the domain name registration without authorized permission

2. _____ Social engineering attack in which a hacker registers a domain name that is similar to a known and trusted website to take advantage of individuals who insert typographical errors when entering a web address

3. _____ Describes the ability of an application to adapt to change dynamically

4. _____ Describes the ability of a program to change how it copes with increased loads and being able to continue functioning as needed

5. _____ Used to protect web applications by monitoring HTTP traffic between applications and the Internet

6. _____ Nonprofit organization that provides free, unbiased information regarding application security

7. _____ Measurement and identification of any changes made to a system in comparison to its baseline

8. _____ Software-based resources utilized to host an application

9. _____ Practice of tracking changes made to a file

10. _____ Key principle for DevOps that provides the functionality of technology without human interaction and can provide the functionality without human interaction through resources, such as files that contain the commands for the technology's functionality

11. _____ Development resources used in application development in which one provides access and resources to members of an organization for their work and the other is used for the removal of the resources when they are no longer needed

Practice 7.5

For each of the following web and application attacks, match the term to its correct description. Be advised, each term will only be used once.

A. cross-site request forgery (CSRF)

B. clickjacking

C. client-side request forgery

D. client-side validation/execution

E. injection attack

F. man-in-the-browser (MITB) attack

G. null pointer exception

H. server-side validation/execution

I. session hijacking

J. SQL injection attack

K. XML injection

1. _____ Malicious attack that tricks a victim into clicking a concealed link

2. _____ Exploits web applications that use Extensible Markup Language

3. _____ Occurs when a victim's Internet browser is hijacked, resulting in alterations to web pages, transaction content, or preferences

4. _____ Occurs when an attacker is able to exploit computer sessions and access data

5. _____ Used as an input validation that is confirmed by a client web browser

6. _____ Used as an input validation that is confirmed by a server

7. _____ Exploits vulnerabilities on a client's device by targeting gaps in a device's web browser

8. _____ Occurs when NULL is stored in a valid memory area sought by hackers to perform buffer overflows or dereference attacks

9. _____ Occurs when an attacker inputs SQL-formatted commands in a user-input field

10. _____ Tricks a web browser into executing unwanted actions of an application to which a user is logged in

11. _____ Attack in which the threat actor is able to provide inputs that will exploit vulnerabilities in an application

Practice 7.6

For each of the following coding techniques, match the term to its correct description. Be advised, each term will only be used once.

A. application development
B. binary
C. camouflaged code
D. compiler
E. data canary

F. dead code/code reuse
G. manual code review
H. obfuscation
I. script

1. _____ Process that entails a user, often a white-hat pen tester, reading every line of a program's code

2. _____ Practice of using code that has been used before for a new application and discarding code that is no longer used or useful

3. _____ File in which content must be interpreted by a program or hardware processor that knows in advance how the file is formatted

4. _____ File capable of performing a variety of automated tasks

5. _____ Tactic to masking something to make it unclear

6. _____ Refers to code written in a way to make it unclear in an effort to prevent reverse engineering

7. _____ Value placed at the end of a buffer space

8. _____ Used to verify whether or not code syntax will execute as planned

9. _____ Process in which a computer program is designed, programmed, tested, and quality controlled

Practice 7.7

For each of the following development model and techniques, choose the term that best completes each sentence. Be advised, each term will only be used once.

agile model	software development life cycle (SDLC)
application security (AppSec)	software diversity
DevOps	waterfall model
software development kit (SDK)	

1. _____ is a philosophy that incorporates security into products and follows the principles of Infrastructure as Code (IaC).

   _____

2. The _____ of software development uses team collaboration to evolve upon their projects.

   _____

3. A collection of development tools that are combined in one package is called a(n) _____.

   _____

4. Developers can ensure software and applications are free from vulnerabilities before they go into production by following the _____ process.

   _____

5. The _____ of software development follows a step-by-step process for project implementations.

   _____

6. _____ is the practice of transferring software into various forms.

   _____

7. The conceptual process used to create, deploy, and maintain software applications is called a(n) _____.

   _____

Practice 7.8

For each of the following terms, match the term to its correct description. Be advised, each term will only be used once.

A. data exposure

B. DLL injection

C. integer overflow attack

D. load balancer

E. normalization

F. server-side request forgery (SSRF)

1. _____ Attack in which an attacker is able to access a server that generates HTTP requests to a targeted website

2. _____ Used to insert code into a running program to force the program to load the DLL

3. _____ Condition in which an operation results in a number that is too large to be stored in memory space allocated for the result

4. _____ Process of organizing data in a database to augment performance

5. _____ Network device that sends requests to multiple servers based on predefined factors

6. _____ Exposure of confidential information to others

CHAPTER 8
Mobile Devices and Embedded Systems

The rise in mobile computing platforms and wireless opportunities presents a unique challenge to ensuring the security posture of an enterprise environment. The increase in mobile, embedded, and specialized devices has resulted in an increase in efforts made to secure them. Addressing security issues in nontraditional systems, such as mobile and specialized systems, is a vital step in data security because these systems typically connect to or interface with an organization's computer network. Due to their unique operational methods, additional layers of security are often needed to support the use of mobile and embedded systems.

To adhere to the passing requirements of the CompTIA Security+ Certification Exam, you should be able to summarize how members of an organization utilize their mobile devices. In this chapter, you will demonstrate your understanding of methods used to secure mobile device usage and determine secure operation of devices in terms of organizational, user, and data safety. Additionally, you will test your knowledge regarding embedded systems and their security needs.

The practice sets in this chapter will help enhance your knowledge of the theories and philosophies presented in the corresponding textbook chapter. As such, complete each of the following activities to the best of your ability. Make note of the questions or terms you find to be the most difficult so you may revisit those concepts at a later date.

Practice 8.1

For each of the following secure mobile solutions and mobile device and connection management methods, choose the term that best completes each sentence. Be advised, each term will only be used once.

Bluetooth	mobile device
bring your own device (BYOD)	mobile device management (MDM)
cellular	remote wipe
choose your own device (CYOD)	USB
company-owned, personally enabled (COPE)	Wi-Fi

1. ____ allows members and guests of an organization to use their personal devices to conduct their work while on the organization's network.

_____

2. A ____ is a device used to conduct business operations remotely.

_____

3. In a ____ model, the organization owns and provides mobile devices their employees use to conduct work.

_____

4. When an organization provides a list of mobile devices their members may use on their network, it is utilizing a ____ deployment model.

_____

5. ____ networks provide connectivity for mobile devices to transfer and obtain data using the same type of connection as a cell phone.

_____

6. When a mobile device is connected to a computer via a ____ port, synchronization of data may occur automatically; as such, it is not encouraged as a data transfer method.

_____

7. ____ is a short-range wireless connectivity method that allows mobile devices to transmit and obtain data from other mobile devices.

_____

8. Most mobile devices are able to connect to an organization's network through ____, which uses radio waves instead of cabling.

_____

9. ____ is a set of software tools that provide a form of single management control to secure devices remotely.

_____

10. A remote-erase feature that, when activated, returns a device to its original factory settings is called ____.

_____

Practice 8.2

For each of the following account management, authentication, and authorization terms, match the term to its correct description. Please be advised, the terms will only be used once.

A. conditional access
B. hardware security module (HSM)
C. impossible travel time restriction
D. lockout
E. password vault

F. time-based login
G. USB OTG
H. Wi-Fi ad-hoc network
I. Wi-Fi direct
J. zero-level formatting

1. _____ Software that contains passwords for various resources but must be installed on each device a user will use

2. _____ Wireless network in which two or more devices connect to one another directly instead of communicating through a wireless router or access point

3. _____ Enables authentication of users by detecting the user's normal login activities and accounts for the user being in different time zones if they travel to various locations

4. _____ Wireless connection that allows device-to-device communication without the use of a centralized network; instead, one device acts as an AP, and the other uses WPS and WPA/WPA2 encryption

5. _____ Safeguard that does not allow a user to obtain access to organizational recourses if the system detects that the user has traveled between locations in a faster time than anticipated

6. _____ Enables multiple mobile devices to be connected without using a computer

7. _____ Process in which new data is written over existing data to destroy the existing data

8. _____ Configuration and control of an organization's devices to determine if the devices will obtain granted access to services and locations

9. _____ Device that employs cryptography to store encryption keys and cryptographic functions and can be implemented into microSD cards for mobile devices

10. _____ Should be utilized after multiple unsuccessful attempts to log into a system

Name _____

◼ Practice 8.3

For each of the following, match the term to its correct description. Please be advised, the terms will only be used once.

A. containerization
B. embedded system
C. jailbreaking
D. Raspberry Pi
E. real-time operating system (RTOS)

F. rooting
G. sideloading
H. static code
I. system control and data acquisition (SCADA)
J. system on a chip (SoC)

1. _____ Combination of hardware and software contained within a larger device used to complete a specific task

2. _____ Low-cost, single-board computer the size of a credit card and powered by a system on a chip

3. _____ Used to authenticate users on devices such as multifunction printers

4. _____ Process of installing applications from one device to another instead of using an official app-distribution method

5. _____ Process of bypassing device restrictions on an Android device to access administrator-level privileges

6. _____ Embedded system that monitors and controls machines and equipment

7. _____ Firmware on a system on a chip in an embedded system

8. _____ Integrated circuit for the central processing unit, memory, storage, and input/output ports on an individual chip

9. _____ Separation of various data types into separate storage pools, called *containers* or *lockers*, so storage can be managed separately

10. _____ Process of allowing an iOS device to bypass device restrictions

Practice 8.4

For each of the following mobile device feature, or service descriptions, choose the term that best completes each sentence. Be advised, each term will only be used once.

carrier unlocking	screen lock
cellular network	Security Enhancements for Android (SEAndroid)
multimedia messaging service (MMS)	short messaging service (SMS)
push notification service	tethering
rich communication services (RCS)	

1. ____ is a text messaging service for cellular devices that allows users to send up to 160 characters but is vulnerable to text-based social engineering techniques.

_____

2. A ____ is a wireless network that transmits over geographical areas called *cells*.

_____

3. A mobile device communication protocol that provides the ability to transmit group-chats and in-call media is called ____.

_____

4. A ____ can be enabled on a computer or mobile device to require a form of authentication to obtain access.

_____

5. A legal process called ____ allows a mobile device user to disconnect the device, primarily a phone, from a specific provider's network.

_____

6. ____ enable mobile device users are able to receive messages with that are managed through an MDM without human intervention.

_____

7. A mobile messaging service called ____ enables message contents to include photos, videos, or audio formats.

_____

8. ____ allows an Internet-enabled mobile device to provide online communications via wireless and Bluetooth connections.

_____

9. ____ is mobile security that is designed for Android devices to prohibit apps from accessing sensitive data and other resources on the device.

_____

Practice 8.5

For each of the following embedded device and system terms, match the term to its correct description. Please be advised, the terms will only be used once.

A. Arduino

B. custom firmware

C. drone

D. firmware OTA update

E. industrial control system (ICS)

F. multifunctional printer (MFP)

G. smart device

H. smart meter

I. smart sensor

J. wearable technology

1. _____ Can record information, such as a user's home electrical use, to provide utility companies a measurement of used power

2. _____ Patch or updates distributed by wireless providers over the air

3. _____ Umbrella term that describes the integrated systems, tools, and instrumentation used to operate industrial processes.

4. _____ IoT devices that are able to connect to wireless networks and can be perceived as a security threat if not monitored and used properly

5. _____ Generated through a third party that provides new functionalities to mobile devices

6. _____ Unmanned, remote-controlled devices that can fly autonomously

7. _____ Autonomous computing devices that can perform context-aware functions

8. _____ Open-source platform and device used to create electrical projects through its single-board microcontroller and software applications

9. _____ Embedded system that can provide data regarding the device's surroundings and changes of environment

10. _____ Device capable of printing, scanning, and faxing documentation

Practice 8.6

For each of the following, match the term to its correct description. Please be advised, the terms will only be used once.

A. application management

B. context-aware authentication

C. facility automation

D. hotspot

E. mobile application management (MAM)

F. mobile client management (MCM)

G. unified endpoint management (UEM)

H. virtualization

I. Voice over IP (VoIP)

J. vulnerable business process

1. _____ Automatic or electronic control for monitoring of systems vital for facility operation, such as lighting, surveillance, energy management, and HVAC systems

2. _____ Control of apps and distribution through centralized tools and services

3. _____ Allows administers to block apps on mobile devices that contain sensitive data

4. _____ Provides an organization control of their mobile devices and how they access data located on company systems

5. _____ Business activities that can be easily exploited by a threat actor

6. _____ Software tools that provide management for multiple device types, including mobile devices, computers, and other Internet-enabled devices

7. _____ Uses situational information to verify a user

8. _____ Provides services via an Internet connection rather than having to install an OS or applications manually

9. _____ Provides Internet access in public locations but often lacks security

10. _____ Enables telephone communications over a network

CHAPTER 9
Introduction to Cryptography

Cryptography is used to secure information using mathematical algorithms to mask data so only those with the decryption key are able to process and understand the message. Data encryption is a vital part of securing data and networks. In the event all physical controls fail, encrypted data will remain encrypted and safe from interception and exploitation.

To adhere to the passing requirements of the CompTIA Security+ Certification Exam, you need to differentiate the theories and philosophies surrounding cryptography and encryption. In this chapter, you will demonstrate your understanding of cryptographic topics, including symmetric encryption, asymmetric encryption, and methods of hiding messages via steganography.

The practice sets in this chapter will help enhance your knowledge of the theories and philosophies presented in the corresponding textbook chapter. As such, complete each of the following activities to the best of your ability. Make note of the questions or terms you find to be the most difficult so you may revisit those concepts at a later date.

Practice 9.1

For each of the following threats and attacks, match the term to its correct description. Be advised, each term will only be used once.

A. man in the middle

B. pass the hash

C. password attacks

D. password crackers

1. _____ Uses dictionary attacks, brute-force attacks, rainbow tables, plaintext, and pass-the-hash practices to obtain a password from a user's login credentials

2. _____ Occurs when a sender's communications are intercepted and a fabricated or forged response is sent back to the sender

3. _____ Programs used on a device or application that compares potential passwords against hashes.

4. _____ Attack in which a hacker intercepts a message, sends it to a remote system, and uses the message's data to appear as an authenticated user

Practice 9.2

For each of the following cybersecurity concepts and implementations, choose the term that best completes each sentence. Be advised, each term will only be used once.

cryptography	data-in-use
data-at-rest	encryption
data-in-transit	masking

1. _____ refers to when data is stored on a computer or network.

_____

2. The transformation of data into a form that only the intended recipient can understand and process is _____.

_____

3. _____ refers to the data transmission over a network during a session.

_____

4. _____ occurs when plaintext data is transformed into ciphertext.

_____

5. The assurance that when data is being transferred amongst entities, it will appear unclear and keep its integrity is called _____ and is utilized in forms of cryptography.

_____

6. _____ refers to data actively being used via a personal computer or system memory.

_____

Practice 9.3

For each of the following cryptographic concepts, match the term to its correct description. Be advised, each term will only be used once.

A. asymmetric
B. cipher suite
C. elliptical-curve cryptography
D. ephemeral
E. hashing
F. homomorphic encryption
G. key exchange
H. key length

I. key stretching
J. perfect forward secrecy
K. post-quantum cryptography
L. quantum computing
M. salting
N. steganography
O. symmetric

1. _____ Combination of message authentication code, encryption, and authentication algorithms that utilize TLS and SSL connections between a browser and server

2. _____ Encryption method that uses a single key to encrypt and decrypt data

3. _____ Process of hiding a message in text, files, or images

4. _____ Number of bits in a cryptographic algorithm's key and determines the ease or difficulty of the key being compromised

5. _____ Augments the difficulty of a password being compromised by adding random numeric values at the end of a password

6. _____ Process in which a cryptographic key is shared between a sender and receiver

7. _____ Cryptographic security feature that changes from one encrypted conversation to another during the data transmission or after the message has been sent

8. _____ Enables computing bits to exist in more than only one state

9. _____ Measure that secures against attacks generated from a quantum computer

10. _____ Security practice in which users make their passwords more complex, longer, and more difficult to crack

11. _____ Mathematical equation that generates a value based on its data

12. _____ Encryption method that uses two mathematically related keys to encrypt and decrypt data

13. _____ Key that is only used once

14. _____ Bases encryption off elliptical curve rather than prime numbers

15. _____ Enables ciphertext to be analyzed, searched, and modified without needing to decrypt the information

◼ Practice 9.4

For each of the following symmetric encryption concepts, match the term to its correct description. Be advised, each term will only be used once.

A. Advanced Encryption Standard (AES)

B. block cipher

C. blowfish cryptography

D. Data Encryption Standard (DES)

E. preshared symmetric key (PSK)

F. Triple DES (3DES) cryptography

1. _____ Encrypts blocks of data in a fixed size at one time, usually 64 or 128 bits.

2. _____ Symmetric block cipher that requires 128-, 192-, or 256-bit keys for encryption

3. _____ Symmetric key algorithm that requires keys to be 56 bits in length and offers 70 quadrillion possibilities

4. _____ Symmetric key block cipher that uses DES encryption but uses two or three keys for a stronger algorithm

5. _____ Free symmetric algorithm originally designed to replace DES

6. _____ Secret value that is previously shared between two parties in symmetric encryption

◼ Practice 9.5

For each of the following asymmetric encryption concepts, match the term to its correct description. Be advised, each term will only be used once.

A. key pair

B. public key

C. private key

1. _____ Key that needs protection

2. _____ Private and public key combination

3. _____ Does not require protection

Practice 9.6

For each of the following encryption concepts and implementations, choose the term that best completes each sentence. Be advised, each term will only be used once.

bcrypt	key-stretching algorithm
ciphertext	nonce
entropy	Password-based Key Derivation Function 2 (PBKDF2)
hash-based message authentication code (HMAC)	substitution cipher
key strength	transposition cipher

1. ____ refers to the degree of randomness with which a key is created.

2. The resiliency of a key's ability to withstand an attack is known as ____.

3. ____ is disguised or encoded information.

4. A(n) ____ provides the cryptographic key and hash for the authentication of the sender.

5. A(n) ____ is a unique number that is only used once in a communication.

6. An algorithm that limits an attacker's ability to decipher passwords due to the increased time to create a digest is considered a(n) ____.

7. ____ refers to key-stretching methods that use pseudorandom functions to add salt to a password.

8. A(n) ____ is a cryptographic algorithm that replaces each letter or character of a word with a different letter or character.

9. A cipher based off the Blowfish cipher used in Linux is ____.

10. A(n) ____ rearranges letters in each word of text.

▰ Practice 9.7

For each of the following password attacks and implementations, choose the term that best completes each sentence. Be advised, each term will only be used once.

brute-force attack	NTLM hash
dictionary attack	password spraying
hash table	plaintext
LM hash	Security Account Manager (SAM)

1. Microsoft's most recent password-encryption method is ____.

_____

2. ____ is a cryptographic attack that attempts to access a large number of user account names with only a few commonly used passwords.

_____

3. During a(n) ____, a threat actor attempts every possible combination of letters, numbers, and special characters.

_____

4. A data set that contains cracked passwords with preconstructed hashes is called a(n) ____.

_____

5. The ____ is a local database of users and groups on a Windows system.

_____

6. ____ is an old method of encrypting local passwords that was used on pre-Windows NT systems.

_____

7. ____ refers to the original form of a message before encryption.

_____

8. In a(n) ____, a threat actor uses software to create a list of words and precomputed hash values to determine a user's password.

_____

Practice 9.8

For each of the following cryptographic attacks, implementations, and limitations, match the term to its correct description. Be advised, each term will only be used once.

A. birthday attack

B. collisions

C. cryptographic attacks

D. downgrade attack

E. high resiliency

F. hybrid cryptography

G. low latency

H. quantum communications

I. quantum cryptography

J. security through obscurity

K. session key

1. _____ Mathematical theory that believes a pair of individuals in a group will share the same day of birth

2. _____ Occurs when a hacker forces a system to switch to a less-secure cryptographic standard

3. _____ Errors that occur when two outputs provide the same message digest

4. _____ Refers to the ability to transfer data via small particles of light through a fiber-optic line

5. _____ Able to merge from both symmetric and asymmetric cryptography

6. _____ Practice of making data not appear as something an attacker would want to decipher

7. _____ Refers to the processing of data with little delays during its transmissions

8. _____ Ability to recovery from a failure quickly

9. _____ Uses quantum mechanics to encrypt data

10. _____ Attacks that attempt to break secrecy of encrypted data

11. _____ Symmetric key used for integrity during a session between a sender and receiver

CHAPTER 10
Public Key Infrastructure

Cryptographic algorithms are useful for protecting data and its confidentiality, but it is not realistic to employ symmetric encryption for data in large organizations or across the Internet. Furthermore, asymmetric encryption can be difficult due to the difficulty in confirming the organization contacting you is the same one providing the key. Public key infrastructure (PKI) utilizes concepts such as certificates in addition to ciphers and cryptographic protocols to help secure transmission of data across public networks.

To adhere to the passing requirements of the CompTIA Security+ Certification Exam, you need to understand cryptographic concepts, implement secure protocols, and apply public key infrastructure. In this chapter, you will demonstrate your understanding of topics such as Transport Layer Security (TLS), digital signatures, and certificates.

The practice sets in this chapter will help enhance your knowledge of the theories and philosophies presented in the corresponding textbook chapter. As such, complete each of the following activities to the best of your ability. Make note of the questions or terms you find to be the most difficult so you may revisit those concepts at a later date.

Practice 10.1

For each of the following, choose the term that best completes each sentence. Be advised, each term will only be used once.

Hypertext Transfer Protocol over SSL/TLS (HTTPS)	Secure Shell (SSH)
IPSec	Secure Sockets Layer (SSL)
Secure/Multipurpose Internet Mail Exchanger (S/MIME)	Transport Layer Security (TLS)
Secure Real-Time Protocol (SRTP)	

1. ____ is a protocol that encrypts data by using cryptographic functions to secure data that is traveling over networks that use the TCP/IP protocol.

_____

2. ____ is a secure extension for Real-Time Transport Protocol (RTP) that protects communications made via Voice over IP (VoIP).

_____

3. An e-mail signing protocol used to increase the security of e-mail transactions is called ____.

_____

4. The ____ protocol uses cryptography to provide data security amongst networked computers.

_____

5. ____ is a secure protocol that uses remote administrative management of servers, routers, switches, and other devices.

_____

6. Authentication can be accomplished between two computers by employing the ____ protocol.

_____

7. An Internet browsing session can be secured using ____.

_____

Practice 10.2

For each of the following terms regarding cryptographic concepts, account management controls, and public key infrastructure (PKI), match the term to its correct description. Be advised, each term will only be used once.

A. blockchain

B. digital certificate

C. digital signature

D. public key infrastructure (PKI)

E. SSH keys

1. _____ Computed value that provides encryption, validity, and trustworthiness during data transmissions

2. _____ Electronic file that is digitally signed to verify that a public key belongs to a person or entity

3. _____ Utilized to link a list of records together using cryptography

4. _____ Set of two keys used to confirm an individual's identity

5. _____ Set of policies, hardware, and procedures necessary to create, store, or revoke public keys used in digital certificates.

Practice 10.3

For each of the following terms regarding certificate formats, match the term to its correct description. Be advised, each term will only be used once.

A. Canonical Encoding Rules Certificate (CER)

B. Distinguished Encoding Rules (DER)

C. Object Identifier (OID)

D. Personal Information Exchange (PFX)

E. PKCS#12

F. PKCS#7

G. Privacy Enhanced Mail (PEM)

H. Public Key Cryptography Standards (PKCS)

I. X.509

1. _____ Certificate type that provides confidentiality to e-mail messages

2. _____ Creates certificates for authentication

3. _____ Defines the file format for private keys that correspond to their public key certificate

4. _____ Encodes data with Base 64 (ASCII characters) to change data

5. _____ Numeric value that identifies a service for which the certificate is being used

6. _____ Set of standards published by RSA security

7. _____ Encodes a public key in binary code

8. _____ Encrypts messages under a PKI

9. _____ Format used for public certificates to guarantee consistent formatting

Practice 10.4

For each of the following terms regarding certificate types, authority, signing request, trust model, and revocation methods, match the term to its correct description. Be advised, each term will only be used once.

A. certificate authority (CA)

B. certificate chaining

C. certificate management

D. certificate-signing request (CSR)

E. certification revocation list (CRL)

F. Online Certificate Status Protocol (OCSP)

G. path validation

H. pinning

I. root certificate

J. trust model

1. _____ Trusted third-party source responsible for the issuing and validating of certificates

2. _____ Process and procedures taken to be sure that digital certificates are current and stored correctly

3. _____ Signed by an issuing CA and is the highest point in the chain of trust for certificate authorities

4. _____ Requests a digital certificate that contains the applicant's public key and integrity information

5. _____ Occurs when one certificate is linked to another for an established trust between them

6. _____ List of all canceled certificates

7. _____ Ensures the public key that is being provided is valid

8. _____ Relationship among parties; uses a hierarchical-trust model in which there is only one master CA

9. _____ Verifies that a digital certificate is safe and will not be revoked

10. _____ Protocol that obtains the status of a certificate

Practice 10.5

For each of the following, choose the term that best completes each sentence. Be advised, each term will only be used once.

Cipher Block Chaining (CBC)	Electronic Codebook (ECB)
common name (CN)	intermediate CA
Counter Mode (CTR)	key escrow
cryptographic modules	PKI management
cryptographic service provider (CSP)	registration authority (RA)

1. ____ is the encryption model that performs randomization on a key.

2. ____ is the managing of certificates, storing and authoring keys, and other tasks that ensure the safety of keys.

3. The hardware or software-based library that encodes and decodes functions so encryption algorithms can be executed is a(n) ____.

4. The ____ consist of hardware, software, and firmware that perform the cryptographic functions.

5. ____ uses block cipher modes of operation to mandate the sender and receiver of a message and generates a new value each time a cipher block is exchanged.

6. A cryptographic mode in which a message is divided into blocks and each block is separately encrypted using the same key is called ____.

7. A trusted third party that manages keys is called a(n) ____.

8. A(n) ____ is capable of validating signatures.

9. The fully qualified domain name (FQDN) of a web server that receives a certificate is also referred to as its ____.

10. A(n) ____ verifies certificate-signing requests and informs a CA to issue a digital certificate.

Practice 10.6

For each of the following terms regarding SSL/TLS, trust models, and blockchains, match the term to its correct description. Be advised, each term will only be used once.

A. distributed-trust model

B. Galois/Counter Mode (GCM)

C. SSL decryptor

D. SSL/TLS accelerator

E. SSL/TLS handshake process

1. _____ Process of verifying digital certificates based on asymmetric encryption

2. _____ Device dedicated to the decryption of SSL traffic, such as a firewall

3. _____ Typically, a hardware card installed on a server and contains dedicated processing capabilities for SSL/TLS transactions

4. _____ Distributes certificates amongst several intermediate CAs

5. _____ Encrypts and process Message Authentication Codes (MACs)

Notes

CHAPTER 11 | Command-Line Interface Management

Managing devices and systems through a command-line interface is an important technical skill. Using the command-line, as opposed to a GUI, often provides more control, functionality, and management options. For example, the Windows **ipconfig** command returns information about a network connection that is not available through the graphical interface.

To adhere to the passing requirements of the CompTIA Security+ Certification Exam, you need to understand command-line interface management. Furthermore, it is important that you understand which commands are specific to Windows and Linux operating systems. In this chapter, you will demonstrate your understanding of command-line utilities, usage of a CLI, and various commands used for security.

The practice sets in this chapter will help enhance your knowledge of the theories and philosophies presented in the corresponding textbook chapter. As such, complete each of the following activities to the best of your ability. Make note of the questions or terms you find to be the most difficult so you may revisit those concepts at a later date.

Practice 11.1

For each of the following, match the term to its correct description. Be advised, each term will only be used once.

A. hard link
B. **ifconfig**
C. **ipconfig**
D. OpenSSL
E. PowerShell
F. Python
G. symbolic link
H. **route**
I. **tracert**
J. wildcard character

1. _____ Used to represent one or more unknown characters in a string of text

2. _____ Open-source command-line tool used by network administrators for cryptographic management

3. _____ Used to display the path a data packet takes across a network in Windows

4. _____ Points directly to the original data

5. _____ Enables you to point to a link, not directly to the original data

6. _____ Multipurpose programming language that allows developers and administrators to create scripts to perform tasks

7. _____ Enables a user to view and modify the local routing table in Windows

8. _____ Able to replace the need of **cmd.exe** and is a powerful command-line shell

9. _____ Displays all current devices connected to a network and its TCP/IP configuration values in Windows

10. _____ Displays all current devices connected to a network and its TCP/IP configuration values in Linux

Practice 11.2

For each of the following, match the term to its correct description. Be advised, each term will only be used once.

A. **arp**

B. **dig**

C. **nslookup**

D. **pathping**

E. **ping**

1. _____ Displays information regarding network latency and the hops between the source and destination in Windows

2. _____ Displays information related to the domain name system in Linux

3. _____ Used to view and modify entries in the Address Resolution Protocol cache in Windows

4. _____ Used to test connections between two networked devices in both Windows and Linux

5. _____ Displays information related to the domain name system in Windows

Practice 11.3

For each of the following, choose the term that best completes each sentence. Be advised, each term will only be used once.

cat	**logger**
chmod	piping
grep	

1. _____ is the act of directing the results of one command into the input syntax of another command.

2. In Linux, a user can use the _____ command to change file and folder permissions.

3. Linux administrators seeking to make notes in the syslog file located in **/var/log** can do so using the _____ command.

4. The command used to view and create files, display contents of multiple files simultaneously, or redirect the contents of multiple files into a single file in Linux is called _____.

5. The _____ is used to search for plaintext data in Linux.

Practice 11.4

For each of the following CLI topics, match the term to its correct description. Be advised, each term will only be used once.

A. alias

B. cmdlets

C. command-line interface (CLI)

D. command prompt

E. method

1. _____ PowerShell instructions that determine the action to be performed on an object

2. _____ Text-based interface used to input and execute commands rather than using a mouse in a GUI environment

3. _____ Provides alternative cmdlet equivalents in a PowerShell environment

4. _____ Originated from DOS and allows a user in a Windows environment to input commands manually

5. _____ Executable programs in PowerShell

Practice 11.5

For each of the following Linux-based command-line items, match the term to its correct description. Be advised, each term will only be used once.

A. forked

B. home directory

C. Linux

D. open-source software

E. shell

1. _____ Location where a user may store personal files

2. _____ Refers to a program that is modified in order to create another program

3. _____ Refers to software that provides a method or running commands to a kernel

4. _____ Enables an administrator to develop scripts and run PowerShell on a Linux operating system

5. _____ Open-source operating system that uses terminal for its command-line interface

▰ Practice 11.6

For each of the following, choose the term that best completes each sentence. Be advised, each term will only be used once.

---

append	object
batch file	Windows Management Instrumentation (WMI)
hexadecimal numbering system	

---

1. A(n) ____ is a self-contained resource that stores information regarding itself in properties and provides program code that is used to interact with it.

    _____

2. ____ is a cmdlet that manages data and operations in a Windows environment.

    _____

3. A set of instructions generated from a list of commands that can be created via the Notepad program in a Windows environment is called a(n) ____.

    _____

4. To ____ data is to use the CLI to add to or modify data in an existing data set.

    _____

5. The ____ uses 16 characters that are generated from the sets of 0–9 and A–F and can be used to produce a background color in a command-line utility.

    _____

Practice 11.7

For each of the following, choose the term that best completes each sentence. Be advised, each term will only be used once.

current directory	property
device driver	provider
distro	service
process	switch

1. _____ refers to data that is embedded into an object.

2. In command-line interface environments, a _____ is a modifier that narrows possible results of a specific parameter.

3. A _____ is software that determines how hardware will operate.

4. A Linux kernel and tools used under the GNU is called a _____.

5. A _____ is a computer program that is actively operating.

6. The features and functionalities of a program are provided by a _____ that runs in the background of an operating system.

7. The present area where a user is interacting and working with data in a command-line interface is called the _____.

8. A _____ is a program that displays and organizes data to provide ease of use.

Practice 11.8

For each of the following command line outputs, match the command to its correct output. Be advised, each term will only be used once.

A. **dig**
B. **ipconfig**
C. **ping**
D. **traceroute**
E. **tracert**

1. _____

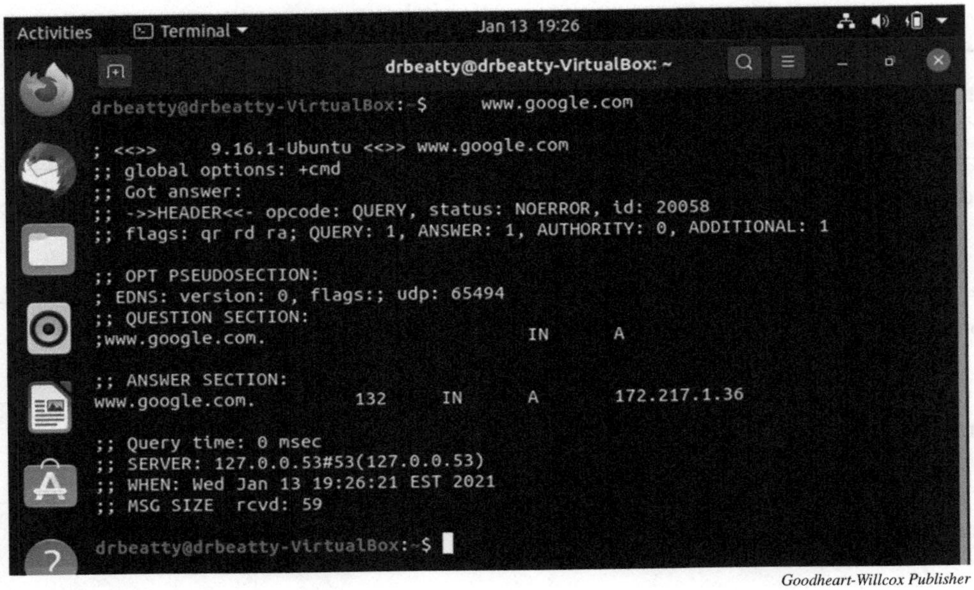

Activities
Terminal
Jan 13 19:26
drbeatty@drbeatty-VirtualBox: ~
drbeatty@drbeatty-VirtualBox:~$ www.google.com
; <<>> 9.16.1-Ubuntu <<>> www.google.com
;; global options: +cmd
;; Got answer:
;; ->>HEADER<<- opcode: QUERY, status: NOERROR, id: 20058
;; flags: qr rd ra; QUERY: 1, ANSWER: 1, AUTHORITY: 0, ADDITIONAL: 1
;; OPT PSEUDOSECTION:
; EDNS: version: 0, flags:; udp: 65494
;; QUESTION SECTION:
;www.google.com. IN A
;; ANSWER SECTION:
www.google.com. 132 IN A 172.217.1.36
;; Query time: 0 msec
;; SERVER: 127.0.0.53#53(127.0.0.53)
;; WHEN: Wed Jan 13 19:26:21 EST 2021
;; MSG SIZE rcvd: 59
drbeatty@drbeatty-VirtualBox:~$

Goodheart-Willcox Publisher

2. _____

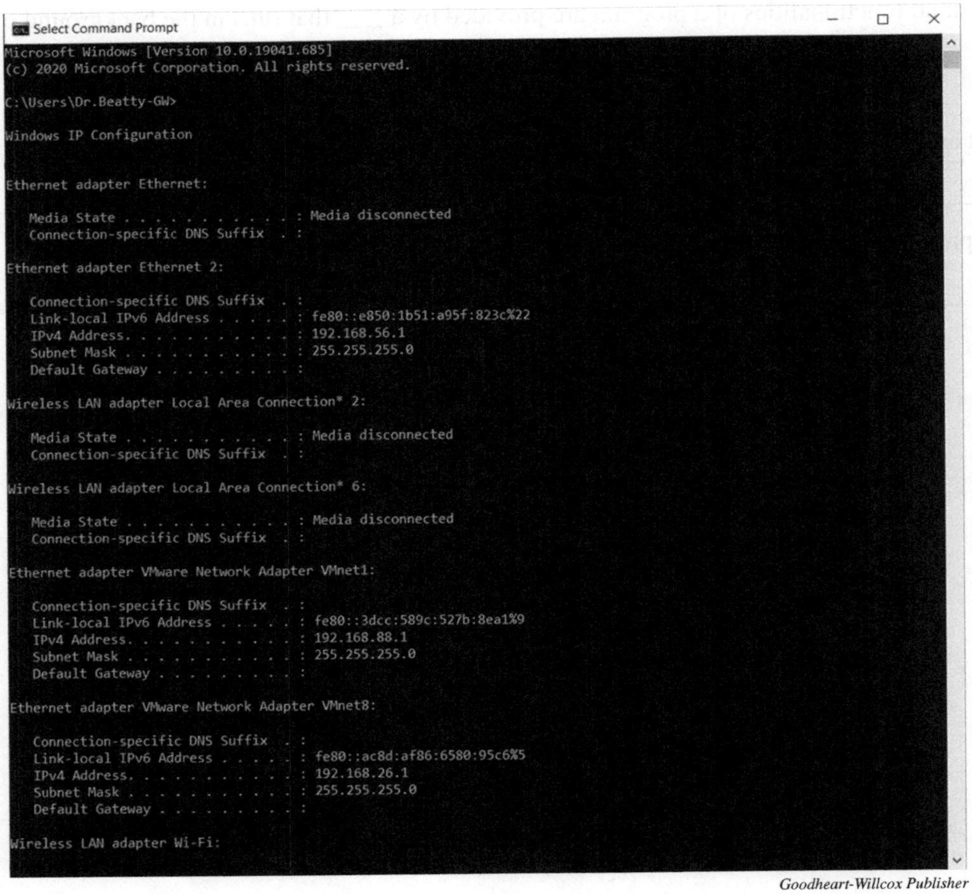

Select Command Prompt
Microsoft Windows [Version 10.0.19041.685]
(c) 2020 Microsoft Corporation. All rights reserved.
C:\Users\Dr.Beatty-GW>
Windows IP Configuration
Ethernet adapter Ethernet:
Media State . . . . : Media disconnected
Connection-specific DNS Suffix . :
Ethernet adapter Ethernet 2:
Connection-specific DNS Suffix . :
Link-local IPv6 Address . . . . . : fe80::e850:1b51:a95f:823c%22
IPv4 Address. . . . . : 192.168.56.1
Subnet Mask . . . . : 255.255.255.0
Default Gateway . . . . :
Wireless LAN adapter Local Area Connection* 2:
Media State . . . . : Media disconnected
Connection-specific DNS Suffix . :
Wireless LAN adapter Local Area Connection* 6:
Media State . . . . : Media disconnected
Connection-specific DNS Suffix . :
Ethernet adapter VMware Network Adapter VMnet1:
Connection-specific DNS Suffix . :
Link-local IPv6 Address . . . . . : fe80::3dcc:589c:527b:8ea1%9
IPv4 Address. . . . . : 192.168.88.1
Subnet Mask . . . . : 255.255.255.0
Default Gateway . . . . :
Ethernet adapter VMware Network Adapter VMnet8:
Connection-specific DNS Suffix . :
Link-local IPv6 Address . . . . . : fe80::ac8d:af86:6580:95c6%5
IPv4 Address. . . . . : 192.168.26.1
Subnet Mask . . . . : 255.255.255.0
Default Gateway . . . . :
Wireless LAN adapter Wi-Fi:

Goodheart-Willcox Publisher

3. _____

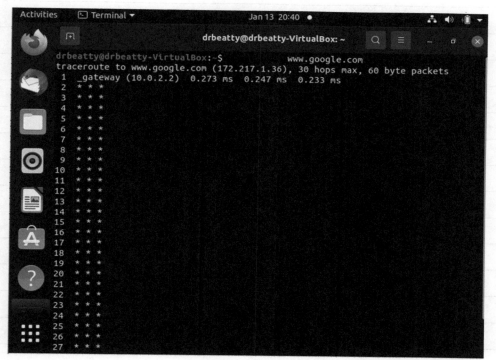

```
Command Prompt                                          −  □  ×
Microsoft Windows [Version 10.0.19041.685]
(c) 2020 Microsoft Corporation. All rights reserved.

C:\Users\Dr.Beatty-GW>        www.google.com

Pinging www.google.com [172.217.1.36] with 32 bytes of data:
Reply from 172.217.1.36: bytes=32 time=39ms TTL=118
Reply from 172.217.1.36: bytes=32 time=47ms TTL=118
Reply from 172.217.1.36: bytes=32 time=35ms TTL=118
Reply from 172.217.1.36: bytes=32 time=32ms TTL=118

Ping statistics for 172.217.1.36:
    Packets: Sent = 4, Received = 4, Lost = 0 (0% loss),
Approximate round trip times in milli-seconds:
    Minimum = 32ms, Maximum = 47ms, Average = 38ms

C:\Users\Dr.Beatty-GW>
```

Goodheart-Willcox Publisher

4. _____

```
Activities     Terminal ▾              Jan 13 20:40 ●

                    drbeatty@drbeatty-VirtualBox: ~     Q  ☰  _  □  ×

drbeatty@drbeatty-VirtualBox:~$          www.google.com
traceroute to www.google.com (172.217.1.36), 30 hops max, 60 byte packets
 1  _gateway (10.0.2.2)  0.273 ms  0.247 ms  0.233 ms
 2  * * *
 3  * * *
 4  * * *
 5  * * *
 6  * * *
 7  * * *
 8  * * *
 9  * * *
10  * * *
11  * * *
12  * * *
13  * * *
14  * * *
15  * * *
16  * * *
17  * * *
18  * * *
19  * * *
20  * * *
21  * * *
22  * * *
23  * * *
24  * * *
25  * * *
26  * * *
27  * * *
```

Goodheart-Willcox Publisher

5. _____

```
Command Prompt                                          −  □  ×
Microsoft Windows [Version 10.0.19041.685]
(c) 2020 Microsoft Corporation. All rights reserved.

C:\Users\Dr.Beatty-GW>        www.google.com

Tracing route to www.google.com [172.217.1.36]
over a maximum of 30 hops:

  1    3 ms    2 ms    2 ms  192.168.0.1
  2    *       *       *     Request timed out.
  3   58 ms   16 ms   13 ms  173-219-252-86.suddenlink.net [173.219.252.86]
  4   30 ms   40 ms   34 ms  173-219-218-150.suddenlink.net [173.219.218.150]
  5   32 ms   30 ms   43 ms  66-76-229-162.suddenlink.net [66.76.229.162]
  6  183 ms   57 ms   37 ms  108.170.246.67
  7   40 ms   43 ms   59 ms  216.239.48.101
  8   93 ms   39 ms   38 ms  209.85.252.46
  9   37 ms  164 ms   39 ms  216.239.63.32
 10   37 ms   46 ms   37 ms  108.170.244.1
 11   41 ms   39 ms   43 ms  216.239.41.161
 12   37 ms   34 ms   32 ms  ord37s07-in-f36.1e100.net [172.217.1.36]

Trace complete.

C:\Users\Dr.Beatty-GW>
```

Goodheart-Willcox Publisher

Notes

CHAPTER 12 / Secure Network Design

Implementation of secure network design can dictate the security of a network and connected devices. Integral devices such as routers and switches can be secured physically and digitally, but it is also important to include dedicated security devices such as firewalls and intrusion-detection or intrusion-prevention systems.

For you to adhere the passing requirements of the CompTIA Security+ Certification Exam, you need to be knowledgeable of secure network design. In this chapter, you will demonstrate your understanding of devices that are commonly encountered on a network, placement and usage of security devices, and basic network segmentation designs. While architecture and design of secure networks are the focus of this chapter, many protocols for a network's security will also be examined.

The practice sets in this chapter will help enhance your knowledge of the theories and philosophies presented in the corresponding textbook chapter. As such, complete each of the following activities to the best of your ability. Make note of the questions or terms you find to be the most difficult so you may revisit those concepts at a later date.

Practice 12.1

For each of the following threats, authentication methods, and authorization methods, choose the term that best completes the sentence. Be advised, each term will only be used once.

Challenge Handshake Authentication Protocol (CHAP)	Microsoft Challenge Handshake Authentication Protocol (MS-CHAP)
Extensible Authentication Protocol (EAP)	
media access control (MAC) flooding	Password Authentication Protocol (PAP)

1. Although it is not as commonly used today due to a lack of encryption, ____ relies on Point-to-Point Protocol (PPP) to validate users.

_____

2. Microsoft's version of the Challenge Handshake Authentication Protocol is called ____.

_____

3. ____ is an authentication protocol framework that outlines secure transport and usage of information and includes data from sources such as smart cards and biometric data.

_____

4. When multiple MAC addresses are assigned to one physical port on a switch, there is an increased risk of ____, which overwhelms the switch due to the number of requests it receives.

_____

5. ____ is a protocol that utilizes an authentication server issuing a challenge to a client after the client has established a connection to the server, and the client and server use a shared secret for authentication.

_____

Practice 12.2

For each of the following terms regarding security concepts and cybersecurity resilience, match the term to its correct description. Be advised, each term will only be used once.

A. configuration management (CM)
B. deception technology
C. geographical considerations

D. non-persistence
E. Secure Sockets Layer (SSL)/Transport Layer Security (TLS) inspection

1. _____ Dictates the constraints of a network's speed and functionality due to the distance between networking devices and considers how constraints could diminish functionality

2. _____ Describes the process of maintaining computers, servers, and applications in a designated area that can provide efficacy regardless of the changes that occur over time

3. _____ Intercepts traffic, decrypts the data, and scans the data for any malicious files or code, and creates a secure connection between a web browser and client

4. _____ Security tools and strategies designed to prevent a threat actor who has already breached a network from causing any damage

5. _____ Refers to actions are taken and configurations implemented to ensure unwanted data is not retained when new devices are added to a network

Practice 12.3

For each of the following secure protocols and network designs, match the term to its correct description. Please be advised, the terms will only be used once.

A. access control list (ACL)
B. aggregators
C. collectors
D. content filter
E. east-west traffic
F. IPSec
G. IPv6
H. jump server
I. Layer 2 Tunneling Protocol (L2TP)
J. load balancer
K. network address translation (NAT) Gateway
L. network segmentation
M. network-based intrusion detection system (NIDS)

N. open-source firewall
O. out-of-band management
P. point-to-point tunneling protocol (PPTP)
Q. port mirroring
R. port security
S. proxy firewall
T. proxy servers
U. Quality of Service (QoS)
V. stateful firewall
W. stateless firewall
X. unified threat management (UTM)
Y. virtual private network (VPN)

1. _____ Encrypts data by using cryptographic functions to secure data traveling over TCP/IP networks but is not able to be used on Windows clients prior to Windows 7 or Server 2008R2.

2. _____ Internet protocol that allows for 128-bit addressing

3. _____ Network connection that provides a way to encrypt data traveling through unsecured public networks

4. _____ Evenly distributes the needs of multiple servers

5. _____ Tunneling protocol used by ISPs to enable VPN operation over the Internet

6. _____ Provides the ability to manage and control infrastructure remotely using an interface separate from the primary connection

7. _____ Method of monitoring traffic by copying data packets from one switch port to another without altering or modifying the original data.

8. _____ Network appliance used to obtain access and manage devices from a separate security zone

9. _____ Device or service provider used to consolidate multiple devices or users via its own functionalities or by forwarding transmissions in a compressed or more efficient approach

10. _____ Act of isolating a network so it is not accessible to unauthorized individuals

11. _____ Security device that gathers information regarding network traffic and is placed where it is able to gather the largest-possible data stream

12. _____ Set of technologies that enable a network to run priority applications and deliver as expected regardless of limited capacity or connectivity

13. _____ Traffic-control feature that prohibits unauthorized devices from forwarding packets

14. _____ Software application that monitors attacks as they happen on the network

15. _____ Acts as a gateway between a local network and the Internet and operates at the application layer

16. _____ Utilized when a router manages traffic using lists of permissions associated with network objects

17. _____ Firewall that monitors packets over a period of time and will only accept previously tracked packets

18. _____ Refers to data that flows from one server to another within an organization's data center

19. _____ Firewall that protects a network based on source and destination addresses

20. _____ Type of firewall that enables users to access its source code

21. _____ Most outdated of the network protocols used to connect to a VPN

22. _____ Technology that is often incorporated in a firewall to monitor Internet traffic and prevent blacklisted websites, files, and services

23. _____ All-in-one security device that allows a network to be managed using one appliance

24. _____ Managed service that provides a connection between a local network and the Internet by translating IP addresses from private to public or public to private

25. _____ Security device that protects a network by filtering a packet's data as well as its header

Practice 12.4

For each of the following deception technologies, authentication methods, and authorization methods, choose the term that best completes the sentence. Be advised, each term will only be used once.

DNS sinkhole	honeynet
fake telemetry	honeypot
honeyfile	

1. A ____ uses a DNS server that prevents the resolution of host names of specific URLs.

_____

2. ____ is a technique that employs deception.

_____

3. A network that is purposefully established and configured to be vulnerable to study an attacker's habits when the network is being attacked is called a ____.

_____

4. A ____ is a fake file that is on a network folder share to observe how and when attackers try to access the file.

_____

5. A computer or server loaded with files or applications that appear to be authentic and placed in a network zone with limited security is called a ____.

_____

Practice 12.5

For each of the following network intrusion-detection, authentication, and authorization methods, choose the term that best completes the sentence. Be advised, each term will only be used once.

anomaly monitoring	out-of-band
heuristic-based monitoring	signature-based monitoring
in-band	

1. ____ detects the anomalies in a network's traffic statistics.

_____

2. Management that if accomplished through an IDS connected to a network is called ____ management.

_____

3. The ____ method utilizes an IDS with an access server connected to a management port on each device.

_____

4. The examination of network traffic to detect patterns and compare them against a signature database is called ____.

_____

5. ____ scans the processes of baseline behaviors to determine if a threat exists.

_____

Practice 12.6

For each of the following secure protocols and methods for networks, match the term to its correct description. Please be advised, the terms will only be used once.

A. aggregation switch

B. demilitarized zone (DMZ)

C. extranet

D. flood guard

E. guest network

F. intranet

G. IP spoofing

H. loop prevention

I. network address translation (NAT)

J. packet-filtering firewall

1. _____ Incorporation of protocols that prohibit a networking switch from creating a continuous loop that can flood a network

2. _____ Firewall that is able to examine every data packet and either forward or drop the packet(s) based off predefined rules

3. _____ Able to combine multiple network connections through one switch

4. _____ Remaps IP address of devices with a private IP address on a public network to public IP addresses

5. _____ Segmentation of certain network resources that border a private network, where public access is blocked

6. _____ Open network that is separated from a primary network and allows anyone to obtain access without authorization or permission

7. _____ Type of intranet that can be accessed by authorized users outside of an organization's network

8. _____ Occurs when an attacker creates a fake IP address for a local, trusted device in order to obtain access to a network

9. _____ Private Internet that is to be used for internal use only

10. _____ Firewall-type feature that limits the amount of memory a switch is able to use and store data for each port

Practice 12.7

For each of the following segregation protocols and methods for networks, match the term to its correct description. Please be advised, the terms will only be used once.

A. authentication header (AH)

B. encapsulating security payload (ESP)

C. Hypertext Markup Language version 5 (HTML5)

D. Internet Key Exchange Protocol version 2 (IKEv2)

E. transport mode

F. tunnel mode

G. tunneling

H. virtual local area network (VLAN)

I. VPN concentrator

J. zero trust

1. _____ Alternative to an Authentication Header (AH) that authenticates the header and encrypts data

2. _____ Security feature that authenticates the sender and determines if any changes need to occur during transmission; cannot be used with NAT

3. _____ IPSec mode that encrypts the IP header of an original packet

4. _____ IPSec mode that only encrypts the data and ESP information

5. _____ Allows remote users to be grouped among switches based on their defined group or functionality of the organization

6. _____ Process of using a VPN to encrypt data before transmitting the data amongst multiple networks

7. _____ Fifth standard for HTML and offers a secure remote access solution

8. _____ Tunneling protocol that uses IPSec tunneling protocol via UDP port 500 to establish a security association

9. _____ Device that collects VPN connections so it can deliver the traffic to the correct VPN node

10. _____ Security model in which no one from inside or outside a network is trusted by default

Practice 12.8

For each of the following, choose the term that best completes the sentence. Be advised, each term will only be used once.

BPDU guard	network interface card (NIC) teaming
broadcast storm	reverse proxy server
correlation engine	

1. A ____ is when there is a high amount of traffic on a network in a short period of time.

2. The combination of multiple network interface cards that functions as one network interface card for increased bandwidth and fault tolerance is called ____.

3. An internal-facing proxy that sits behind a firewall is considered a ____.

4. A software application that is programmed to understand relationships of a system is called a ____.

5. A ____ uses switch features such as STP/RSTP to prevent the sending of its methods.

Name _____

Practice 12.9

For each of the following, match the term to its correct description. Please be advised, the terms will only be used once.

A. antispoofing

B. Dynamic Host Configuration Protocol (DHCP) snooping

C. forward proxy server

D. microsegmentation

E. network TAP

F. north-south traffic

G. round-robin scheduling

H. security zone

I. virtual IP (VIP) address

J. VLAN access control list (VACL)

1. _____ Rotation of time permitted for a process to run that results in equal amounts of time applied to each process in a cyclic fashion without any priority

2. _____ Devices installed inside of a network to monitor traffic

3. _____ Flow of traffic from an organization's data center to an outside location

4. _____ Device identifiers that do not correspond to physical devices in a network

5. _____ Permissions set for packets that travel inside and outside of a VLAN

6. _____ Able to prohibit devices suspected of having fake addresses

7. _____ Internet-facing proxy that intercepts forward requests from a local network to the Internet

8. _____ Security technique that allows administrators to split a network's attack surface by dividing network segments based on workloads

9. _____ Layer-2 technology in a switch that prevents unauthorized servers from assigning IP addresses to devices on a network

10. _____ Section of a network that is segmented and has limited access to an organization's internal network

◼ Practice 12.10

For each of the following terms, choose the term that best completes the sentence. Be advised, each term will only be used once.

active-active configuration
active-passive configuration
affinity scheduling

Secure Socket Tunneling Protocol (SSTP)
security configuration management (SCM)

1. The process of distributing loads based on which device is best fit to handle a given load is called _____.

2. _____ is the management of configurations for a system to manage a risk.

3. The operational modality in which all load balancers are actively operating is called _____.

4. _____ is an operational modality in which one load balancer is responsible for distributing traffic and the other operates passively unless the first balancer fails.

5. _____ is a VPN tunneling protocol that supports traffic over an SSL/TLS encrypted connection.

Secure Network Administration

Many common services vital to network usage are inherently vulnerable. These services provide functionality such as logging in; accessing the Internet; and requesting or obtaining data, files, or resources. As such, it is of the utmost importance to ensure proper network administration. This often includes utilizing secure versions of essential protocols and identifying vulnerabilities and symptoms of network attacks.

To adhere to the passing requirements of the CompTIA Security+ Certification Exam, you should be able understand the items that are needed for secure network administration, know the common network attacks, and what data sources are utilized to support an investigation. In this chapter, you will demonstrate your understanding of secure network administration and the required resources to administer a network securely.

The practice sets in this chapter will help enhance your knowledge of the theories and philosophies presented in the corresponding textbook chapter. As such, complete each of the following activities to the best of your ability. Make note of the questions or terms you find to be the most difficult so you may revisit those concepts at a later date.

Practice 13.1

For each of the following secure protocols and secure network designs, choose the term that best completes the sentence. Be advised, each term will only be used once.

Domain Name System (DNS)	network access control (NAC)
file integrity monitor (FIM)	packet sniffer
monitoring services	

1. A ____ is a security control method that monitors modifications made to files on a computer and validates the integrity of the software including the operating system of the computer.

   _____

2. On both Windows and Linux, the ____ allows users to input a domain name for a website or resource instead of the website's or resource's IP address for access and connectivity.

   _____

3. Raw data traveling on network media is captured through an NIC by using a ____.

   _____

4. Also known as a *host health check*, ____ provides endpoint security to a host is the host meets the minimum standards to connect to a network.

   _____

5. A software utility that observes a device or network for hardware errors, interruptions, or performance issues, and directs the faulty activity or outages to a network administrator is called a ____.

   _____

Practice 13.2

For each of the following potential indicators that are associated with network attacks, choose the term that best completes the sentence. Be advised, each term will only be used once.

Address Resolution Protocol (ARP) poisoning

distributed denial of service (DDoS) attack

Domain Name System (DNS) poisoning

MAC cloning

malicious code

1. ____ is an attack that produces a spoofed—yet trusted—address that is sent into the LAN to have the network's traffic sent to the attacker.

   _____

2. ____ occurs when an entry in a victim's cache will redirect a legitimate URL to an incorrect IP address.

   _____

3. *Spoofing*, or ____, occurs when an attacker configures a host using an address of a separate validated host to obtain access to a network and its resources.

   _____

4. A(n) ____ utilizes multiple hosts to contribute to the scope of the attack in an effort to prevent users from accessing a system.

   _____

5. An automated task that is produced and executed via scripts and performs harmful activity on a network and its devices is called ____.

   _____

Practice 13.3

For each of the following tools for assessing organizational security, match the term to its correct description. Be advised, each term will only be used once.

A. Cuckoo

B. **curl**

C. **dnsenum**

D. **hping**

E. IP scanner

F. Nessus

G. **netcat**

H. **netstat**

I. nmap

J. **scanless**

K. sn1per

L. SSH

M. **tcpdump**

N. **theHarvester**

O. universal resource locator (URL) redirection

1. _____ Command used to transfer data to and from a server using various protocols and analyze the resulting information

2. _____ Vulnerability scanner used to gather information regarding vulnerabilities of the devices in an organization

3. _____ Command used to scan and analyze ports, conduct network security audits, and test firewalls

4. _____ Command used in Linux systems to gather information such as e-mails, subdomains, employees name, IP addresses, open ports from public sources, and other forms of data

5. _____ Used to reroute one domain to another

6. _____ Text-based protocol analyzer that can scan networks, discover hosts, discover services, and other port information all while generating estimates as to which operating systems are being utilized

7. _____ Command-line utility that displays TCP and UDP connections

8. _____ Kali Linux command that displays DNS information and retrieves DNS servers and entries of an organization

9. _____ Python-based command lint utility that conducts port scanning on websites

10. _____ Text-based solution that functions as a packet sniffer in Linux

11. _____ Open-source malware analysis system that enables a user to run malware in a sandbox environment to study how malware operates and compromises data

12. _____ Tool that searches a network's IP addresses and information regarding the network devices

13. _____ Kali Linux tool for collecting information regarding WHOIS records, HTTP headers, DNS, TCP, and UDP enumeration

14. _____ Secure protocol used to provide remote administrative management of servers, routers, switches, and other devices

15. _____ Versatile utility used to read and write data using TCP/IP

Practice 13.4

For each of the following data sources, match the term to its correct description. Please be advised, the terms will only be used once.

A. bandwidth monitor

B. log file

C. NetFlow

D. sFlow

E. SIEM dashboard

1. _____ Captures the metadata of packets

2. _____ Network protocol generated by Cisco that collects and monitors IP traffic as it flows in and out of a network interface card

3. _____ Displays data into a display of simple security monitoring

4. _____ Network tool that enables administrators to monitor device traffic and usage

5. _____ Record of events that occur during server or computer operation

Practice 13.5

For each of the following protocols, match the term to its correct description. Please be advised, the terms will only be used once.

A. Dynamic Host Configuration Protocol (DHCP)

B. File Transfer Protocol (FTP)

C. File Transfer Protocol/SSL (FTPS)

D. Internet Mail Access Protocol (IMAP)

E. Post Office Protocol (POP)

F. Secure File Transfer Protocol (SFTP)

1. _____ Protocol that enables file transmissions among Internet-connected devices

2. _____ Added an extension of SSH to provide secure file transfers while using a Secure Shell tunnel to encrypt data-in-transit; now considered an obsolete protocol

3. _____ Legacy e-mail protocol that enables users to obtain incoming messages

4. _____ E-mail protocol considered to be a remote e-mail protocol since messages are neither deleted from a server nor downloaded to a user's computer once they are obtained

5. _____ Extension of FTP that added SSH functionality for secure file transmissions

6. _____ Assigns IP address to devices that automatically connect to a network

Practice 13.6

For each of the following secure network assessment methods, choose the term that best completes the sentence. Be advised, each term will only be used once.

exploitation framework	packet capture
network security assessment	packet replay

1. A(n) ____ is a software package that contains apps used to analyze and replicate attacks for vulnerability assessments.

_____

2. The review of data packets that have been previously captured is called ____.

_____

3. ____ refers to the real-time interception of data packets in transit.

_____

4. The auditing process that provides a review of computer and network security is called a(n) ____.

_____

Practice 13.7

For each of the following network administration topics, match the term to its correct description. Be advised, each term will only be used once.

A. DNS attack
B. DNS Security Extensions (DNSSEC)
C. ICMP echo requests
D. IP Flow Information Export (IPFix)

E. network administration
F. System Health Agent (SHA)
G. URL redirection attack

1. _____ Query messages sent to destination machines to establish connectivity

2. _____ Cyberattack in which vulnerabilities within an organization's Domain Name System are exploited

3. _____ Network attack that redirects a victim to a malicious copy of the website they are attempting to access

4. _____ Standard responsible for the collection and analysis of data that exports information regarding the network flow of devices

5. _____ Performs a self-check on a client

6. _____ Suite of specifications that require responses from a DNS server to be digitally signed to verify they have been obtained from a valid and authorized source

7. _____ Operational tasks needed for a network to run efficiently

Notes

CHAPTER 14

Wireless Network Security

Wireless networks enable devices to connect via radio waves instead of copper-core or fiber-optic cabling. This presents significant security challenges as the risk of data interception or manipulation is increase exponentially when wireless communications are used. As such, IT staff must be prepared to support various wireless connections types and modes with security protocols and cryptography.

To adhere to the passing requirements of the CompTIA Security+ Certification Exam, you should be able to differentiate the theories and philosophies of wireless network security. In this chapter, you will demonstrate your understanding of various topics, including wireless installations, attacks, vulnerabilities, and authentication.

The practice sets in this chapter will help enhance your knowledge of the theories and philosophies presented in the corresponding textbook chapter. As such, complete each of the following activities to the best of your ability. Make note of the questions or terms you find to be the most difficult so you may revisit those concepts at a later date.

Practice 14.1

For each of the following attacks, wireless authentication, and wireless authorization methods, choose the term that best completes the sentence. Be advised, each term will only be used once.

802.1X

Counter Mode with Cipher Block Chaining Message
   Authentication Code Protocol (CCMP)

Extensible Authentication Protocol (EAP)

Remote Authentication Dial-In Service (RADIUS)

replay

---

1. ____ is an identity and access authentication server that operates on wired and wireless networks.

   _____

2. A wireless networking protocol for determining how a message should be formatted is ____.

   _____

3. A(n) ____ attack occurs when a hacker obtains credentials to log in to a system to initiate an attack, stores them, and uses them at another time.

   _____

4. The standard often used by organizations for wireless authentication is ____, which provides more security than other wireless protocols as utilizes port-based security.

   _____

5. A wireless encryption standard designed to be used with wireless LANs is called ____.

   _____

Practice 14.2

For each of the following network design and mobile solution terms, match the term to its correct description. Be advised, each term will only be used once.

A. ANT
B. Bluetooth
C. cellular
D. infrared
E. near-field communication (NFC)

F. radio-frequency identification (RFID)
G. Wi-Fi Protected Access II (WPA2)
H. Wi-Fi Protected Access III (WPA3)
I. Wi-Fi Protected Setup (WPS)
J. Zigbee

1. _____ Generation of Wi-Fi security that provides advanced security protocols to the communication of wireless transmissions

2. _____ Wireless technology that utilizes electromagnetic fields to identify or track tags that are attached to objects

3. _____ Network security setting and standard for wireless networks released in 2007

4. _____ Wireless communication standard that enables transmissions using electromagnetic fields amongst devices that are in a close proximity

5. _____ Telecommunication network standard based on IEEE's 802.15.4 personal area network standard

6. _____ Wireless protocol utilized at short distances and typically used for mobile devices to share data

7. _____ Generation of WPA that provides stronger security protections and better control of network access; replaced the RC4 cipher with AES encryption and added Counter Mode with Cipher Block Chaining Message Authentication Code Protocol

8. _____ Wireless communication that relies on a short- and medium-length communication option to transmit signals and data via line-of-site

9. _____ Proprietary wireless technology that allows devices to communicate with each other wirelessly over short distances

10. _____ Type of wireless network enables communications for mobile devices by using a system of stations and transceivers.

Practice 14.3

For each of the following wireless design and solution terms, match the term to its correct description. Be advised, each term will only be used once.

A. captive portal

B. channel overlay

C. controller-based access point (controller-based AP)

D. fat access point

E. RADIUS Federation

F. stand-alone access point (stand-alone AP)

G. thin access point

H. Wi-Fi analyzer

I. wireless access point (WAP)

J. wireless LAN controller (WLC)

K. wireless local area network (WLAN)

1. _____ Devices that can locate wireless signals and signal strength in physical locations

2. _____ Allows users to connect and authenticate to one network while using credentials from another network

3. _____ Provides resiliency in wireless networks by diminishing dead zones with overlapping network coverage

4. _____ Access point managed by a wireless LAN controller (WLC) that receives and transmits wireless traffic

5. _____ Network technology that uses a wireless signal for the transmission of data for a network

6. _____ AP that receives and transmits wireless data

7. _____ Responsible for management of multiple wireless access points in a network

8. _____ Web page users must view before accessing a wireless network; often provides information regarding network policies and requires acceptance of an organization's terms of use

9. _____ Device that provides network access between a wireless network and a physically cabled network

10. _____ Networking device that is independent from other devices and manages authentication, encryption, and other necessary wireless functions

11. _____ WAP that must obtain the configurations for its functionality but is able to accept and transmit data to devices

For each of the following wireless and network attack methods, choose the term that best completes the sentence. Be advised, each term will only be used once.

bluejacking	jamming
bluesnarfing	rogue access point (rogue AP)
disassociation attack	session replay attack
evil twin router	wireless crackers

1. A(n) ____ uses the same SSID of a desired AP a victim is seeking.

_____

2. ____ is the act of purposely interfering, interrupting, or eliminating of a wireless signal's strength and data transmissions.

_____

3. The distribution of unwanted messages over a Bluetooth connection is called ____.

_____

4. In a(n) ____ attack, hackers are able to steal data via the Bluetooth connection.

_____

5. A(n) ____ is a type of denial of service attack where an attacker disconnects a victim from their wireless connection(s).

_____

6. ____ are designed to break the encryption methods and protections of a WLAN.

_____

7. An unauthorized AP that enables an attacker to work around an organization's network security is called a(n) ____.

_____

8. A(n) ____ occurs when an attacker intercepts a session ID and reuses it to impersonate an authorized user.

_____

Practice 14.5

For each of the following wireless devices, security, and access methods, match the term to its correct description. Be advised, each term will only be used once.

A. baseband

B. cell

C. narrowband (NB)

D. subscriber identity module (SIM) card

E. Wi-Fi Protected Access (WPA)

F. Wi-Fi Protected Access II (WPA2)

G. Wi-Fi Protected Access III (WPA 3)

H. Wi-Fi survey

I. wireless network security

J. wireless router

K. wireless site survey

1. _____ Second generation of wireless protection that offers more security than its predecessor by utilizing AES encryption methods

2. _____ Refers to a wireless signal's frequency range before it has been converted via modulation

3. _____ Has the same features as an AP as well as the ability to provide functionality for wireless connections within LANs or WANs

4. _____ Security method that replaced WEP by providing augmented security via keys and user authentication

5. _____ Describes a mobile device network, its base stations, and the confined geographical area where it provides coverage

6. _____ Describes the process of enabling security on a wireless local area network

7. _____ Radio communication method that uses a band of frequencies within a given communication channel

8. _____ Newest form of security for wireless and provides advanced security protocols for wireless transmission

9. _____ Integrated circuit that stores a mobile user's international mobile subscriber identity (IMSI) device number and related key

10. _____ Refers to the planning, designing, and the documentation of a wireless network environment and implementation

11. _____ Provides a network engineer's analysis of the devices needed to deploy wireless in given locations

Practice 14.6

For each of the following wireless and network access and security methods, choose the term that best completes the sentence. Be advised, each term will only be used once.

EAP over Transport Layer Security (EAP-TLS)	predictive site survey
EAP Tunnel Transport Layer Security (EAP-TTLS)	pre-shared key (PSK)
EAP-Flexible Authentication via Secure Tunneling (FAST)	Protected EAP (PEAP)
	Simultaneous Authentication of Equals (SAE)
open security	

1. ____ refers to wireless connections that do not require authentication or provide encryption.

_____

2. ____ is a password-based authentication method that replaced the PSK used in WPA2.

_____

3. The ____ authentication method was created by Cisco to replace LEAP.

_____

4. Also called a *wireless heat map*, a(n) ____ is a visual representation of wireless signal strength.

_____

5. ____ is an open-standard authentication protocol created via the collaboration of Cisco, Microsoft, and RSA in order to protect EAP communications.

_____

6. ____ provides certificate-based authentication.

_____

7. ____ allows communications to be sent via a protected tunnel.

_____

8. An authentication method used for WLAN security that requires a key value before granting access to an AP is called ____.

_____

CHAPTER 15 / Cloud Computing

A cloud-based approach to networking and storing resources is advantageous for organizations of all sizes. In fact, cloud computing has become one of the most prevalent forms of data distribution. However, due to its remote nature, cloud computing has several security concerns. As such, it is important not only to ensure security protocols are in place but also plans for attack mitigation, data recovery, and managing legalities based on the location of the cloud server(s).

To adhere to the passing requirements of the CompTIA Security+ Certification Exam, you should be able to demonstrate knowledge regarding cloud computing. In this chapter, you will demonstrate your understanding of cloud computing advantages and disadvantages, cloud service types, and virtualization.

The practice sets in this chapter will help enhance your knowledge of the theories and philosophies presented in the corresponding textbook chapter. As such, complete each of the following activities to the best of your ability. Make note of the questions or terms you find to be the most difficult so you may revisit those concepts at a later date.

Practice 15.1

For each of the following vulnerabilities and cloud-computing disadvantages, choose the term that best completes the sentence. Be advised, each term will only be used once.

access control	outages
availability	personal cloud
Clarifying Lawful Overseas Use of Data (CLOUD) Act	private cloud
confidentiality	public cloud
dependence	poor authentication
integrity	software-defined networking (SDN)
off-premises model	software-defined visibility (SDV)
on-premises model	

1. _____ is an approach to management of a network using the application of code.

_____

2. When utilizing cloud computing, the Internet is a requirement to obtain resources, so if a user does not have an Internet connection, the _____ of an organization's data is negatively impacted.

_____

3. _____ policies are a cloud-computing vulnerability as they determine the rights or abilities a user has to the service being provided, whereas having and controlling all data and services on-site provides an organization and their users more control.

_____

4. A cloud-computing resource owned and managed by a single private organization is called a(n) _____.

_____

5. ____ is a vulnerability in an organization's network, as the organization must rely on the cloud-computing company's operations, support, and security.

_____

6. One disadvantage of cloud computing is users' concerns for ____ and data privacy.

_____

7. ____ measures act as a cloud-computing vulnerability since user accounts could be compromised.

_____

8. Cloud-computing ____ are considered a predictable disadvantage, as communication issues between the IT staff and vendor could lead to a misconfiguration or other forms of implementation error.

_____

9. Cloud-computing ____ is considered a disadvantage, as users cannot be sure whether data has been altered.

_____

10. The ____ provides oversight into data storage on cloud providers.

_____

11. A(n) ____ is when an organization access and stores data in an off-site location.

_____

12. An organization accessing and storing data on-site is using a(n) ____.

_____

13. A cloud-computing resource that allows a user to manage their own cloud service to store files or offer services within a household is a(n) ____.

_____

14. A(n) ____ is a cloud-computing resource that provides services to anyone.

_____

15. ____ allows automation between software programs through a set of open, RESTful APIs, which allow them to interact directly.

_____

Practice 15.2

For each of the following cloud-computing security designs and concepts, match the term to its correct description. Be advised, each term will only be used once.

A. Anything as a Service (XaaS)

B. Cloud Access Security Broker (CASB)

C. Cloud Security Alliance (CSA)

D. data sovereignty

E. Firewall as a Service (FWaaS)

F. Infrastructure as a Service (IaaS)

G. Platform as a Service (PaaS)

H. Security as a Service (SECaaS)

I. Software as a Service (SaaS)

J. virtualization

1. _____ Cloud-computing technology that eliminates the need to install software locally and is one of the most utilized forms of cloud computing

2. _____ Nonprofit organization that offers frameworks for best practices in cloud computing

3. _____ Method of delivering a firewall and other advanced security tools to the cloud environment

4. _____ Form of cloud computing provided by a vendor when the vendor provides infrastructure over the Internet

5. _____ Concept that states digital data is subject to jurisdiction and laws of the country of where the storage device is located

6. _____ Form of cloud computing provided by a vendor when the vendor allows customers to develop, run, and manage their applications in the cloud

7. _____ Cloud-computing practice that allows resources to be distributed via virtual machine instead of users having computer resources installed on their physical machine

8. _____ Business model that integrates security services into the infrastructure of an organization

9. _____ Entity often implement into organizations' cloud-computing systems to utilize a set of software tools that enable enterprise security policies to extend to data stored on the cloud

10. _____ Refers to the delivery of any service through the Internet

Practice 15.3

For each of the following cloud-computing service and security concepts, match the term to its correct description. Be advised, each term will only be used once.

A. cloud application security

B. cloud audit

C. cloud infrastructure

D. cloud security

E. cloud service provider (CSP)

F. community cloud

G. container

H. container security

I. managed security service provider (MSSP)

J. managed service provider (MSP)

1. _____ Vendors that provide the information technology services via the Internet

2. _____ Vendor that manages a customer's information technology operations environment

3. _____ Method of providing executable software that contains applications and uses the host OS in a virtualized environment

4. _____ Cloud-computing method that allows the sharing of resources among everyone affiliated with an organization

5. _____ Processes. policies, and procedures implemented to ensure containers run as designed

6. _____ Vendor that manages the customer's information technology security environment

7. _____ Provides remote location operation for hardware, software, and other components needed to implement required infrastructure

8. _____ Methods used to protect data transmissions and storage and harden a cloud environment against vulnerabilities and attacks

9. _____ Products such as Microsoft Office 365 utilize this method, which advises the policies and procedures governing data used in a cloud environment

10. _____ Examines cloud service controls to analyze and report its security and performance

Practice 15.4

For each of the following cloud-computing methods and concepts, match the term to its correct description. Be advised, each term will only be used once.

A. cloud backup

B. cloud governance

C. cloud instance

D. cloud model

E. edge computing

F. fog computing

G. hypervisor

H. thin client

I. virtual machine (VM) escape

J. virtual machine (VM) sprawl

1. _____ Software program that monitors and manages an organization's virtual operating systems

2. _____ Decentralized model that ensures computing activities can take place with devices not physically close but connected via a LAN

3. _____ Model that collects information and processes it on devices in close proximity to one another in a network

4. _____ Determines how a cloud infrastructure will be used

5. _____ Occurs when virtual deployments are abundant and not properly managed

6. _____ Occurs when a program breaks out of the virtual environment and interacts directly with a host

7. _____ Devices, such as computers, that do not contain internal storage and are used to run virtual environments

8. _____ Practice of backing up an organization's data to a cloud-based server

9. _____ Policies and procedures used in an organization to manage its association and processes with their cloud-computing methods

10. _____ Virtualized server installation that takes place within a cloud-computing environment

◼ Practice 15.5

For each of the following concepts, choose the term that best completes the sentence. Be advised, each term will only be used once.

cloud storage	microservice
high availability	resource policy
host operating system	serverless architecture
hosted service	transit gateway
hybrid cloud	uptime

1. ____ is the measurement that is expressed as a percentage of the time that a cloud storage system is working and functioning properly.

_____

2. A cloud infrastructure's ability to function without interruption is called ____.

_____

3. The use of remote servers hosted on the Internet to store and process and organization's data is called ____.

_____

4. A(n) ____ is the operating system installed that interacts with a device's hardware.

_____

5. A(n) ____ is a software application-development method compiled of reusable components used in a cloud-native application.

_____

6. A(n) ____ provides on-demand software in a cloud-computing environment.

_____

7. ____ can help with cloud environment management processes by specifying who can access and act on resources such as networks, applications, storage, services, and servers.

_____

8. A(n) ____ is the development method where data servers, storage devices, and networking resources are used in a remote setting.

_____

9. Cloud-computing hardware consists of a ____, which uses a transit hub to interconnect an organization's virtual private cloud (VPC) and on-premises network.

_____

10. The combination of public, private, or community clouds is called a(n) ____.

_____

Practice 15.6

For each of the following terms mentioned below, choose the term that best completes the sentence. Be advised, each term will only be used once.

guest operating system	secrets management
next-generation secure web gateway (SWG)	security group
reference architecture	services integration

1. A ____ is software installed on a machine to run in a virtual system.

2. ____ is the use of specific tools and procedures to ensure confidentiality and availability of information via digital authentication.

3. A cloud-based method for prohibiting malware, protecting data, and detecting threats is a ____.

4. ____ refers to the cloud tools and technologies that connect information technology environments to provide real-time exchanging of information.

5. The documentation that provides recommendations for the integration of information technology products and solutions is called ____.

CHAPTER 16 — Governance, Risk, and Compliance

As organizations become more reliant on digital storage and access of data, the need to ensure information is protected becomes increasingly important. Plans must be enacted not only to secure data but also to prove compliance to regulations or standards as well as prepare for associated risks. The potential for risk occurs on a number of levels, and proper risk management—including assessment, response, and prediction—is essential.

To adhere to the passing requirements of the CompTIA Security+ Certification Exam, you should have an understanding of governance, risk, and compliance in the realm of digital information security. It is equally important to understand how members of an organization are brought into an organization upon hire, how they exit an organization at the end of their employment, and organizational expectations of technology usage during employment. In this chapter, you will demonstrate your understanding of relevant organizational security and policies.

The practice sets in this chapter will help enhance your knowledge of the theories and philosophies presented in the corresponding textbook chapter. As such, complete each of the following activities to the best of your ability. Make note of the questions or terms you find to be the most difficult so you may revisit those concepts at a later date.

Practice 16.1

For each of the following risk management processes and concepts, match the term to its correct description. Be advised, each term will only be used once.

A. intellectual property (IP)

B. man-made disaster

C. risk analysis

D. risk management strategies and security controls

E. third-party risk management (TPRM)

1. _____ Refers to the likelihood and severity of a person or event disrupting productivity in an organization

2. _____ Refers to an organization's ideas, inventions, or processes

3. _____ Practice used when an organization contemplates faulty transactions when conducting business with vendors outside of the organization

4. _____ Refers to events caused by accidental or deliberate actions that result in organizational errors, safeguards, or negligence

5. _____ Practice used by organizations to mitigate situations that could prohibit productivity

Practice 16.2

For each of the following tools, policies, and producers, match the term to its correct description. Be advised, each term will only be used once.

A. acceptable use policy (AUP)
B. background check
C. credential policies
D. data sanitization
E. employee user training
F. job rotation

G. mandatory vacation
H. offboarding
I. onboarding
J. separation of duties
K. social media analysis

1. _____ Occurs when an organization collects data from sources such as Facebook, monitors information being posted online regarding their organization, and looks to avoid forms of social engineering attacks

2. _____ Occurs when an employee is made aware of an organization's security policies after they are hired

3. _____ Tactic used by organizations in which employees are moved to a different department so they understand additional roles

4. _____ Common practice of training members of the importance of data security

5. _____ Employee policy in which multiple people are required to complete a job or task

6. _____ Permanent removal of data from a system

7. _____ Employee process of recovering identification or digital access keys after the employment has ended

8. _____ Forces a user to step away from organizational duties for a short period of time

9. _____ Confirms an applicant's work history, references, and existence of criminal history

10. _____ Controls the user authentication process and confirm user access to given resources and locations

11. _____ Provides information to members of an organization regarding what they can and cannot do with organizational technology

Name _____

Practice 16.3

For each of the following, choose the term that best completes the sentence. Be advised, each term will only be used once.

inherent risk	risk posture
policy violation	risk register
residual risk	risk transfer
risk avoidance	threat assessment
risk awareness	vulnerability assessment

1. ____ enables security practitioners to focus on their organization's most common threats.

   _____

2. A tool used to list, categorize, and provide instructions for managing risks is a(n) ____.

   _____

3. The risk that remains after mitigation controls are implemented is called a(n) ____.

   _____

4. ____ is the practice of eliminating a risk by the avoidance of the agents that are known to cause the risk(s).

   _____

5. The practice of shifting a risk to another party is called ____ and often involves purchasing insurance.

   _____

6. The process consists of finding weaknesses in an organization's network is called a(n) ____.

   _____

7. A(n) ____ is one that would occur if controls were not implemented to mitigate the risk.

   _____

8. ____ is the overall protection that a cybersecurity program offers an organization.

   _____

9. The steps taken to identify and determine the potential threats an organization may be presented with a(n) ____.

   _____

10. A(n) ____ occurs when a member of an organization does not adhere to the security policies effectively.

   _____

Practice 16.4

For each of the following risk analysis methods, match the term to its correct description. Be advised, each term will only be used once.

A. annualized loss expectancy (ALE)

B. annualized rate of occurrence (ARO)

C. heat map

D. qualitative assessment

E. quantitative assessment

F. risk control self-assessment

G. risk impact

H. single loss expectancy (SLE)

1. _____ Analysis that uses numbers or monetary values

2. _____ Monetary value of a damaged asset

3. _____ Analysis based on subjective opinion rather than data

4. _____ Estimated consequences or losses caused by a risk

5. _____ Expected number of times an incident will happen in one year

6. _____ Process of examining risks and the degree to which controls are effective

7. _____ Organizes risks into defined impact levels

8. _____ Monetary value anticipated to be lost based on frequency of loss in a given year

Practice 16.5

For each of the following concepts related to data governance, choose the term that best completes the sentence. Be advised, each term will only be used once.

data anonymization	data minimization
data clearance	data retention policy
data compliance	Information Rights Management (IRM)
data governance	personally identifiable information (PII)
data life cycle	pseudoanonymization
data masking	

1. A(n) ____ is a de-identification procedure where personal identification information fields are replaced with artificial identifiers.

   _____

2. ____ is data that can be used to pinpoint a specific person, such as a Social Security number.

   _____

3. A(n) ____ dictates how long an organization must retain their data, in case it is needed for an investigation or evidence in the organization's future.

   _____

4. A(n) ____ is the processes that protect data such as health records and other various sensitive forms of data from unauthorized access.

   _____

5. The stages data goes through from its creation to its archival or deletion is called a(n) ____.

   _____

6. ____ is the practice of following regulations as it applies to data management to ensure the data's accountability.

   _____

7. The policies and procedures that an organization uses for the managing of its data assets is called ____.

   _____

8. ____ refers to the measures performed by an organization to limit the amount of personal data that is collected to ensure it relates to the specific tasks needed to accomplish said tasks.

   _____

9. ____ is a data security technique that copies data while obfuscating sensitive data.

   _____

10. The authorization that permits access to security data is called ____.

    _____

11. ____ is the sanitization and removal of personally identifiable information (PII).

    _____

Practice 16.6

For each of the following personal policies, match the term to its correct description. Be advised, each term will only be used once.

A. data owner

B. executive user

C. privileged user

D. role-based awareness training

E. system owner

F. user

1. _____ Type of elevated user with increased access to data resources

2. _____ Role focused on data protection and backups along with the related policies and implementations

3. _____ Assigns the role and provides training for the individuals in an organization based on their position in the organization

4. _____ Account assigned to anyone who operates an application on an organization's network

5. _____ Individual responsible for the overall usage of a given application and making decisions regarding the data usage

6. _____ Individual responsible for data compliance, policy management, and privilege usage

Practice 16.7

For each of the following, choose the term that best completes the sentence. Be advised, each term will only be used once.

asset life cycle	IT asset management (ITAM)
asset management	risk acceptance
change control	risk assessment
change management	risk mitigation
critical asset	

1. ____ requires that assets needing to be purchased are planned for effective use and tracked through their life cycles for a financial decision to be made.

   _____

2. The process or plan that describes the policies and practices of an organization's preparedness, equipment, and trainings they provide their members to implement technology changes is called ____.

   _____

3. A(n) ____ is one needed for an organization to sustain its operations.

   _____

4. The informed decision of assuming a risk is called ____.

   _____

5. ____ is the systematic approach of identifying risks due to vulnerabilities and then ranking the risk that would cause the most harm to assets as the risk that should be tended to most.

   _____

6. The act of taking steps in order to reduce the impacts of a risk an organization may experience is called ____.

   _____

7. When managing changes, ____ ensures changes are necessary, documented, and integrated as seamlessly as possible.

   _____

8. ____ tracks the information technology assets of an organization including its hardware and software systems.

   _____

9. The ____ is the method that is implemented in managing an asset from its purchase until it is discarded.

   _____

Practice 16.8

For each of the following terms below, match the term to its correct description. Be advised, each term will only be used once.

A. clean-desk policy

B. employment contract

C. environmental disasters

D. managerial control

E. operational control

1. _____ Caused by humans due to their damaging of the environment, such as staring a fire

2. _____ Security controls that uses administrative processes to measure performance and take corrective actions when needed

3. _____ Agreement between a member of an organization and the organization itself

4. _____ Security controls implemented by individuals who carry out day-to-day operations in an organization

5. _____ Human resource policy that determines how a member of an organization should leave their desk when they are not physically present at their desk

CHAPTER 17 Incident Response and Digital Forensics

It is important for an organization to be proactive, as opposed to reactive, in terms of incident response. This means that plans should exist long before an incident takes place. An incident-response plan outlines the appropriate or necessary actions an organization must take in the event a cyberattack occurs. These plans provide a structured response to enable organizations to mitigate or minimize the impacts of an incident. These plans also provide guidance for data- or business-recovery practices.

To adhere to the passing requirements of the CompTIA Security+ Certification Exam, you should be able to understand incident response in the cybersecurity field. Furthermore, you need to understand how digital forensics is applied in the field of cybersecurity. In this chapter, you will demonstrate your understanding of topics such as digital forensics, data acquisition, and forensics reporting.

The practice sets in this chapter will help enhance your knowledge of the theories and philosophies presented in the corresponding textbook chapter. As such, complete each of the following activities to the best of your ability. Make note of the questions or terms you find to be the most difficult so you may revisit those concepts at a later date.

Practice 17.1

For each of the following cybersecurity forensics tactics and incident response methods, choose the term that best completes the sentence. Be advised, each term will only be used once.

configuration changes	incident response (IR)
Cyber Kill Chain	metadata
cybersecurity resilience	order of volatility
digital forensics	stakeholder management
documentation and evidence	tabletop exercise

1. ____ is data about data and provides information such as the data creator and what day and time the data was created and modified.

   _____

2. In digital forensics, ____ are vital for verifying events that took place as well as when and where they occurred.

   _____

3. A(n) ____ offers members of an organization an opportunity to discuss a real or hypothetical problem(s) and how the organization will solve the problem(s).

   _____

4. ____ is defined as acting against and recovering from a cybersecurity incident.

   _____

5. ____ is the ability to prepare for, respond to, and recover from cybersecurity attacks.

   _____

6. The process of meeting the needs of individuals that impact security from both inside and outside an organization is referred to as ____.

   _____

7. The ____ lists a series of steps that follow a cyberattack and was created by members of Lockheed Martin.

_____

8. The recovery, analysis, and protection of digital evidence from a crime scene to present in court is called ____.

_____

9. ____ are precautious taken to mitigate cybersecurity incidents.

_____

10. The order or sequence in which digital evidence is collected is defined by the organization's ____

_____

▰ Practice 17.2

For each of the following incident response and plan methods, match the term to its correct description. Be advised, each term will only be used once.

A. containment

B. eradication

C. incident response plan (IRP)

D. incident response process

E. quarantine

1. _____ Process of evaluating the damages, removing a root cause, and repairing an organization's systems, after a threat has been contained

2. _____ Placing a file that is or could be infected with malware in a separate area to be sure it is not accessible

3. _____ Written document that provides instructions needed to be followed if an incident occurs

4. _____ Outline of steps to be taken when an incident occurs and requires the need of an IRP

5. _____ Actions that will limit further damage from an incident that has occurred to ensure any evidence is protected and cannot be destroyed

▰ Practice 17.3

For each of the following data acquisition methods, match the term to its correct description. Be advised, each term will only be used once.

A. artifacts

B. cloud forensics

C. data acquisition

D. data dump (dd)

E. memory dump

F. mirror image backup

G. screenshot

1. _____ Image that provides what is currently displayed on a GUI of a device

2. _____ Data acquisition method that stores content from a device's RAM so it can be analyzed

3. _____ Pertains to the investigation practices of a cloud environment as opposed to a physical environment

4. _____ Replication of a hard drive, including any hidden files or data that was on the hard drive

5. _____ Refers to any objects that could contain forms of evidence

6. _____ Process of collecting any volatile and non-volatile data in the collecting of evidence

7. _____ Disk image file that is a replica of a hard drive that is being investigated

◼️ Practice 17.4

For each of the following, choose the term that best completes the sentence. Be advised, each term will only be used once.

chain of custody	strategic intelligence
counterintelligence	time offset
legal hold	time stamp
preservation of evidence	work-hour
segmentation	

1. A ____ prohibits members of an organization from destroying any documentation or other evidence that is relevant to an investigation.

_____

2. The difference in time in comparison to Coordinated Universal Time (UTC) is called ____.

_____

3. The documentation that identifies who will maintain unaltered and complete control over the evidence in a case is called ____.

_____

4. ____ is the gathering of information regarding the extent to which a cybercriminal is able to obtain data from a system.

_____

5. The division of an affected asset's components, such as network recourses and software, from other components is called ____.

_____

6. A ____ is the digital record of when a specific event occurred.

_____

7. ____ refers to organizational policy processes for investigations that include the evaluation, analysis, and evidence procedures.

_____

8. The practices taken to ensure evidence has not been altered is ____.

_____

9. ____ is the amount of work a member of an organization performs in an hour's time.

_____

Notes

CHAPTER 18 | Business Continuity and Disaster Recovery

Despite all security controls in place in an organization, situations or events can arise that create risk or cause losses. For example, natural disasters are one of the most impactful events on business operations, causing approximately $232 billion in loss worldwide. Additionally, man-made disasters, such as cyberattacks, terrorism, or human error, cause disruption to business operations. As such, the existence of plans that carefully outline recovery strategies for ongoing business continuity is vital. These plans include business-impact analyses (BIAs) and disaster recovery plans (DRPs).

To adhere to the passing requirements of the CompTIA Security+ Certification Exam, you should be able to grasp the concepts of business continuity and disaster recovery (BCDR). Understanding BCDR will also augment your planning skills for situations that require an organization to stop their productivity due to a move or disaster. In this chapter, you will demonstrate your understanding of disaster recovery and business resilience.

The practice sets in this chapter will help enhance your knowledge of the theories and philosophies presented in the corresponding textbook chapter. As such, complete each of the following activities to the best of your ability. Make note of the questions or terms you find to be the most difficult so you may revisit those concepts at a later date.

Practice 18.1

For each of the following, match the term to its correct description. Be advised, each term will only be used once.

A. backups

B. business continuity plan (BCP)

C. business-impact analysis (BIA)

D. disaster recovery plan

E. high availability

F. recovery site

G. redundancy

H. replication

I. resilience

J. restoration order

1. _____ Refers to capabilities of a system being able to recover from a disruption in an appropriate amount of time

2. _____ Process of copying data to sources such as an off-site server in either incremental or differential methods in case the date needs to be retrieved

3. _____ Determines the order in which services will be put back into operation

4. _____ Location from which a business can operate temporarily until the business site is up and running again

5. _____ Duplication of systems to augment dependability

6. _____ Determines how an organization will function if a disaster occurs and functionality or data is lost

7. _____ Data backup in which data is copied and stored on-site

8. _____ Comprehensive, proactive plan that outlines the steps needed to keep an organization functioning before, during, and after a disaster or unplanned stoppage of productivity

9. _____ Ability of systems to remain active without any interruptions

10. _____ Detailed process that dictates the consequences of organizational distributions and uses data to generate recovery strategies

Practice 18.2

For each of the following reliability methods, match the term to its correct description. Be advised, each term will only be used once.

A. generator

B. multipathing

C. power distribution unit (PDU)

D. power surge

E. RAID 0

F. RAID 1

G. RAID 1+0

H. RAID 5

I. single point of failure (SPOF)

J. uninterruptible power supply (UPS)

1. _____ Employs two hard drives in such a way that each hard drive makes a copy of the other hard drive

2. _____ Utilizes disk striping to ensure multiple hard drives are synchronized with each other while the retrieval of data occurs

3. _____ Battery-based device that provides users with the ability to continue operations if electricity fails during their work

4. _____ Fluctuation of electrical voltage that lasts longer than three seconds

5. _____ Combines the performance of RAID 0 with fault tolerance

6. _____ Risk that occurs when a system part fails and causes the entire system to stop working

7. _____ Alternative routes among a server and storage devices

8. _____ Device responsible for distributing electrical power

9. _____ Combination of RAID 1 and RAID 0

10. _____ Provides long-term power when electricity is not available

Practice 18.3

For each of the following, choose the term that best completes the sentence. Be advised, each term will only be used once.

archive bit	hot site
cold site	incremental backup
copy backup	IT contingency plan (ITCP)
data backups	storage area network (SAN)
differential backups	warm site
full backup	

1. A(n) ____ is a facility with the minimal amount of equipment to allow an organization to resume its operations.

   _____

2. A network that allows access to consolidated storage devices is a(n) ____.

   _____

3. ____ consist of the copying of data from one location to another medium.

   _____

4. A fully functional site that serves as a complete duplication of an organizational setting is a(n) ____.

   _____

5. ____ start from a full backup and then create other backups based on files that have been changed or created since the last full backup.

   _____

6. A(n) ____ is the supplemental plan that takes place if the DRP does not prove successful.

   _____

7. The bit in a file that determines whether it has or has not backed up is a(n) ____.

   _____

8. Also called a backup file, a(n) ____ copies designated files but does not clear archive bits.

   _____

9. A(n) ____ is a location that provides office space for an organization but does not have operational equipment.

   _____

10. When an organization uses a(n) ____ method, they copy all files regardless of when they were first made or when they were altered.

    _____

11. A(n) ____ is a series of backups where the first day begins with a full backup, and the remaining day in the backup cycle creates copies of the files that have been changed or created since the last backup.

    _____

Practice 18.4

For each of the following business continuity and impact analysis methods, choose the term that best completes the sentence. Be advised, each term will only be used once.

business continuity	mission-critical functions and systems
failover	recovery point objective (RPO)
failover cluster	recovery time objective (RTO)
fault tolerance	

1. The group of servers that coordinate to provide availability of resources to an organization is called a ____.

2. ____ provides an organization the ability to function without interruption when one or more system components fail.

3. A ____ provides the means of switching from primary equipment to secondary equipment without human interaction and ensures high availability for an organization.

4. The ability for an organization to be operational before, during, and after a catastrophic event is called ____.

5. The target time by which applications and services must be restored to avoid unacceptable consequences once a disaster occurs is called ____.

6. A ____ refers to the maximum amount of data an organization can afford to lose after operations have stopped.

7. ____ are essential functional and systems need to keep an organization operational.

CHAPTER 19

Employment and Soft Skills

It is common knowledge that employers typically seek candidates with the best skills for the job. However, those skills are not always technical or job-specific skills. Employers also want to hire those with the ability to function effectively as a member of a team, interact professionally with coworkers and customers, and perform their work with a high degree of accuracy with minimal downtime.

While the CompTIA Security+ Certification Exam does not assess one's ability to find, obtain, or retain employment, these are important topics for any professional to have. Without an understanding of the job-search, job-application, or hiring processes, you will find it quite difficult to obtain gainful employment and begin your career as a security professional. In this chapter, you will demonstrate your understanding of important employment documents, interviewing preparation, and essential soft skills sought by most, if not all, employers.

The practice sets in this chapter will help enhance your knowledge of the theories and philosophies presented in the corresponding textbook chapter. As such, complete each of the following activities to the best of your ability. Make note of the questions or terms you find to be the most difficult so you may revisit those concepts at a later date.

Practice 19.1

Match each of the following interview questions to its corresponding question type. Be advised, question types will be used more than once.

A. behavioral question

B. common question

C. hypothetical question

1. _____ How would you respond to a situation in which a coworker fails to show up for their scheduled shift, relieving you of yours?

2. _____ Can you give me an example of a time you took a leadership role in your current occupation and the results of your leadership?

3. _____ What about this position or company interests you?

4. _____ Where do you see yourself five years from now?

5. _____ How do you handle mistakes?

Practice 19.2

For each of the following statements about soft skills, choose the term that best completes the sentence. Be advised, each term will only be used once.

active listening	confidence
attitude	conflict resolution
collaboration skills	

1. Being certain about one's own abilities and judgment is called ____.

_____

2. ____ is fully processing what a person says.

_____

3. The process of resolving disputes is called ____.

_____

4. A person's ____ describes their personal thoughts or feelings that affect their outward behavior.

_____

5. Behaviors that enable a person to work effectively with others are called ____.

_____

Practice 19.3

Match each of the following to its corresponding description. Be advised, each term will only be used once.

A. critical-thinking skills	F. integrity
B. decision-making	G. leadership
C. diversity awareness	H. morals
D. empathy	I. problem-solving
E. ethics	J. professionalism

1. _____ Ability to embrace the unique traits of others

2. _____ Ability to influence others to reach a goal

3. _____ Ability to share someone else's emotions and show understanding of how the other person is feeling

4. _____ Act of exhibiting appropriate character, judgment, and behavior by a person trained to perform a job

5. _____ Process of taking a course of action after weighing the benefits and costs of alternate actions

6. _____ Honesty of a person's actions

7. _____ Rules of behavior based on a group's ideas about what is right and wrong

8. _____ Provide the ability to make sound judgments

9. _____ Process used to evaluate a situation and find a solution

10. _____ Individual's ideas of what is right and wrong

Name _____

Practice 19.4

For each of the following statements about employment, choose the term that best completes the sentence. Be advised, each term will only be used once.

cover message	mock interview
employment verification	networking
job-acquisition skills	portfolio
job application	reference
lifelong learning	résumé

1. Talking with people you know and making new relationships that can lead to potential career or job opportunities is called ____.

   _____

2. A(n) ____ is a letter or e-mail that introduces and summarizes why an applicant is applying for a job.

   _____

3. A(n) ____ is a form that includes an applicant's contact information, education, and work experience.

   _____

4. Practices conducted with another person to prepare for an employment screening is called a(n) ____.

   _____

5. ____ is the voluntary attainment of knowledge or information through the course of a person's life.

   _____

6. A document that outlines a person's career goals, education, and work experience to prove an application have the necessary experience for a job is called a(n) ____.

   _____

7. A person who knows an applicant's skills, talents, or personal traits and is willing to recommend the individual is called a(n) ____.

   _____

8. ____ is an employment process through which information provided on an applicant's documentation is checked to confirm its accuracy.

   _____

9. Skills used to gain employment are called ____.

   _____

10. A(n) ____ is a selection of related materials that are collected and organized to show the qualifications, skills, and talents that support an individual's career or personal goals.

   _____

Practice 19.5

Match each of the following interview questions to its corresponding question type. Be advised, question types will be used more than once.

A. office politics

B. resilience

C. teamwork

D. time management

E. work ethic

1. _____ Cooperative efforts of team members to reach a goal

2. _____ Believe that honest work is a reward on its own

3. _____ Behaviors that individuals practice to gain advantage over others in the workplace

4. _____ Person's ability to cope with and recover from change or adversity

5. _____ Practice of organizing time and work assignments to increase personal efficiency

Instructions for Using the CompTIA Security+ Reference Guide

The CompTIA Security+ Reference Guide is designed to assist you as you study and prepare for the CompTIA Security+ Certification Exam. The following information is intended for individuals to use as a reference as they complete the prior portions of this Study Guide or as they practice for an upcoming CompTIA Security+ exam.

While implementing the CompTIA Security+ Reference Guide into a preparation and study system, it is advised to document the objectives you think you have mastered as well as the objectives you find challenging. Organizing exam objectives based on your perception of difficulty enables you to focus on the domain(s) and section(s) you need to practice to earn a CompTIA Security+ Certification. Each objective includes the full language of the Security+ objective for organizational or referential purposes.

This Reference Guide is divided into five domains that match those found in the CompTIA Security+ Exam Objectives. Within each domain, the corresponding objectives are discussed individually. Domain names have been contracted into acronyms, and one will appear as part of the title on each reference page, for ease of use. The acronyms for the CompTIA Security+ domains are as follows:

1.	Attacks, Threats, and Vulnerabilities	ATV
2.	Architecture and Design	AD
3.	Implementation	IMP
4.	Operations and Incident Response	OIR
5.	Governance, Risk, and Compliance	GRC

Each acronym is followed by an objective number and the relevant topics to the material. These relevant topics are noted and listed with alphabetical identifiers. For example, ATV-1.1C refers to the third substandard (*Vishing*) in Objective 1.1 (*Compare and contrast different types of social engineering techniques*) in Domain 1 (*Attacks, Threats, and Vulnerabilities*):

1.0 Attacks, Threats, and Vulnerabilities: **ATV**

- **1.1** Compare and contrast different types of social engineering techniques
  - Phishing (A)
  - Smishing (B)
  - **Vishing** (C)
  - Spam (D)

Each domain, section, and topic for the CompTIA Security+ SY0-601 Exam Objectives will be presented in this section of your text. Therefore, it is recommended, and encouraged, that you use these pages to make notes of what you do and do not understand about each objective. Noting your progress and identifying areas in which you need additional studying will increase the efficacy of your studying methods, as well as the likelihood of obtaining a CompTIA Security+ Certification.

Phishing

Description

Phishing is the fraudulent practice of sending e-mails to victims that appear to be from an actual organization, such as the victim's bank. The contents of the e-mail often ask the victim to supply credentials in order to verify their account via e-mail. However, the links embedded in the e-mail message do not direct to the victim's banking website; instead, they redirect the victim to a spoofed web page where the attacker is able to collect the victim's username and password. Once an attacker has these, they can access the victim's banking account.

There are numerous methods for detecting if an e-mail is legitimate or a form of phishing. Common methods include reviewing the sender's e-mail address, the subject title of the email, and hovering over the link to see the website's address. Nonetheless, it is important to advise users that they should not open an e-mail from a sender they do not recognize, along with verifying that organizations will not send e-mails asking users to supply their username and passwords via transmitted link.

Example

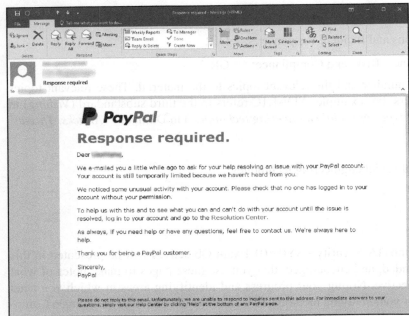

Goodheart-Willcox Publisher

Related Concepts

- Smishing—ATV-1.1B
- Vishing—ATV-1.1C
- Spear phishing—ATV-1.1F
- Pharming—ATV-1.1I
- Whaling—ATV-1.1L
- Credential harvesting—ATV-1.1P
- Personnel—GRC-5.3A

Security+ Objective

1.1: Compare and contrast different types of social engineering techniques.

Smishing

Description

Smishing is a form of phishing that uses text messaging or short message service (SMS) to obtain private information from a victim. Smishing attacks are often conducted by sending a message to a victim's mobile phone that asks the victim to verify the delivery of a product ordered online by providing personal information, including name, address, e-mail address, or the credit card used to make the purchase. Like phishing, it is difficult to *prevent* this type of attack. However, as long as the user simply deletes the message without responding or taking action, there is no real threat.

Example

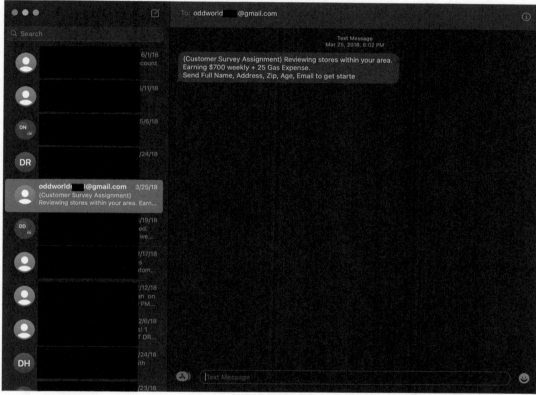

Goodheart-Willcox Publisher

Related Concepts

- Phishing—ATV-1.1A
- Vishing—ATV-1.1C
- Spear phishing—ATV-1.1F
- Pharming—ATV-1.1I
- Whaling—ATV-1.1L
- Credential harvesting—ATV-1.1P

Security+ Objective

1.1: Compare and contrast different types of social engineering techniques.

Vishing

Description

Vishing occurs through a phone call. With a vishing attack, the attacker's goal is to use a telephone to obtain data that can be later used for a cyberattack. Often, the attack poses as an authentic individual, such as someone who needs to have their password reset to an online bank account. Furthermore, the attackers will advise that they do not have access to the e-mail account on file and will ask the individual on the phone to forward the link to reset the bank account password to an alternate e-mail. If the scheme of this example were successful, the attacker receives a reset link for a victim's bank account, which can be used to steal money or make fraudulent purchases.

Example

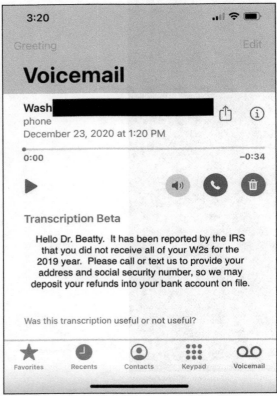

Goodheart-Willcox Publisher

Related Concepts

- Phishing—ATV-1.1A
- Smishing—ATV-1.1B
- Spear phishing—ATV-1.1F
- Pharming—ATV-1.1I
- Whaling—ATV-1.1L
- Credential harvesting—ATV-1.1P

Security+ Objective

1.1: Compare and contrast different types of social engineering techniques.

Spam

Description

Spam is unsolicited e-mails that attackers send in bulk to a complied recipient list; it is often referred to as *junk mail*. Spam e-mails are typically used for commercial purposes, but they can also include malicious links that direct the recipient to a website an attacker has generated. Once there, the attacker may be able to intercept data or harvest credentials.

Example

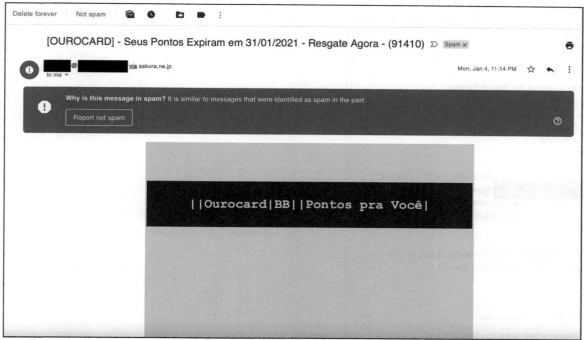

Goodheart-Willcox Publisher

Related Concepts

- Phishing—ATV-1.1A
- Spam over Internet messaging (SPIM)—ATV-1.1E

Security+ Objective

1.1: Compare and contrast different types of social engineering techniques.

ATV-1.1E   Spam over Internet Messaging (SPIM)

Description

Similar to the concept of spam and its relationship to e-mail messages, *spam over Internet messaging (SPIM)* is unsolicited messages obtained through forms of instant messaging. For example, messages received from an attacker through forms of Facebook Messenger may include links that purport to be about information regarding a certain product or article. However, the link actually directs the victim to a malicious site that could steal information or install malware onto the user's device.

Example

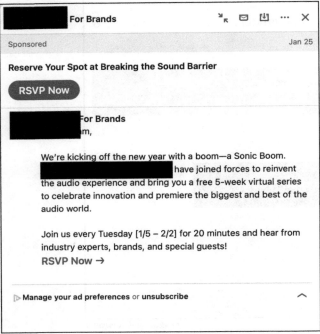

Goodheart-Willcox Publisher

Related Concepts

- Spam—ATV-1.1D

Security+ Objective

1.1: Compare and contrast different types of social engineering techniques.

Spear Phishing

Description

Spear phishing is a phishing campaign that targets a particular victim or group of victims. While phishing e-mails are normally sent to a large list of addresses, spear phishing attempts to collect information about victims. Often, the attacker masquerades as someone the victim knows and can trust. Therefore, these e-mails appear to be legitimate, professional, and collaborative in nature but actually direct victims to a malicious site where the victim provides credentials or information. For example, an attacker may spoof the e-mail address of an executive in a company and send e-mails to employees asking for confidential information about the company such as purchase orders or banking information. Often, a simple review of the sender's e-mail address can determine the validity of the e-mail.

Example

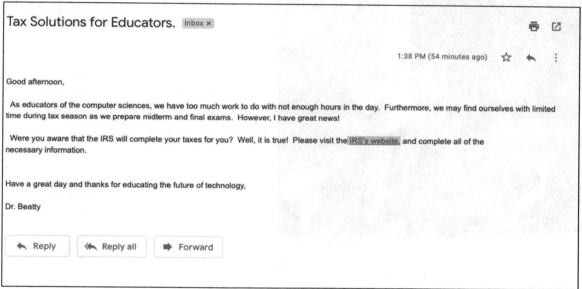

Goodheart-Willcox Publisher

Related Concepts

- Phishing—ATV-1.1A
- Smishing—ATV-1.1B
- Vishing—ATV-1.1C
- Pharming—ATV-1.1I
- Whaling—ATV-1.1L
- Credential harvesting—ATV-1.1P

Security+ Objective

1.1: Compare and contrast different types of social engineering techniques.

Dumpster Diving

Description

Dumpster diving occurs when an attacker searches for information in a dumpster used by an organization they wish to attack. Typically, the goal is to find information from disposed paper that has not been shredded, optical or disk drives that have been discarded without reformatting, or any other entity that could house confidential or valuable information.

Example

Goodheart-Willcox Publisher

Related Concepts

- Reconnaissance—ATV-1.1R

Security+ Objective

1.1: Compare and contrast different types of social engineering techniques.

ATV-1.1H Shoulder Surfing

Description

Shoulder surfing is a social engineering attack in which an attacker looks over a victim's shoulder to observe keystrokes or information entered onto a display. This type of attack is often conducted in an effort to determine usernames, passwords, or personally identifiable information such as Social Security numbers. Shoulder surfing is more prevalent in high-crowded areas, such as an airport, and users should be aware of the viewpoints an individual may have while being behind them. Screen filters can be used to prevent shoulder surfing.

Shoulder surfing can be accomplished with relative ease. Imagine a scenario in which a threat actor approaches an employee working at an information or reception desk. The threat actor can ask for information, such as a person's direct phone number or office location, and when the employee conducts a search for the requested data, the threat actor can view the employee's keyboard or screen to identify keystrokes or confidential information. With this information, the threat actor may be able to bypass security measures or gain access to the organization's network. *Screen filters*, also known as *content filters*, can be helpful in mitigating shoulder surfing.

Related Concepts

- Tailgating—ATV-1.1J
- Credential harvesting—ATV-1.1P
- Reconnaissance—ATV-1.1R

Security+ Objective

1.1: Compare and contrast different types of social engineering techniques.

ATV-1.1I Pharming

Description

A *pharming* attack occurs when a victim's Domain Name Service (DNS) has been compromised. In most pharming attacks, a victim attempts to access a known website, such as a financial institution site, but is instead redirected to a spoofed site. Once on this malicious site, any credentials or information entered are sent to the attacker.

Example

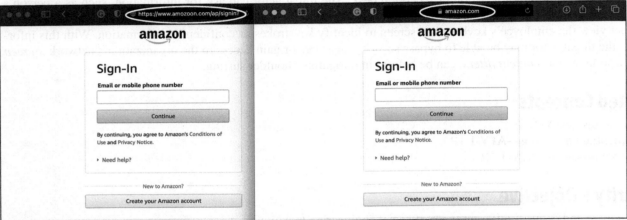

Goodheart-Willcox Publisher

Related Concepts

- Phishing—ATV-1.1A
- Smishing—ATV-1.1B
- Vishing—ATV-1.1C
- Spear phishing—ATV-1.1F
- Whaling—ATV-1.1L
- Credential harvesting—ATV-1.1P
- Domain name system (DNS)—ATV-1.4E

Security+ Objective

1.1: Compare and contrast different types of social engineering techniques.

Tailgating

Description

Tailgating is a social engineering attack in which an individual who does not have access to a physical premise follows closely behind an individual that has access to a physical premise.

Example

A common example of tailgating is an attacker holding a door for and entering after authorized personnel. Often, the authorized individual uses a near-field communication (NFC) badge to open a door. Once the door is unlocked, the attacker either opens the door for the individual or sneaks in before the door closes and locks.

Related Concepts

- Shoulder surfing—ATV-1.1H
- Mantraps—AD-2.7B
- Visitor logs—AD-2.7Q

Security+ Objective

1.1: Compare and contrast different types of social engineering techniques.

ATV-1.1K Eliciting Information

Description

Eliciting information is a social engineering tactic used by an attacker to obtain information from a victim through nontechnical means.

Example

One of the primary methods of eliciting information is through personal conversations in which an attacker gains their victim's trust. Once trust is obtained, the victim will be more likely to share private, personal, or confidential information about themselves, others, or data.

Related Concepts

- Prepending—ATV-1.1M
- Credential harvesting—ATV-1.1P
- Reconnaissance—ATV-1.1Q
- Impersonation—ATV-1.1S

Security+ Objective

1.1: Compare and contrast different types of social engineering techniques.

Whaling

Description

Whaling attacks are similar to spear phishing attacks in that they target a specific person. However, whaling attacks normally target high-ranking members of an organization, such as a CEO.

Example

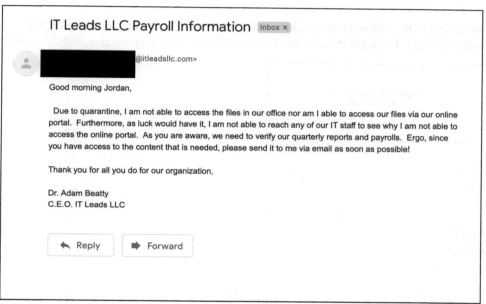

IT Leads LLC Payroll Information Inbox ×

@itleadsllc.com>

Good morning Jordan,

   Due to quarantine, I am not able to access the files in our office nor am I able to access our files via our online portal. Furthermore, as luck would have it, I am not able to reach any of our IT staff to see why I am not able to access the online portal. As you are aware, we need to verify our quarterly reports and payrolls. Ergo, since you have access to the content that is needed, please send it to me via email as soon as possible!

Thank you for all you do for our organization,

Dr. Adam Beatty
C.E.O. IT Leads LLC

◀ Reply   ➡ Forward

Goodheart-Willcox Publisher

Related Concepts

- Phishing—ATV-1.1A
- Smishing—ATV-1.1B
- Vishing—ATV-1.1C
- Spear phishing—ATV-1.1F
- Pharming—ATV-1.1I
- Credential harvesting—ATV-1.1P

Security+ Objective

1.1: Compare and contrast different types of social engineering techniques.

Prepending

Description

Prepending is a social engineering technique in which characters are added to the beginning of a text string, phrase, word, or other input. The goal is often to influence how a user receives or interprets a message. Prepending can also result in manipulation of the Autonomous Systems-Path (AS-Path) of a Border Gateway Protocol (BGP) route.

Example

A good example of prepending can be seen in the following image, in which a threat actor has attempted to mimic the US Internal Revenue Service (IRS) Twitter account. The legitimate Twitter handle, @IRStaxpros, is spoofed as @IRSdotcom.

Authentic Twitter Account
@IRStaxpros

Prepending Twitter Account
@IRSdotcom

Goodheart-Willcox Publisher

Related Concepts

- Eliciting information—ATV-1.1K
- Credential harvesting—ATV-1.1P
- Reconnaissance—ATV-1.1Q
- Impersonation—ATV-1.1S

Security+ Objective

1.1: Compare and contrast different types of social engineering techniques.

Identity Fraud

Description

Identity fraud is an illegal action in which an attacker obtains, stores, and then uses a victim's personal identity information to pose as that person or commit financial fraud.

Examples

The following are considered the most typical forms, and uses, of identity fraud:

1. An attacker opening lines of credit through their victim's identity

2. Attackers making purchase via their victim's identity and financial information

3. Attackers selling their victim's identity and financial information to other attackers on the dark web

Related Concepts

- Invoice scam—ATV-1.1O
- Impersonation—ATV-1.1S

Security+ Objective

1.1: Compare and contrast different types of social engineering techniques.

Invoice Scams

Description

Invoice scams occur when an attacker sends a phony invoice to a company with the goal of receiving payment for services or goods. Many times, companies pay invoices they receive without investigating the source or work performed. In this capacity, invoice scams can be surprisingly effective. False invoices are primarily sent via e-mail, but physical invoices can still be effective. Another method of invoice scams occurs when an attacker sends a digital invoice that appears to be from a legitimate vendor and requires the victim to create or input a username and password into a malicious website that harvests financial data.

Examples

Goodheart-Willcox Publisher

Related Concepts

- Identity fraud—ATV-1.1N
- Credential harvesting—ATV-1.1P
- Impersonation—ATV-1.1S

Security+ Objective

1.1: Compare and contrast different types of social engineering techniques.

Credential Harvesting

Description

Credential harvesting occurs when an attacker tricks a victim into entering their username and password into a malicious website so the attacker can steal the victim's credentials. Credential harvesting is commonly utilized in phishing and man-in-the-middle (MITM) attacks. Additionally, credential harvesting is often the goal of other social engineering attacks and cyber incidents.

Example

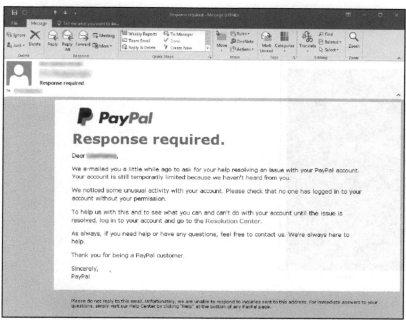

Goodheart-Willcox Publisher

Related Concepts

- Phishing—ATV-1.1A
- Smishing—ATV-1.1B
- Vishing—ATV-1.1C
- Spear phishing—ATV-1.1F
- Dumpster diving—ATV-1.1G
- Shoulder surfing—ATV-1.1H
- Pharming—ATV-1.1I
- Eliciting information—ATV-1.1K
- Whaling—ATV-1.1L
- Prepending—ATV-1.1M
- Invoice scams—ATV-1.1O
- Watering hole attack—ATV-1.1T

Security+ Objective

1.1: Compare and contrast different types of social engineering techniques.

Reconnaissance

Description

Reconnaissance is a process in which an attacker collects information about their victims before implementing an attack. Reconnaissance can be *active*, which involves acquiring data through tools and utilities that interact with a system, or *passive*, which is the acquisition of data without the target knowing it is occurring. In addition to reconnaissance conducted by an attacker, authorized penetration testers, vulnerability testers, or white hat hackers can also conduct reconnaissance.

Examples

1. Port Scanning

Goodheart-Willcox Publisher

2. Phishing

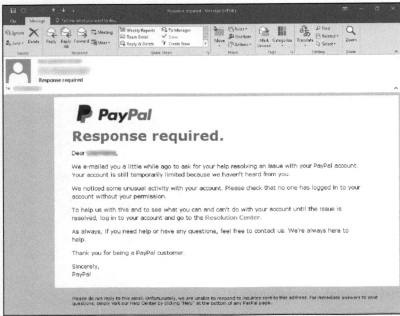

Goodheart-Willcox Publisher

3. Ping Sweeping

```
Command Prompt

Microsoft Windows [Version 10.0.19041.746]
(c) 2020 Microsoft Corporation. All rights reserved.

C:\Users\Dr.Beatty-GW>for /l %i in (1,1,254) do @ping -n 1 -w 100 192.%i

Pinging 192.0.0.1 with 32 bytes of data:
Request timed out.

Ping statistics for 192.0.0.1:
    Packets: Sent = 1, Received = 0, Lost = 1 (100% loss),

Pinging 192.0.0.2 with 32 bytes of data:
Reply from 173.219.152.193: TTL expired in transit.

Ping statistics for 192.0.0.2:
    Packets: Sent = 1, Received = 1, Lost = 0 (0% loss),

Pinging 192.0.0.3 with 32 bytes of data:
Request timed out.

Ping statistics for 192.0.0.3:
    Packets: Sent = 1, Received = 0, Lost = 1 (100% loss),

Pinging 192.0.0.4 with 32 bytes of data:
Request timed out.

Ping statistics for 192.0.0.4:
    Packets: Sent = 1, Received = 0, Lost = 1 (100% loss),

Pinging 192.0.0.5 with 32 bytes of data:
Request timed out.

Ping statistics for 192.0.0.5:
    Packets: Sent = 1, Received = 0, Lost = 1 (100% loss),

Pinging 192.0.0.6 with 32 bytes of data:
Reply from 173.219.152.193: TTL expired in transit.

Ping statistics for 192.0.0.6:
    Packets: Sent = 1, Received = 1, Lost = 0 (0% loss),

Pinging 192.0.0.7 with 32 bytes of data:
Reply from 173.219.152.193: TTL expired in transit.

Ping statistics for 192.0.0.7:
    Packets: Sent = 1, Received = 1, Lost = 0 (0% loss),

Pinging 192.0.0.8 with 32 bytes of data:
Reply from 173.219.152.193: TTL expired in transit.
```

Goodheart-Willcox Publisher

Related Concepts

- Prepending—ATV-1.1M

Security+ Objective

1.1: Compare and contrast different types of social engineering techniques.

Hoax

Description

A *hoax* is a falsehood that people believe to be genuine. Hoaxes often take the form of *scareware*, which consists of Internet pop-ups informing users that their devices are infected with malware when they are actually not. Another example of a hoax is when an attacker exploits a victim's gullibility to obtain the victim's personal information, username and password, or money.

Example

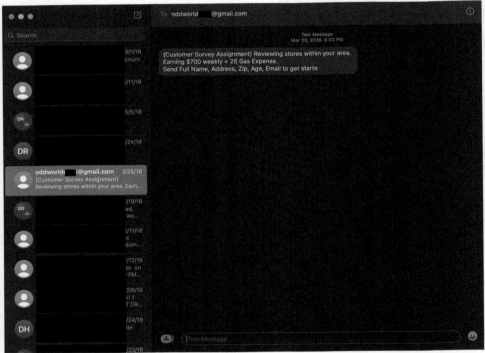

Goodheart-Willcox Publisher

Related Concepts

- Prepending—ATV-1.1M
- Influence campaign—ATV-1.1V

Security+ Objective

1.1: Compare and contrast different types of social engineering techniques.

Impersonation

Description

Impersonation is used by an attacker when they attempt to portray themselves as a trustworthy individual affiliated with the victims or organizations they seek to attack. If effective, impersonation attacks may lead to obtaining personal information or the transferring of funds.

Example

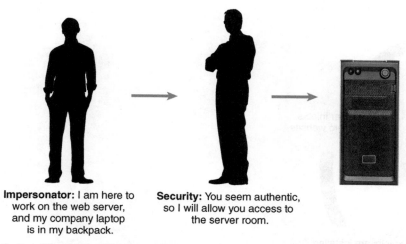

Impersonator: I am here to work on the web server, and my company laptop is in my backpack.

Security: You seem authentic, so I will allow you access to the server room.

Goodheart-Willcox Publisher; (silhouette icons) Rawpixel.com/Shutterstock.com; (server) Den Rozhnovsky/Shutterstock.com

Related Concepts

- Eliciting information—ATV-1.1K
- Prepending—ATV-1.1M
- Identity fraud—ATV-1.1N
- Invoice scams—ATV-1.1O

Security+ Objective

1.1: Compare and contrast different types of social engineering techniques.

Watering Hole Attack

Description

Attackers use *watering hole attacks* by hacking into a website they know their victims visit frequently. Once the attacker has hacked their victim's frequently visited website, the attacker may utilize credential harvesting or other rogue activities.

Example

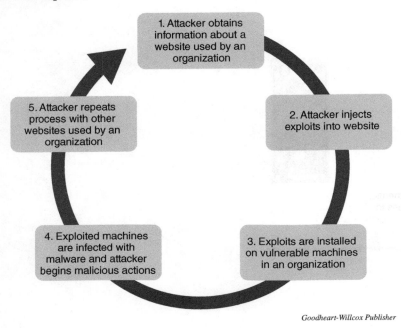

1. Attacker obtains information about a website used by an organization

2. Attacker injects exploits into website

3. Exploits are installed on vulnerable machines in an organization

4. Exploited machines are infected with malware and attacker begins malicious actions

5. Attacker repeats process with other websites used by an organization

Goodheart-Willcox Publisher

Related Concepts

- Credential harvesting—ATV-1.1P

Security+ Objective

1.1: Compare and contrast different types of social engineering techniques.

ATV-1.1U Typo Squatting

Description

Typo squatting, also commonly referred to as *URL hijacking*, occurs when an attacker establishes a website with a URL that is syntactically similar to a website the victim attempts to access. The attacker is relying on the victim performing a typographical error when inputting the website URL in their browser.

Example

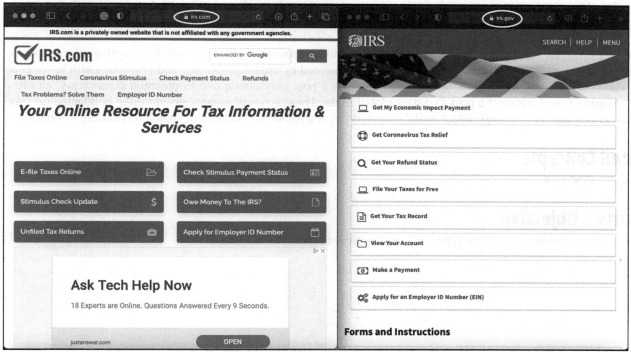

Goodheart-Willcox Publisher

Related Concepts

- Domain name system (DNS)—ATV-1.4E

Security+ Objective

1.1: Compare and contrast different types of social engineering techniques.

Influence Campaigns

Description

Influence campaigns are designed to sway the public's opinion regarding political and social issues. They are often conducted in one of two methods: hybrid warfare and social media influence.

Examples

Hybrid warfare refers to military strategy that combines political, conventional, and cyberwarfare to disseminate false information. It can include tactics used in political warfare to persuade an elected official's decision regarding military use as well as strategies used to present false, misleading, or fabricated news. A common example of hybrid warfare is the use of social media websites to persuade and influence elections.

Social media influence campaigns weaponized social media sites in an effort to launch disruptive information or psychological campaigns. These campaigns can be implemented by creating, sharing, and promoting articles or user posts. The post itself, along with the augmented attention a post may obtain due to potential controversy, elevates the information found within the post to a near global scale. These types of campaigns are often conducted on fake accounts, called *burner accounts*, which make it difficult to determine who created or shared misleading information.

Related Concepts

- Hoax—ATV-1.1R

Security+ Objective

1.1: Compare and contrast different types of social engineering techniques.

ATV-1.1W — Principles (Reasons for Effectiveness)

Description

In general, there are seven principles that make social engineering attempts effective. These principles include authority, intimidation, consensus, scarcity, familiarity, trust, and urgency. It is important to note that the reasons for effectiveness are largely based on the psychological tactics used for the social engineering attacks, not the technology used.

Examples

Authority refers to an attacker presenting as some type of power or influence over the victim or an attacker taking the authority and rights of their victims. For example, the attacker may state they are from an organization's help desk and need to confirm the credit card or banking information used for tech support. The victim, due to the authority of the attack, may provide the information without question.

Intimidation is when an attacker instills some level of fear or concern in their victim. For example, an attacker may tell a victim that they owe money to a bank and failure to provide a credit card or account number will result in additional financial penalties. The victim may feel intimated that if they do not offer the information, they will be responsible for financial penalties or fines.

Consensus, also termed as *social proof*, is when an attacker makes a request appear as a common occurrence. For example, the attacker may tell the victim that the prior employee in their role provided this information in the past. Since that individual is not there to state whether it is true, the victim may believe that the information can be provided.

Scarcity is when an attacker emphasizes to their victims that there is a lack of supply of something and, therefore, its value has increased. For example, an attacker may notify the victim that their antivirus software license is set to run out, and more licenses must be needed to avoid unprotected systems. As a result, the victim may provide financial information to the attacker, intending to purchase additional licenses, which is used to make fraudulent transactions.

Familiarity is a social engineering tactic where the attacker leads the victim to believe they are friends. Doing so will leave the victim vulnerable to the attacker, and the victim will not think the attacker will use the information for malicious purposes.

Trust is a key concept in social engineering, and attackers rely on their victims trusting them. Once the attacker has gained their victims' trust, they will lead them to believe their issues can be resolved as long as they provide the requested information.

Urgency is utilized by attackers to convey a sense of immediate action or attention. For example, they may tell their victims that their software is set to expire at the end of the year in an effort to get the victim to act fast and provide financial data. This is often successful through distracting their victims from thinking as to whether or not they should share the information, through the urgency of the circumstances.

Security+ Objective

1.1: Compare and contrast different types of social engineering techniques.

Malware

Description

Malware is malicious software created by attackers to disrupt the functionality of a victim's computer, obtain unauthorized access to a system, and render the victim's computer unable to retrieve or use data. If you choose to work with malicious programs in an effort to further your studies, it is strongly advised that you utilize virtual machines and have proper supervision and instruction from an instructor. There are many forms of malware, including the following.

Examples

Ransomware is most often implemented by locking a computer and sending a message or screen prompt instructing the victim to send funds to the attacker; otherwise, the device will remain locked, and the victim will lose access to data. In recent years, the FBI MoneyPak Ransomware, also called Reveton Ransomware, encrypts the data on a target machine so the user cannot access it. The following is an example of one form of ransomware.

1. Attacker generates ransomware and attaches it to a file or web page

4. Attacker demands payment, often in cryptocurrency, to provide a key

2. Victim unknowingly downloads ransomware and is not able to access data due to encryption

3. Data cannot be decrypted without key

Goodheart-Willcox Publisher; (silhouette icon) Rawpixel.com/Shutterstock.com; (computer) Den Rozhnovsky/Shutterstock.com

A *Trojan*, also termed as a *Trojan horse*, is a program that presents itself as legitimate software but is in fact malware. Once a Trojan is installed into a victim's machine, it has as much access to the victim's system as the user. The following image is a visualization of a Trojan discovered by Windows Defender.

Trojans may enable computers to appear as though they are operating without error when they are actually infected with malware running in the background.

Over time, performance is impacted

Attackers may be able to access and obtain data or personal information

Trojan may enable attacker to connect to other devices remotely

Goodheart-Willcox Publisher; (clock) NEGOVURA/Shutterstock.com; (compact disk) Yuliia Markova/Shutterstock.com; (computers) Den Rozhnovsky/Shutterstock.com

Worms are malware that do not need victims to perform any actions, as they are able to operate, replicate, and spread to other systems with no user interaction. This type of malware self-propagates and spreads to other systems rapidly using the victim's network as a transmission medium. Due to the inherent difficulty of catching worms, intrusion-detection systems (IDSs) and intrusion-prevention systems (IPSs) are often employed to assist in containing their spread.

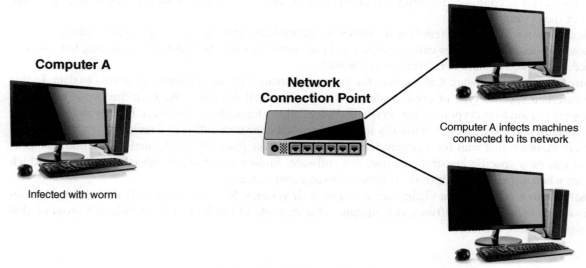

Goodheart-Willcox Publisher; (switch) Romvo/Shutterstock.com; (computers) Den Rozhnovsky/Shutterstock.com

Potentially unwanted programs (PUPs) are programs that are unwanted by a user but have been approved for download. Often, these programs are built into downloadable software. For example, a user may download a web browser but be unaware that the web browser is packaged with a trial-basis antimalware program. Not all PUPs are malware, but they do utilize system resources and can be a drain on a device and its network.

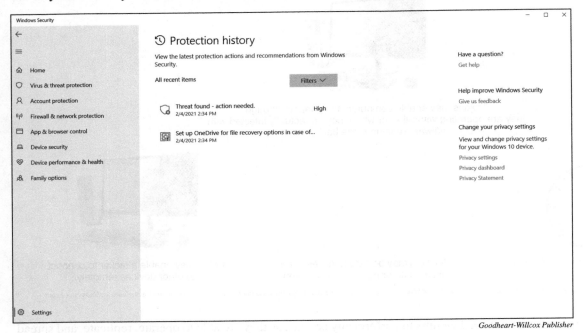

A *fileless virus* is malware that uses a computer's system files or applications to launch malware. Often, these viruses rely on exploits within legitimate programs to install malware on a victim's system.

Command and control (C&C) attacks are malware attacks that configure a machine to signal the attacker's server for instruction. The server is configured to send commands to a victim's system and is widely used to steal data and disrupt services of the system.

Bots are devices within a victim's system that are infected with malware that enables an attacker to take control of the system remotely. Bots are sometimes called *zombies* and can spread to millions of devices, including IoT hosts. A series of infected, networked devices is referred to as a *botnet*.

Cryptomalware is a type of malware that requires the use to cryptocurrency for the return or access to data. In this regard, ransomware is a specific type of cryptomalware. The fundamental difference between the two is that while ransomware may only claim to encrypt files, true cryptomalware follows through on that threat. Furthermore, since the ransom must be paid in cryptocurrency, it is usually impossible to trace the transaction to a recipient.

Logic bombs are malware that wait for a certain series of events to take place before the malware actions are activated. The event can be a specific keystroke or installed software. Similar to a logic bomb is a *time bomb*, which launches malware when a specific day or time, as opposed to an event, occurs.

Spyware is malware that watches what victims are doing on their systems. Spyware is typically downloaded by victims due to the victims believing the software is legitimate. One example of this is the CoolWebSearch program that monitors your web browsing activities.

Keyloggers record the keys a victim types on their keyboard. Once collected, a script of keystrokes entered while the keylogger was active on a system is provided to the attacker.

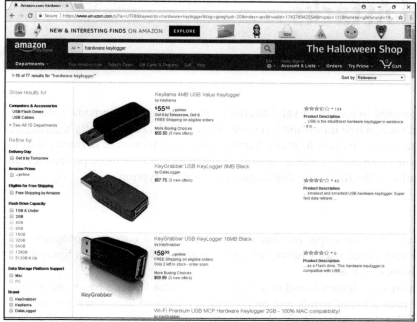

Goodheart-Willcox Publisher

A *remote access Trojan (RAT)* software downloaded on a victim's machine that enables attackers to connect and take control of a victim's system remotely. The following is an image that displays a widely used RAT called DarkComet.

Rootkit malware is one of the most difficult types of malware to detect and remove from a system. This is due to the software residing in the kernel of an operation system. An example of rootkit malware is the ZeuS virus, which can collect passwords from a protected storage location.

Backdoors create access to a victim's computer. This access does not require authentication to access the victim's machine either.

Related Concepts

- Malicious code or script execution—ATV-1.4G
- Endpoint protection—IMP-3.2A

Security+ Objective

1.2: Given a scenario, analyze potential indicators to determine the type of attack.

ATV-1.2B Password Attacks

Description

For most authentication methods, a user is required to provide a valid username and password. Usernames are often easier to guess, as most system utilize a pattern such as first initial and last name. For example, Adam Beatty's username is abeatty. Passwords can be much more complex for hackers to guess. Furthermore, usernames are normally sent in clear text, but passwords are usually hashed when transmitted over a network. Since password are more protected than usernames, attackers often launch attacks similar to the following that target password encryption.

Examples

Spraying is an attack method in which hackers input an ample number of usernames into a computer program that loops through the usernames and attempts to guess each user's password with a number of possibilities. Spraying is often achieved through dictionary attacks or brute-force attacks.

Dictionary attacks involve a hacker using words or phrases found in a dictionary to break a user's password. Often, these attacks are conducted via software that uses a list of words and precomputed hashes to help determine a password. While most Group Policy Objects (GPOs) do not permit simple passwords, it is important to remember that words and simple phrases are often used when hackers attempt to hack a user's account. Dictionary attacks can be mitigated through the use of lockout policies.

Brute-force attacks occur when hackers try to guess a user's password by attempting every scenario they deem as a possibility that could be your password. Although hackers may have access to a user's password hash, including various forms of case, numbers, and special characters, this is not the best method of password hacking due to the amount of time used to guess a password and the possibility of an account being locked out and a notification sent to the account owner. There are two forms of brute force attacks of which a cybersecurity professional should be aware:

- *Offline* brute-force attacks consist of a hacker trying to access a password hash without the risk of being discovered since they are not actually trying to log on an application server.
- *Online* brute-force attacks require a hacker to interact with an application server to obtain access.

Rainbow tables consist of pre-built hashes, their calculations, and the possibilities of passwords that are already completed. Rainbow tables are a database of collected hashes that consist of possible passwords Also, rainbow tables are significant when trying to hack long passwords. However, a rainbow table must have a table for each hashing method.

Plaintext/unencrypted attacks may occur when a hacker obtains passwords form a database that stores a user's password in plaintext. Since the password is not encrypted, the hacker could possibly obtain passwords with relative ease.

Related Concepts

- Account policies—AD-3.7C
- Authentication management—AD-3.8A
- Password crackers—OIR-4.1G

Security+ Objective

1.2: Given a scenario, analyze potential indicators to determine the type of attack.

Physical Attacks

Description

Physical attacks in the cybersecurity sector are based on manipulation of physical entities attackers are able to access or circumvent.

Examples

Malicious universal serial bus (USB) cables are capable of compromising a connected device in a short amount of time. Often, these cables inject keystrokes that enable an attacker to install malware. These attacks typically go unnoticed until unusual activity is discovered. Once connected, attackers can execute commands on not only the connected device but also other devices networked to the targeted machine.

Malicious flash drives contain a virus. Once the malicious drive is inserted into a system, the virus will install on the machine due to the plug-and-play nature of flash drives. Drives infected with malware typically contains backdoors, ransomware, Trojans, or browser hijacking tools.

Card cloning occurs when an attacker makes a copy of the information that is provided on a card such as a credit card. This information is then transferred to a blank card, which is used to make fraudulent purchases or gain access to a secured area. To obtain this information, attackers often use a card skimmer.

Skimming is the process of installing a device, called a *skimmer*, on card-based transaction systems such as ATMs or point-of-sale (PoS) devices. When a card is inserted into the ATM or PoS device, the skimmer reads the information on the card and transmits the data to an attacker's system. Once a card's information is obtained, the data can be used to create a clone. Skimmers often go undetected on most devices; however, they can be identified by opening the transaction system or by attempting to pull the card reader away from the system.

Related Concepts

- Dumpster diving—ATV-1.1G
- Shoulder surfing—ATV-1.1H
- Tailgating—ATV-1.1J
- Explain the importance of physical security controls—AD-2.7

Security+ Objective

1.2: Given a scenario, analyze potential indicators to determine the type of attack.

Adversarial Artificial Intelligence (AI)

Description

Adversarial AI refers to machine learning techniques that create dangerous outcomes due to accidental or purposeful malicious errors in a machine's input. Although there are various factors as to how this may occur, there are two attributes that are the most effective in this act.

Examples

Tainted training data for machine learning (ML) can be an AI defect, as the AI systems rely on training data for functionality. Tainted training data MI can effectively poison AI algorithms and result in attacks or alteration of AI coding. The *security of machine learning algorithms* can be altered by an attacker, as ML learns directly from the data it collects or is given.

Security+ Objective

1.2: Given a scenario, analyze potential indicators to determine the type of attack.

ATV-1.2E Supply Chain Attacks

Description

A *supply chain attack* is an external threat in which a threat actor gains access to a system using the access of a partner or vendor in a supply chain. In this type of attack, a vendor or partner's credentials are stolen and used to access a system as opposed to an organizational employee's credentials.

Example

A good example of a supply chain attack is one in which a third-party vendor is used for payroll information, such as Paychex. Assume Paychex suffered a network breach and an attacker is now able to create a spoofed e-mail. The spoofed e-mail is sent to organizations that use Paychex and requests that organizations download a software update in order to maintain functionality. When the organization downloads the software to its workstation(s), the attack may be able to access the organization's network and workstations remotely.

In this example, the attacker did not attack the organization directly. Rather, the organization was impacted as a result of an attack committed against a partner, vendor, or affiliate.

Related Concepts

- Vectors—ATV-1.5C
- Third-party risks—ATV-1.6D
- Third-party risk management—GRC-5.3C

Security+ Objective

1.2: Given a scenario, analyze potential indicators to determine the type of attack.

Cloud-Based vs. On-Premises Attacks

Description

Cloud-based technologies offer organizations cost-effective methods while having their data stored offsite. However, due to data and storage devices being accessible via an Internet connection, cloud-based systems are perceived to be more prone to breaches and attacks. Therefore, while cost and convenience are luxuries of cloud-based storage, many organizations may prefer to utilize on-premises storage means.

On-premises technologies offer more control and security compared to cloud-based technologies. However, it should not be implied that there are no risks for on-premises technologies, as attacks can target on-premises technologies as well, such as physical damage and malicious code, for example.

Examples

A cloud vector is an attack vector that originates through cloud providers, operations, technologies, or software. Examples of cloud vectors include shared services, supply-chain attacks, DoS attacks, hijacking attacks, and attempts to gain credentials through social engineering.

On-premises attacks are typically easier to defend against since they occur within an organization's physical campus. These include physical attacks and manual injection of code through macros, input, or malicious USB drives. Theft or damage can also constitute an on-premises attack.

Related Concepts

- Cloud-based vs. on-premises vulnerabilities—ATV-1.6A
- On-premises vs. off-premises—AD-2.2D
- Cloud vs. on-premises requirements—AD-2.4E
- On-premises vs. cloud—AD-2.5C
- On-premises vs. cloud—OIR-4.5C

Security+ Objective

1.2: Given a scenario, analyze potential indicators to determine the type of attack.

ATV-1.2G **Cryptographic Attacks**

Description

Cryptographic attacks refer to attacks in which a threat actor attempts to break the encryption on data they have retrieved or intercepted. In other words, they are trying to discover the key and hash used to decipher the encrypted data. If successful, the attack results in the reveal of plaintext data.

Examples

- A *birthday attack* is a cryptographic attack that seeks to exploit the birthday paradox, which is a mathematical theory that states in a set of randomly chosen people, some pair of them will have the same birthday. These attacks work better on networks that have a high number of collision due to probability that there will be multiple results with the same output. A collision is a data transmission error that occurs when two different inputs produce the same message digest.
- A *collision attack* is a cryptographic attack that exploits collisions by comparing two hashes. The hacker must be in control of the input to the hash function and generates a high volume of traffic in an attempt to duplicate the hash digest.
- A *downgrade attack* is a cryptographic attack in which a hacker forces a system to switch to a less-secure cryptographic standard. The hacker does not attempt to break encryption keys; instead, they force the system to use less-secure cryptography so cracking encryption is not necessary.

Related Concepts

- Diversity—AD-2.5H
- Constraints—AD-2.6M
- Summarize the basic of cryptographic concepts—AD-2.8
- Cryptographic protocols—IMP-3.4A

Security+ Objective

1.2: Given a scenario, analyze potential indicators to determine the type of attack.

ATV-1.3A — Privilege Escalation

Description

Privilege escalation is an attack that exploits a vulnerability, such as a coding error, design flaw, or oversight, to obtain higher levels of access than originally intended.

Examples

In general, there are two types of privilege escalation:

- *Vertical privilege escalation* occurs when a user exploits a system to gain access to data restricted to accounts with higher-elevated permissions.
- *Horizontal privilege escalation* involves a user accessing a different user's account that has the same permission level but different file access.

Related Concepts

- Penetration testing—ATV-1.8A

Security+ Objective

1.3: Given a scenario, analyze potential indicators associated with application attacks.

Cross-Site Scripting (XSS)

Description

Cross-site scripting (XSS) is an attack in which scripts are injected into pages within a trusted website. Once placed, the scripts enable information entered on the website to be shared with the attacker. One of the most common methods for executing XSS attacks is to inject scripts in website search boxes.

Example

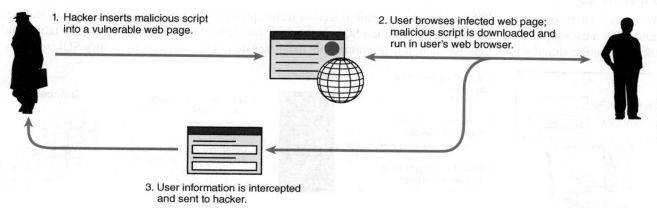

1. Hacker inserts malicious script into a vulnerable web page.

2. User browses infected web page; malicious script is downloaded and run in user's web browser.

3. User information is intercepted and sent to hacker.

Goodheart-Willcox Publisher; (silhouettes) Rawpixel.com/Shutterstock.com

Related Concepts

- Injections—ATV-1.3C
- Error handling—ATV-1.3H
- Improper input handling—ATV-1.3I
- Malicious code or script execution—ATV-1.4G
- Application security—IMP-3.2D

Security+ Objective

1.3: Given a scenario, analyze potential indicators associated with application attacks.

Injections

Description

Injections occur when data is inserted into a program that, by programming and application design, should not be able to accept the data insertion. These programming flaws allow attackers to inject code or scripts into programs and applications such as SQL, DLL, LDAP, and XML.

Examples

Structured query language (SQL) injections are code-injection techniques in which SQL-formatted commands are entered in a user-input field. These injections, called SQL statements, can direct SQL databases to display tables and the information stored within that. As such, it is important that databases do not allow a user to modify SQL requests.

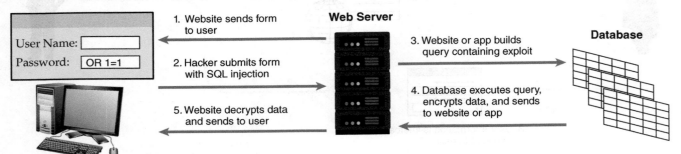

Goodheart-Willcox Publisher; (computers) romvo/Shutterstock.com; (servers) Sujith RS/Shutterstock.com

Dynamic link library (DLL) injections take place when a user inserts running code in the address space of a running process to force it to load another DLL. In DLL injections, users rewrite DLL code in such a way that effects all applicants reliant on the library. The best defense against DLL injection is to make configuration adjustments to limit administrator rights and maintain up-to-date antimalware programs.

1.	Process X	Attach Process Y
2.	Process X	Allocate Memory Process Y and Allocated Memory
3.	Process X	Copy DLL Process Y and Injected DLL

Goodheart-Willcox Publisher

Lightweight directory access protocol (LDAP) injections enables users to obtain sensitive user information that is meant to be secure via LDAP. LDAP injections spoof interpreters to obtain permissions that allow them to query databases without requiring a password.

Extensible markup language (XML) injections modify XML applications or services. If the injection is successful, a user is able to interfere with the XML data being processed by an application or service. XML injections include XML statements being inserted into user input fields, resulting in unexpected commands and security exploits.

Related Concepts

- Cross-site scripting—ATV-1.3B
- Improper input handling—ATV-1.3I
- Malicious code or script execution—ATV-1.4G

Security+ Objective

1.3: Given a scenario, analyze potential indicators associated with application attacks.

Pointer/Object Dereference

Description

A *pointer* is a variable in memory that stores the address of another variable and redirects, or points, the memory to the appropriate locations. A *pointer dereference error*, also called an *object dereference*, is a vulnerability in which a value is not obtained from the correct area. Dereference attacks access and manipulate data that is controlled in memory. Thus, wherever variables of code point to determines how the code will execute, along with any modifications that may persist while executing.

Example

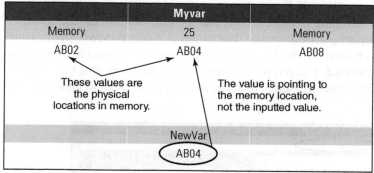

	Myvar	
Memory	25	Memory
AB02	AB04	AB08

These values are the physical locations in memory.

The value is pointing to the memory location, not the inputted value.

NewVar
AB04

Goodheart-Willcox Publisher

Related Concepts

- Buffer overflows—ATV-1.3E
- Integer overflow—ATV-1.3K
- Resource exhaustion—ATV-1.3N
- Memory leak—ATV-1.3O

Security+ Objective

1.3: Given a scenario, analyze potential indicators associated with application attacks.

Directory Traversal

Description

Directory traversal is the process of accessing content on a web server that is not to be displayed or shared, such as the web server's directories. Attackers often use injections to obtain this type of information.

Example

Imagine a clothing website. When you browse the website, you see pictures of the various articles of clothing. Each image is likely displayed with an HTML tag such as <img src="/loadImage?filename=cardigan.jpg">. In this example, the loadImage command queries the filename parameter and displays the **cardigan.jpg** file. The image is stored on a web server, and an API is used to locate the file's exact file path. If the API does not have any type of error handling and input validation, a hacker could use the browser navigator to enter a URL that uses the loadImage command to navigate to a root folder, such as https://www.clothingsite.com/loadImage?filename=../../../etc/passwd. In the same way the loadImage command is able to navigate a web server to display an image, it is now being used to navigate to a root folder (**../../..**) and display the contents of **etc/passwd**, which typically stores registered users on a Unix server.

See an attempted directory traversal in the following screen capture. Note, the attempt resulted in an undiscovered page.

Goodheart-Willcox Publisher

Related Concepts

- Injections—ATV-1.3C

Security+ Objective

1.3: Given a scenario, analyze potential indicators associated with application attacks.

Buffer Overflow

Description

Buffer overflows occur when more data exists in a buffer than the memory can handle. A *buffer* is a component of physical memory used for temporary storage of data. When overflows occur, applications are overloaded, and the remaining contents are sent to other memory areas. Although this is not an easy exploit for attackers to discover, once they do, they can take control of a system's memory. *Buffer-overflow attacks* involve a hacker exploiting an overflow and including executable instructions or overwriting other areas of memory.

Example

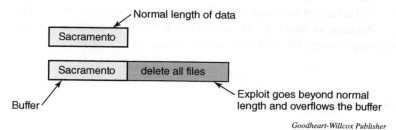

Goodheart-Willcox Publisher

Related Concepts

- Integer overflow—ATV-1.3K
- Memory leak—ATV-1.3O

Security+ Objective

1.3: Given a scenario, analyze potential indicators associated with application attacks.

ATV-1.3G Race Conditions

Description

Race conditions are programming flaws that cause programming functions to occur simultaneously. As a result, this can cause data from one of the functions not to have any outcomes while the other function obtains all of the calculated data. A *race condition attack* exploits the existence of a race condition and takes advantage of the gap in time between initiation and execution of a service.

Example

Race conditions are able to create time-of-check to time-of-use bugs. A *time-of-check to time-of-use (TOCTOU)* is a race condition in which one incident occurs in the time it takes for software to verify the state of a resource before the resource is used. A TOCTOU creates a vulnerability because an attacker can manipulate a file or resource in the gap of time between verification and execution, and the compromised file will be used unknowingly.

Related Concepts

- Application programming interface (API) attacks—ATV-1.3M

Security+ Objective

1.3: Given a scenario, analyze potential indicators associated with application attacks.

Error Handling

Description

Error handling is an important aspect of input validation in which measures are taken to ensure an application can respond to or recover from errors instead of locking up or crashing. Programs and applications need to implement error handling; otherwise, they will have faulty functionality, often in the form of error messages, such as the one shown in the following example.

Example

Goodheart-Willcox Publisher

Related Concepts

- Improper input handling—ATV-1.3I

Security+ Objective

1.3: Given a scenario, analyze potential indicators associated with application attacks.

Improper Input Handling

Description

Improper input handling is a vulnerability that occurs when a software developer does not provide a method of input validation in the software. As a result, an injection of malicious code can alter the functionality of the software. SQL injections are often successful due to improper input handling.

Examples

In-Band SQL Injections:

- *Error-based injections* involve a hacker entering SQL commands to produce error messages. The attacker then uses information found in the error messages to obtain information about the database.
- *Union-based injections* take advantage of the **UNION** SQL command, which combines multiple SQL statements to generate a single HTTP response, which can contain information valuable to a hacker.

Blind SQL Injections:

- *Boolean injections* occur when an attack queries an SQL database, which prompts an application to return the result—depending on if the query is true or false. The attacker can then use the resulting HTTP information to determine if the message was a true or false result.
- *Time-based injections* occur when an SQL query is sent to a database, which waits before responding. The attacker records the time it takes for the database to respond and whether the query was true or false.

Out-of-Band SQL Injections:

- *Out-of-band injections* are used when attackers are not able to use one channel for launching an attack and receiving information. This is also used if a server is unable to withstand the actions being performed.

Related Concepts

- Cross-site scripting—ATV-1.3B
- Injections—ATV-1.3C
- Error handling—ATV-1.3H
- Malicious code or script execution—ATV-1.4G
- Application security—IMP-3.2D

Security+ Objective

1.3: Given a scenario, analyze potential indicators associated with application attacks.

Replay Attacks

Description

Replay attacks consist of attackers obtaining data from network packets via rogue sources such as ARP poising or MitM attacks. Once the packets are obtained by an attacker, the attacker resends the packets to obtain authorized access.

Example

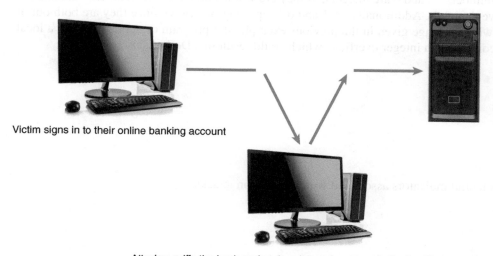

Victim signs in to their online banking account

Attacker sniffs the hash and replays it to gain access to the banking account.

Goodheart-Willcox Publisher; (computer and server) Den Rozhnovsky/Shutterstock.com

Related Concepts

- Man in the middle—ATV-1.4B
- Man in the browser—ATV-1.4C
- Packet capture and replay—OIR-4.1D

Security+ Objective

1.3: Given a scenario, analyze potential indicators associated with application attacks.

Integer Overflow

Description

Integer overflows occur when an integer extends beyond its boundaries. *Boundaries* for integers normally have low-end and high-end ranges.

Example

Imagine a range of −6 to 6. The numbers −6 and 6 are integers, as they are whole numbers. The numbers −6.1 and 6.1 are *not* integers because they have decimals. Additionally −6.1 and 6.1 represent overflows since they are both out of the specified range. Continuing with the range given in the previous example, if a program or application has a local variable equal to 10.2, it would constitute an integer overflow, which could result in a DoS attack.

Related Concepts

- Buffer overflow—ATV-1.3F
- Memory leak—ATV-1.3O

Security+ Objective

1.3: Given a scenario, analyze potential indicators associated with application attacks.

Request Forgeries

Description

Request forgeries take advantage of the trust a website has for the user visiting the website. When a user inputs their login credentials to access resources on a website, they are utilizing authentication. Thus, the user and the website have now established a form of trust, and the website will share its recourses to the user. However, attackers often take advantage of this trust and perform request forgeries, such as the following.

Examples

Server-side request forgery	The attacker bypasses open ports or is provided access through firewall rules. After bypassing or authenticating through external resources and security, the attacker is able to access internal data. *Goodheart-Willcox Publisher; (computer and server) Den Rozhnovsky/Shutterstock.com*
Client-side request forgery	1. Attacker sends an e-mail with a link to a valid site on which they have inserted malicious code or scripts 3. Victim is able to access valid website and use device as anticipated; device is vulnerable to attacker 2. Victim opens e-mail, selects the link, and malicious code or script is executed 4. Attacker disables security features on victim's device *Goodheart-Willcox Publisher; (computer) Den Rozhnovsky/Shutterstock.com*
Cross-site request forgery	1. User logs into bank account. Trust relationship established. Evil Script 2. Script sends commands to bank server. Bank server accepts due to trust relationship. Evil Script *Goodheart-Willcox Publisher; (servers) Sujith RS/Shutterstock.com; (computers) romvo/Shutterstock.com*

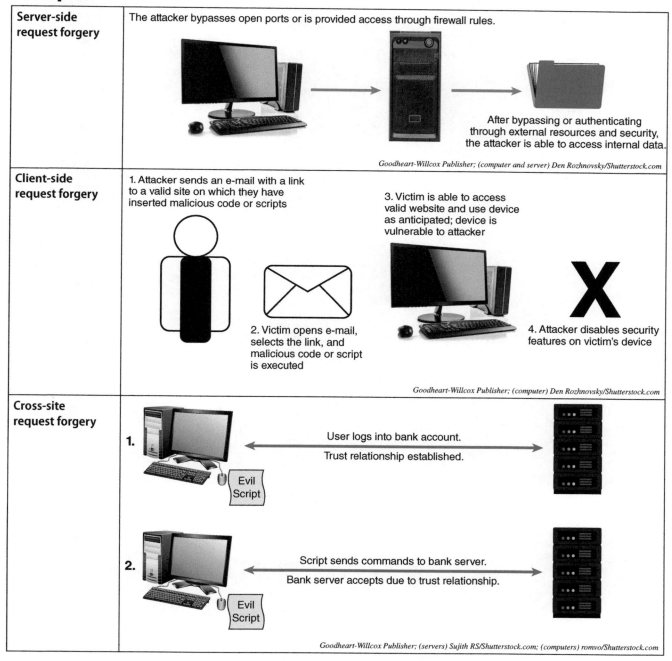

Related Concepts

- Error handling—ATV-1.3H
- Improper input handling—ATV-1.3I
- Replay attack—ATV-1.3J

Security+ Objective

1.3: Given a scenario, analyze potential indicators associated with application attacks.

Application Programming Interface (API) Attacks

Description

An *application programming interface (API) attack* is the use of malicious code or exploitation of vulnerable code within an API to attack the API's endpoint. These types of commands often redirect control of tasks to the attacker and can potentially allow an attacker to access data outside the API. One of the most common methods of this attack is via DoS and DDoS attacks.

Example

A simple example of an API attack is accomplished with a script injection. The threat actor injects malicious script into an API that does not enforce input handling, and that script runs on the user's web page. This specific example is also an example of cross-site scripting (XSS).

Related Concepts

- Injections—ATV-1.3C
- Buffer overflows—ATV-1.3F
- Error handling—ATV-1.3H
- Improper input handling—ATV-1.3I
- Integer overflow—ATV-1.3K
- Malicious code or script execution—ATV-1.4G

Security+ Objective

1.3: Given a scenario, analyze potential indicators associated with application attacks.

Resource Exhaustion

Description

Resource exhaustion refers to attacks or exploits that cause a system to be unusable, inactive, or inaccessible. This is often the result of insufficient memory or deliberately accomplished via DoS or DDoS attacks.

Example

A common example of a resource exhaustion attack is called the *billion laughs attack*. Billion laughs is a DoS attack that targets XML-parsing software. In this attack, entries of code are written that define 10 entities, and each entity consists of 10 previous entities. Additionally, the code includes a single appearance of the largest entity, essentially expanding to one billion copies of the initial entry. These entries are inputted using the text string lol. When the parsing software loads the document, it reads a text string, for example lol6, but lol6 is defined as 10 strings of lol5. This process repeats, with lol5 being defined as 10 strings of lol4, and so on. If coded successfully, a small block of XML code that should normally be less than one kilobyte actually consists of roughly one billion lol entries that take up nearly three gigabytes of memory.

Related Concepts

- Memory leak—ATV-1.3O
- Distributed denial of service (DDoS)—ATV-1.4F

Security+ Objective

1.3: Given a scenario, analyze potential indicators associated with application attacks.

Memory Leak

Description

Memory leaks occur when a program or application does not allocate the memory correctly. When a program completes running, the memory allocated for it should be freed from the program and reallocated to other programs. If object references stay in memory when they are not needed any longer, memory can become exhausted, leading to lockup, crashes, or exploitation of the memory leak.

Examples

Memory leaks are often the result of

- memory values not being deleted from allocated memory;
- objects stored in memory cannot be accessed by code; or
- DoS attack.

Related Concepts

- Pointer/object dereference—ATV-1.3D
- Buffer overflows—ATV-1.3E
- Integer overflow—ATV-1.3K
- Resource exhaustion—ATV-1.3N

Security+ Objective

1.3: Given a scenario, analyze potential indicators associated with application attacks.

Secure Sockets Layer (SSL) Stripping

Description

Secure sockets layer (SSL) stripping occurs when a user provides information, such as login credentials, via an HTTP proxy instead of the intended HTTPS site. Since HTTP does not have security or encryption, attackers are able to obtain and use the user's credentials to access their account, provided the credentials are not changed after the attack.

Example

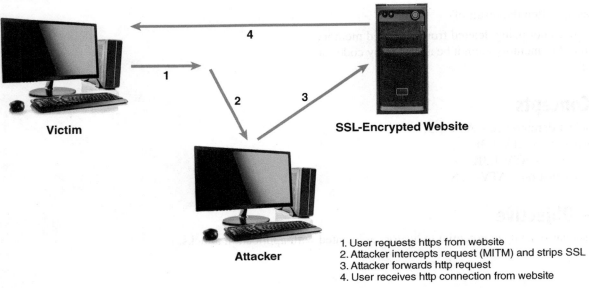

Victim

SSL-Encrypted Website

Attacker

1. User requests https from website
2. Attacker intercepts request (MITM) and strips SSL
3. Attacker forwards http request
4. User receives http connection from website

Goodheart-Willcox Publisher; (computers and server) Den Rozhnovsky/Shutterstock.com

Related Concepts

- Man in the middle—ATV-1.4B
- Man in the browser—ATV-1.4C

Security+ Objective

1.3: Given a scenario, analyze potential indicators associated with application attacks.

Driver Manipulation

Description

Driver manipulation often occurs via malware installed with a computer's drivers. Since drivers provide the communication between a computer and its operating system, they are normally trusted. As such, they can often be targets for attackers. Manipulation is typically conducted in one of two ways: shimming and refactoring.

Examples

Think of *shimming* as a type of intermediary, as shims allow you to decide if you would like to employ backward capability. If users decide to use a Windows shim, known to most users as *Compatibility Mode*, an attacker could simply create a shim that appears to be legitimate but actually installs malware on the user's Windows machine.

Refactoring is the process of modifying or restructuring code without affecting external behavior. Similar to shimming, refactoring is a common process that often improves aspects of software. However, refactoring can be used maliciously since it provides insight into code vulnerabilities.

Related Concepts

- Improper or weak patch management—ATV-1.6E
- Boot integrity—IMP-3.2B
- Enforcement and monitoring of—IMP-3.5D

Security+ Objective

1.3: Given a scenario, analyze potential indicators associated with application attacks.

Pass the Hash

Description

Pass-the-hash attacks occur when an attacker is able to authenticate to a remote server by using the Windows NT LAN Manager (NTML) hash of the administrative user's password. Since the attacker possesses an intercepted hash, there is no need for brute force or any other cracking attempts. The best defense against this type of attack is diligence, defense-in-depth, intrusion-detection systems, intrusion-prevention systems, firewalls, least privilege, secure patches, and use of IPSec.

Examples

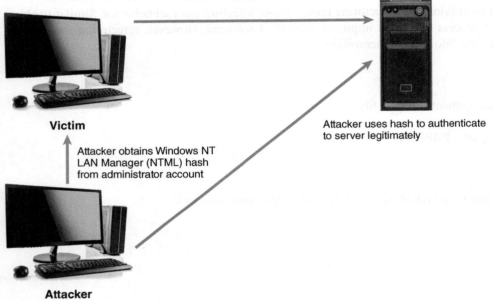

Victim

Attacker obtains Windows NT LAN Manager (NTML) hash from administrator account

Attacker uses hash to authenticate to server legitimately

Attacker

Goodheart-Willcox Publisher; (computers and server) Den Rozhnovsky/Shutterstock.com

Related Concepts

- Hashing—AD-2.1I
- Hashing—AD-2.8E
- Database—IMP-3.2C
- Integrity—OIR-4.5D

Security+ Objective

1.3: Given a scenario, analyze potential indicators associated with application attacks.

ATV-1.4A Wireless

Description

Due to the growing prevalence of wireless communications and networks, wireless-based attacks are becoming more commonplace. *Wireless* attacks are often conducted with the same goal(s) as traditional attacks, but the methodology varies due to the nature of wireless communications. The following examples describe some of the most common forms of wireless vulnerabilities and attacks.

Examples

An *evil twin* is simply an unauthorized access point. Evil twin implementation occurs when an attacker purchases a standard wireless access point, connects it to a network, and configures it with the same SSID and security settings as the genuine network or AP. Furthermore, if the evil twin access point is closer to a victim than the organization's wireless network access point, the evil twin access point may overpower the signal of the organization's legitimate access point, increasing the likelihood of victims unknowingly joining an evil twin. Evils twins are a specific type of rogue access point.

Rogue access points are APs that are plugged into a network without a network administrator's knowledge and can be controlled by a malicious user. These devices also have the ability to enable wireless sharing via their operating system. All evil twins are rogue access points, but not all rogue access points are evil twins. The fundamental difference between a general rogue access point and an evil twin is that evil twins are configured to replicate specific legitimate APs and typical rogue APs are not.

Bluesnarfing is a Bluetooth attack in which hackers are able to export data such as e-mails and contacts via a Bluetooth connection. Additionally, malware could be injected into a device via bluesnarfing.

Bluejacking is a Bluetooth attack where attackers send unsolicited messages via a Bluetooth connection. Not all examples of bluejacking are malicious. For example, retailers may distribute advertisements to Bluetooth-enabled devices within a certain proximity of a store. This is still technically bluejacking, and quite possibly spam, but not necessarily malicious.

Disassociation is a wireless attack in which attackers launch a DoS attack on a wireless network and disconnect users. This is often accomplished via 802.11 management frames.

Jamming, also referred to as *wireless jamming*, is disrupting the radio frequency (RF) of a wireless network. Wireless jammers are illegal in the United States.

Radio frequency identification (RFID) attacks occur when there is interference or spoofing between an RFID and the transmitter it is trying to reach.

Near-field communication (NFC) requires two devices to be near each other. NFC attacks are often conducted via remote capture, which requires the attacker to be within ten meters (roughly 10 feet) of the active devices. NFC attacks can also be performed as man-in-the-middle attacks.

Initialization vector (IV) attacks are wireless attacks that modify the IV during wireless transmission. Recall that an initialization vector (IV) is a randomly generated number of variables added to an encryption key each time a transmission occurs. These types of attacks enable the attacker to read packets in plaintext.

Related Concepts

- Vectors—ATV-1.5C
- Cryptographic protocols—IMP-3.4A
- Authentication protocols—IMP-3.4B
- Methods—IMP-3.4C
- Installation considerations—IMP-3.4D

Security+ Objective

1.4: Given a scenario, analyze potential indicators associated with network attacks.

Man in the Middle

Description

Man-in-the-middle (MITM) attacks occur when an attacker monitors their victim's activity, intercepts communication, and sends a fictitious response to the sender. These attacks require the ability to monitor activity without being discovered and are often accomplished through methods such as eavesdropping via ARP poisoning or spoofing while on the same subnet, NFC interceptions, or by attackers portraying themselves as a web server from which the victim wishes to obtain a connection.

Example

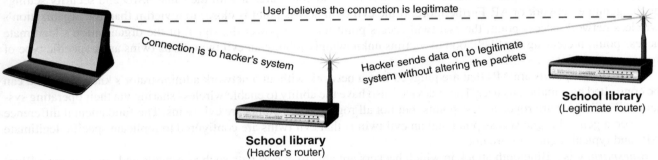

User believes the connection is legitimate

Connection is to hacker's system

Hacker sends data on to legitimate system without altering the packets

School library
(Legitimate router)

School library
(Hacker's router)

Goodheart-Willcox Publisher; (tablet) romvo/Shutterstock.com; (routers) RealVector/Shutterstock.com

Related Concepts

- Replay attack—ATC-1.3J
- Secure Sockets Layer (SSL) stripping—ATV-1.3P
- Man in the browser—ATV-1.4C

Security+ Objective

1.4: Given a scenario, analyze potential indicators associated with network attacks.

Man in the Browser

Description

Man-in-the-browser (MITB) attacks act similarly to MITM attacks. The difference between the two is that MITB attacks do not require the attacker to be on the victim's network. Instead, malware is installed on the victim's machine, and data transmitted via the browser is sent to the attacker.

Example

SSL stripping is a specific type of MITB attack.

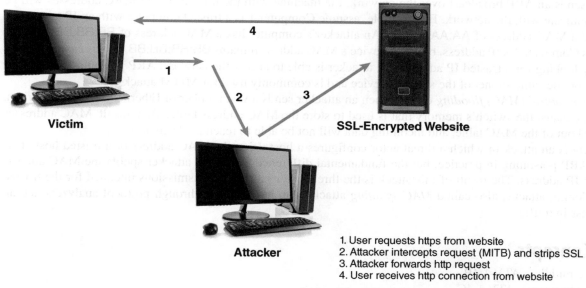

Victim

SSL-Encrypted Website

Attacker

1. User requests https from website
2. Attacker intercepts request (MITB) and strips SSL
3. Attacker forwards http request
4. User receives http connection from website

Goodheart-Willcox Publisher; (computers and server) Den Rozhnovsky/Shutterstock.com

Related Concepts

- Replay attack—ATC-1.3J
- Secure Sockets Layer (SSL) stripping—ATV-1.3P
- Man in the middle—ATV-1.4B

Security+ Objective

1.4: Given a scenario, analyze potential indicators associated with network attacks.

Layer 2 Attacks

Description

Layer 2 attacks are attacks that take place in the Data Link Layer of the OSI model. These attacks alter the transmission of frames from devices on a local area network (LAN). There are multiple examples of layer 2 attacks, including the following.

Examples

Address resolution protocol (ARP) poisoning is used to convert a trusted IP address to a MAC address on a switch. When a host sends an ARP broadcast over the network, the machine with the trusted IP and MAC addresses will be able to communicate with the network. For example, assume Computer 1 is a trusted computer with an IP address of 192.0.0.1 and a MAC address of AA:AA:AA:AA. An attacker's computer has a MAC address of BB:BB:BB:BB. The attacker steals Computer 1's IP address, but their device's MAC address remains BB:BB:BB:BB. In this case, since the switch is only looking for a trusted IP address, the attacker is able to access the network. ARP poisoning requires an attacker to be on the same subnet of the spoofed device and is commonly used for MITM attacks.

Media access control (MAC) flooding occurs when an attacker sends a vast number of Ethernet frames to a switch. Doing so will exhaust the switch's memory that is used to store the MAC address table. As a result, MAC addresses will be pushed out of the MAC table, and incoming data will not be able to reach its destination.

MAC cloning is an attack in which a threat actor configures a host using the MAC address of a trusted host. This is similar to ARP poisoning in practice, but the fundamental difference is that the attacker spoofs the MAC address instead of the IP address. The result of this attack is the threat actor receiving transmissions intended for the trusted host. MAC cloning attacks, also called *MAC spoofing* attacks, can be identified through protocol analyzers and an unexpected loss in traffic.

Related Concepts

- Man in the middle—ATV-1.4B
- Man in the browser—ATV-1.4C

Security+ Objective

1.4: Given a scenario, analyze potential indicators associated with network attacks.

ATV-1.4E Domain Name System (DNS)

Description

Domain name system (DNS) is a networking service that allows users to access a website using a domain name instead of the website's IP address. While IP addresses can be used to access a website, most users either do not know a website's IP address or are simply unaware that IP addresses can be used for navigation. However, many threat actors are aware of IP-based navigation as well as the fact that most users do not know how to perform such navigation. As such, DNS services are frequent targets for hackers. Attacks on DNS include the following.

Examples

Domain hijacking occurs when an attacker obtains access to the domain registration in an attempt to transfer the ownership of the domain from the rightful owner. The domain registration is where the primary DNS information is stored.

DNS poisoning is linking domain names to illegitimate IP addresses. In a DNS poisoning attack, the attacker redirects legitimate URLs to incorrect IP addresses often with the goal of installing malware or manipulating a system's local host file, which is used to populate the local DNS cache when a system is booted.

Universal resource locator (URL) redirection occurs when a user is directed to a website that is different from the website the user wants to access. URL redirections are not always malicious. Many times, organizations redirect URLs that are close to an organizations domain to account for user errors. However, malicious redirections can lead to phishing campaigns that often go unnoticed until an administrator reviews site traffic or analytics. These attacks are normally executed via proxy and can be prevented through stringent practices, such as the inclusion of web application firewalls, scanners, and maintaining up-to-date software and code.

Domain reputation refers to the trust that if a domain, such as www.google.com, changes its IP address, DNS will redirect a user to the new, correct IP address when access to the domain is attempted.

Related Concepts

- Protocols—IMP-3.1A
- Use cases—IMP-3.1B
- Types of certificates—IMP-3.9B

Security+ Objective

1.4: Given a scenario, analyze potential indicators associated with network attacks.

Distributed Denial of Service (DDoS)

Description

Distributed denial of service (DDoS) attacks are executed when multiple systems attack a server, website, or other data transmission medium to cause a widespread outages for users trying to obtain access to systems. These types of attacks are capable of shutting down an entire network. Often, DDoS attacks target the following.

Examples

Network DDoS attacks cause a network to experience more traffic than it can control. As a result, the communications of every device on the network may not be able to send or receive data.

DDoS attacks that target *network applications* cause disruption to programs that function at the Application layer of the OSI model. Attacks on applications make them unstable or unusable.

Operational technology (OT) refers to equipment located within a network. This includes cameras, sensors, IoT devices, or the network itself. Attacks on these technologies can lead to a complete stop in operations. These attacks typically include a network of bots (called a *botnet*) spamming services with illegitimate requests.

Related Concepts

- Resource exhaustion—ATV-1.3N

Security+ Objective

1.4: Given a scenario, analyze potential indicators associated with network attacks.

Malicious Code or Script Execution

Description

Malicious code or script execution can be generated on many platforms. Recall that scripts are small programs created to run automated tasks. Imagine a scenario in which a script designed to launch illegitimate requests to a server is executed. The result could be a widespread DoS attack that shuts down a network. The following provides examples of common software development environments, command-line tools, and insertions that can be placed into documents for attack methods.

Examples

PowerShell:

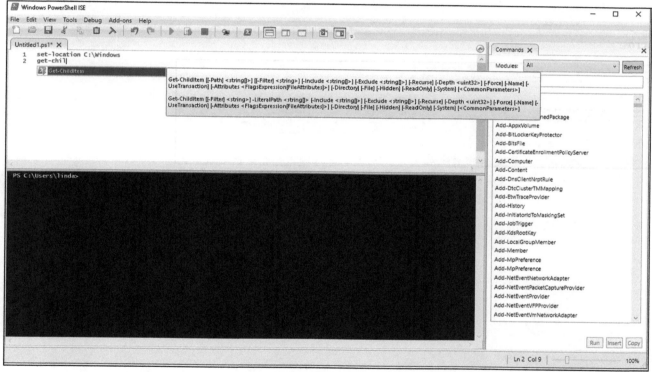

Goodheart-Willcox Publisher

Python:

```
Basic Math.py - /Users/adambeatty/Desktop/Basic Math.py (3.9.1)
#Step One: Let's go over some of the basics of addition (which ones work, which ones do not, and why?):


print(1+2)

print(1+1+1)



#Step Two: Same concept as step one, but let's go a little more in depth and use multiplication (*) and exponentiation (**:


print(10*10)

print((10)*(10))

print(10**10)
```

```
IDLE Shell 3.9.1
Python 3.9.1 (v3.9.1:1e5d33e9b9, Dec  7 2020, 12:10:52)
[Clang 6.0 (clang-600.0.57)] on darwin
Type "help", "copyright", "credits" or "license()" for more information.
>>>
=============== RESTART: /Users/adambeatty/Desktop/Basic Math.py ===============
3
3
100
100
10000000000
>>> |
```

Goodheart-Willcox Publisher

Macros:

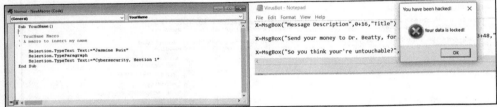

Goodheart-Willcox Publisher

Virtual Basic Applications (VBA):

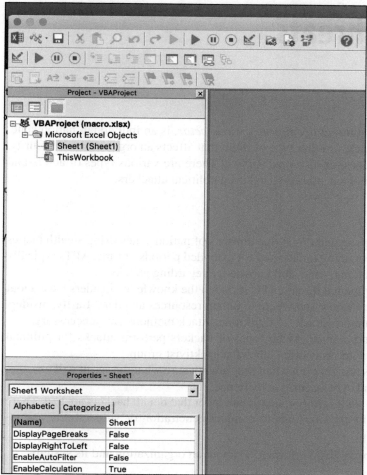

Goodheart-Willcox Publisher

Related Concepts

- Malware—ATV-1.2A
- Cross-site scripting—ATV-1.3B
- Injections—ATV-1.3C
- Application Programming Interface (API) Attacks—ATV-1.3M
- Actors and threats—ATV-1.5A
- Automation/scripting—AD-2.3G
- Shell and script environments—OIR-4.1C

Security+ Objective

1.4: Given a scenario, analyze potential indicators associated with network attacks.

Actors and Threats

Description

In regard to cybersecurity, a *threat actor*, also called a *threat agent* or *malicious actor*, is an individual, nation state, or organization responsible for a security incident, attack, or other type of event that affects an organization's security. The actions of threat actors result in stolen data, outages, or disrupted service. There are various types of actors and threats, and they vary from experienced attackers, to novice attackers, and even political attackers.

Examples

An *advanced persistent threat (APT)* is a highly sophisticated threat that consists of nation states using stealth tactics to gain unauthorized access to systems or networks remaining undetected for extended periods of time. APTs typically have numerous individuals with ample amounts of funding, time, and knowledge regarding attacks.

An *insider threat* is considered one of the most detrimental threats. This is due to the knowledge insiders have about their organization, the organization's operations, such as how and where to obtain resources and data. Lastly, insiders may already have access to the system they are planning to attack, so traditional attack methods are unnecessary.

Hacktivist is a term that is derived from *hacker* and *activist*. These types of hackers perform attacks for political reasons or as a form of social justice. The group Anonymous is often labeled a hacktivist group.

Script kiddies refer to premade scripts that attackers utilize, even when they are not sure what the script will execute. This type of attacker normally lacks programming and cybersecurity experience.

Hackers are often included as a type of threat actor, but it is important to remember that not all hackers are bad. There are also welcoming forms of hacking requested from organizations to conduct penetration or vulnerability assessments. Example of hacker types include the following.

- *White-hat hackers* are ethical hackers who have been given information about an organization and its systems. They are not malicious.
- *Black-hat hackers*, often termed as *crackers*, are malicious, unethical hackers who have not been given permission by an organization to perform any form of hacking.
- *Gray-hat hackers* often seek vulnerabilities that could lead to potential exploits but do not exploit the vulnerabilities as a black-hat hacker would. While gray-hat hackers are not technically malicious, they do not always obtain permission from an organization before attempting to hack it.

Shadow IT refers to the use of information systems, devices, hardware, software, or services without the approval of an organization's IT department. The installation of unapproved devices threatens an organization's security posture in a number of ways. For example, assume a user inserts a personal flash drive to take files home over the weekend. If the flash drive is infected with malware, the user's work computer is at risk for infection.

Competitors are often seeking methods to diminish or eliminate the productivity of their retail competitor. These types of attacks include espionage, DoS attacks, and customer or client persuasion.

Related Concepts

- Attributes of actors—ATV-1.5B
- Vectors—ATV-1.5C

Security+ Objective

1.5: Explain different threat actors, vectors, and intelligence sources.

Attributes of Actors

Description

Attributes are characteristics a person possesses. Many attributes may enable an actor to launch attacks successfully. Common examples of attributes include the following.

Examples

Actors can be internal or external. *Internal* actors are those inside of an organization that pose a threat or vulnerability. *External* actors are those outside of an organization that commit cybercrimes upon an organization.

Some actors may be *sophisticated*, meaning they have experience and knowledge. An actor's level of sophistication and capability determines the *resources* and *funding* they may or may not have. Furthermore, this attribute dictates whether an attack will be advanced or rely on free tools obtained via the Internet.

Threat actors often have differing *intents* or *motivations* for launching attacks. Often, the motivation behind an attack has to do with a political agenda, desire for financial gain or attention, or revenge.

Related Concepts

- Actors and threats—ATV-1.5A
- Vectors—ATV-1.5C

Security+ Objective

1.5: Explain different threat actors, vectors, and intelligence sources.

Vectors

Description

Vectors are the trajectory methods used to bypass an organization's defense. To put it simply, they are the means by which a threat actor attempts to access a system. Vectors are not the goal of the hacker; rather they serve as pathways used to launch attacks.

Examples

Direct access vectors include the physical and remote capabilities for an attacker to disrupt or obtain access to a system. It is recommended that authentication methods be employed for physical and remote access, including cloud-based access, for any system; this will help to prevent attacks and deny access to anyone who does not comply with the proper authentication methods.

Wireless vectors include an initialization vector (IV) that changes a wireless key stream each time it is used. However, if the IV is not significantly large and the same keys are reused, the encryption of the key can be decrypted, and an attacker can obtain the confidential data.

E-mail and removable media vectors are often used when a user disables or does not update their antivirus software. As a result, e-mails and files from removable devices will not be scanned or quarantined.

Supply chain vectors often occur as an end-to-end process of a vendor supplying and releasing of their products. These products may include chips for systems that receive firmware updates. Thus, only trustworthy vendors should be used. Otherwise, it is possible that their products contain a vulnerable backdoor to the device.

Social media vectors vary as the popularity of social media platforms fluctuates. Since individuals place an ample amount of information on their public profile, including information about their organization, attackers use these sites to conduct multiple rounds or forms of reconnaissance with the presented via social media profiles. Furthermore, pictures of the inside of an organization are a common source of information for attackers to utilize in physical attacks.

Related Concepts

- Supply chain attacks—ATV-1.2E
- Given a scenario, analyze potential indicators associated with network attacks—ATV-1.4
- Actors and threats—ATV-1.5A
- Attributes of actors—ATV-1.5B
- Third-party risks—ATV-1.6D
- Hardening—IMP-3.2E
- Third-party risk management—GRC-5.3C

Security+ Objective

1.5: Explain different threat actors, vectors, and intelligence sources.

ATV-1.5D Threat Intelligence Sources

Description

Threat intelligence sources assist cybersecurity professionals in defending their systems from well-known and potentially new threats. Popular examples of threat intelligence sources often include the following.

Examples

Open-source intelligence (OSINT) includes organizations that work together to provide information about attacks they have experienced or researched, as well as how to defend from attacks. Platforms used to obtain this information include YouTube and social media analytical software such as Maltego; however, these are not the only examples of OSINT platforms. Open-source intelligence also offers *vulnerability databases* that provide information about known vulnerabilities and relevant groups that share information.

Closed/proprietary sources are commercial products that require an account and payment in order to access or extract information. Proprietary sources are incredibly reliable, as they employ dedicated specialized tools to gather and report minute details and information about threats. These sources also tend to be more trusted since the sources have agreements with the organizations that rely on them and the resources used to populate these intelligence sources are generally not available to public.

An *information sharing center (ISC)* is an industry-specific group of business owners and IT employees working collectively to gather, analyze, and distribute data about cyber threats. When information is collected, the rapid notification and distribution of data is often critical in preventing widespread attacks. One of the most commonly used ISCs is the Cyber Information Sharing and Collaboration Program (CISCP), which is sponsored by the US Department of Homeland Security.

The *dark web* contains websites and services that can only be obtained via a dark net browser, such as the TOR browser. The dark web largely consists of illegal activity and information, but it is also a community frequently used by cybercriminals. Therefore, it can double as a source of valuable counterintelligence information.

Indicators of compromise (IoC) are the digital footprints of a threat. IoCs are typically found or discovered during a review of syslog and other various system files and log entries. Information security professionals often form communities to share potential or industry-relevant threats and their trajectories, as proven by a system's data.

The Department of Homeland Security's *Automated Indicator Sharing (AIS)* program is a free resource that provides the sharing of cyber threat indicators between DHS and private organizations. Like an ISC, AIS produces timely information about cyber threat indicators that are vital in preventing widespread attacks. AIS functions through two standards.

- *Structured Threat Information eXpression (STIX)* is a standardized language developed by the MITRE Corporation and the OASIS Cyber Threat Intelligence (CTI) technical committee to discuss cyber threat information. STIX includes the scope and structure of threats and enables consistency in information sharing.
- *Trusted Automated Exchange of Indicator Information (TAXII)* defines the method of information exchanges, including data formatted with STIX standards.

Predictive analysis refers to the examination of data to determine the likelihood of a cyber threat. It relies on technology that combines machine- and self-learning analytics with detection techniques to monitor network activity and compare it to baseline or historical data to predict a breach before it occurs.

Threat maps are visual representations of cyber threats. The maps are often displayed as a country or world map with known threats and targets identified by location. Threat maps enable security professionals to make accurate predications based on their location and relative vulnerability to a given threat.

File/code repositories are used in application development to store code that is proven to be secure or will be used repeatedly. These repositories are often targets for threat actors, though, since manipulation of code in a repository can ultimately impact future iterations of applications. As such, repositories can be a valuable source of threat intelligence. Reviewing code stored in a repository can provide insight to the types of injections or vulnerabilities that are often targeted by hackers.

Related Concepts

- Research sources—ATV-1.5E
- Threat hunting—ATV-1.7A

Security+ Objective

1.5: Explain different threat actors, vectors, and intelligence sources.

ATV-1.5E Research Sources

Description

Research sources are excellent for obtaining intelligence about current and potential threats. Although experience is a great teacher, utilizing proper research methods will provide you with information regarding attacks that you have yet to experience firsthand. It also can help prevent new attacks. Examples of valuable research sources include the following.

Examples

Vendor websites may provide you with information regarding attacks they have experienced on their products, how they recovered from the attacks, along with how they were able to prevent attacks.

Conferences and *academic journals* provide scholarly resources regarding attacks. These are among the most valid and trustworthy sources, as individuals must be qualified to speak at a conference, and academic journals must be peer-reviewed.

Requests for comments (RFCs) provide an abundance of information regarding attacks and other information about information technology. Each RFC has a reference number for ease of location based on the topic of discussion. The Internet Engineering Task Force's web page for RFCs is available at https://tools.ietf.org/html/.

Local industry groups are organizations founded by businesses that operate in a given industry. These groups often provide relevant information to communities and similar organizations. This is often the quickest way to push information to professionals and provide timely information about threats and links for further engagement.

Social media can be a reliable source of information for cyber threats. Often, groups of hackers will communicate through social media feeds to discuss vulnerabilities, exploits, or attempted targets. However, even more useful can be the social media feeds of employees. Often, users will accept a friend request from someone who ultimately uses the information shown on a social media profile to launch a social engineering attack. Social media pages belonging to a company should be secured as much as possible, and information posted should be limited to vague, general information that does not provide a potential attacker with data that could help launch an attack.

Threat feeds are real-time data streams that provide detailed information about known threats, including IP addresses, malware signatures, and domain names. These streams enable security professionals to obtain real-time information about pending threats and vulnerabilities.

Adversary tactic, techniques, and procedures (TTP) are knowledge bases that provide publicly available information about tactics and techniques used by hackers to conduct their attacks. These articles enable security professionals to get insight into *how* hackers behave and initiate attacks so they can learn to lock down potential avenues of attack.

Related Concepts

- Threat intelligence sources—ATV-1.5D
- Threat hunting—ATV-1.7A

Security+ Objective

1.5: Explain different threat actors, vectors, and intelligence sources.

ATV-1.6A   Cloud-Based vs. On-Premises Vulnerabilities

Description

Cloud-based vulnerabilities are, as their name implies, vulnerabilities exclusive to cloud-based connections. These vulnerabilities surpass the number of *on-premises vulnerabilities*, which consist of vulnerabilities exclusive to local, physical connections. One reason for this increased number of cloud-based vulnerabilities is due to an off-site server or vendor managing the data and applications for an organization. Thus, the responsibility of security exceeds that of an on-site security team. Additionally, a security team has far less control of cloud-based technologies, which also accounts for the higher volume of cloud vulnerabilities.

Examples

Examples of similar vulnerabilities include the following.

- Poor authentication policies
- Users with more permission or privilege than they should have
- Outages caused by misconfigurations

Examples of vulnerabilities unique to the cloud include the following.

- Risks associated with cloud vectors
- Shared service that allows multiple customers to share hardware and resources
- Supply-chain attacks
- DoS attacks

Related Concepts

- Cloud-based vs. on-premises attacks—ATV-1.2F
- On-premises vs. off-premises—AD-2.2D
- Cloud vs. on-premises—AD-2.4E
- On-premises vs. cloud—AD-2.5C
- On-premises vs. cloud—OIR-4.5C

Security+ Objective

1.6: Explain the security concerns associated with various types of vulnerabilities.

ATV-1.6B | Zero-Day

Description

Zero-day vulnerabilities are those that exist within an application or device before a patch is released to resolve or prevent an exploit. Although authentic individuals will notify software companies regarding vulnerabilities, attackers often exploit zero-day vulnerabilities as soon as they are discovered, which often occurs prior to patch creation. Furthermore, zero-day vulnerabilities may be unknown for a significant amount of time and require significant coding time and abilities to create a suitable patch.

Example

One of the most well-known zero-day vulnerabilities is Stuxnet. The Stuxnet virus was sophisticated malware that exploited four different vulnerabilities within Windows 7 to cause considerable damage to Iran's nuclear enrichment programs.

Related Concepts

- Weak configurations—ATV-1.6C
- Improper or weak patch management—ATV-1.6E
- Legacy platforms—ATV-1.6F
- Endpoint protection—IMP-3.2A
- Application security—IMP-3.2D

Security+ Objective

1.6: Explain the security concerns associated with various types of vulnerabilities.

ATV-1.6C | Weak Configurations

Description

Weak configurations are inadequate security controls within a device or system that can lead to attackers exploiting vulnerabilities. Weak configurations cover a great deal of settings from unprotected privileged user accounts, overly permissive rules, use of unsecured protocols, and failure to recognize vulnerable settings. In general, weak configurations are avoidable, as these settings can be modified to harden a system.

Examples

- *Open permissions* are permissions that provide unlimited access to open or modify files.
- *Errors* are weak configurations attackers are able to study. Once attackers have analyzed the error, along with any code via an error screen, they can learn how to exploit the vulnerability.
- *Weak encryption* may lead to an attacker being able to decipher keys and be able to read data in its original format. Systems with weak encryption are particularly vulnerable to brute-force attacks.
- *Default settings* are weak configurations because it means there has not been any host hardening techniques applied. Default vulnerabilities that exist within devices are often known to hackers, such as default usernames and passwords. Therefore, it is important to modify and harden default security settings of devices and applications in an effort to secure them.
- *Open ports and services* are the ports and services that can be utilized in an organization's network. Some ports and services are required for basic computer operation, but all nonessential ports and services should be restricted. Attackers often use open ports or services as an entryway to a network.

Related Concepts

- Zero day—ATV-1.6B
- Improper or weak patch management—ATV-1.6E
- Legacy platforms—ATV-1.6F
- Hardening—IMP-3.2E

Security+ Objective

1.6: Explain the security concerns associated with various types of vulnerabilities.

Third-Party Risks

Description

Third-party risks are vulnerabilities that stem from a security issue with an outside vendor or service. An organization does not have control over these vulnerabilities. As such, the organization must assume the risk and try to verify the third party is operating securely.

Examples

Vendor management is the process of procuring and managing services from a third party. This is an important task, as the organization cannot control how the vendor operates. Therefore, due diligence is key, and efforts should be made to vary the vendors employed so there is no one single point of failure within a supply chain or system. Two primary concerns within vendor management include the following.

- *System integration* is the process of linking various IT systems, services, and software. Vendors often need access to an organization in order to provide services. This presents a potential risk as if the vendor's system is compromised, it can put your organization at risk as well. Vendor accounts should follow the principle of least privilege and be created only as needed.
- *Vendor support* is the act of a vendor providing training, help, or follow-up services. A lack of vendor support is considered a vulnerability because if issues arise with a service and vendor support is not provided, the organization may suffer from downtime or loss of functionality.

A *supply chain* risk is a very real possibility, as supply chains are responsible for the end-to-end process of products and services for customers and clients. If a vulnerability exists within a supply chain, the organization and its products are at risk to attack or manipulation.

Outsourced code development can often expedite the development of software for an organization, but it presents some risk. When outsourcing coding practices, the owner of the code should be clearly detailed in the contract between the two parties. Additionally, programmers hired by the third party should be properly vetted to prevent additional vulnerabilities or risk. If the third party is to use its own personnel instead of hiring a subcontractor, that too should be specified in some type of binding agreement.

Data storage plans should be included as part of vendor management. When third parties require access to data, measures must be taken to protect its integrity and confidentiality. Cloud-based storage is a popular option for providing third parties access to data, but as with any cloud use, the services and securities must be review to ensure data is protected against theft or manipulation.

Related Concepts

- Supply chain attacks—ATV-1.2E
- Vectors—ATV-1.5C
- Third-party risk management—GRC-5.3C

Security+ Objective

1.6: Explain the security concerns associated with various types of vulnerabilities.

Improper or Weak Patch Management

Description

Improper or *weak patch management* is a vulnerability that attackers often seek to exploit. Outdated firmware or unpatched software usually results in holes in security that enable threat actors to access a system or network. Three critical areas to monitor for weak or improper patching include the following.

Examples

Recall that *firmware* is software that enables communication between hardware and a computer system. Firmware that is not updated properly creates the possibility of device vulnerabilities being exploited. Furthermore, there are vendors of firmware that may only update their firmware during certain life cycles, which can also leave your device(s) vulnerable to exploits.

An *operating system (OS)* and the *applications* installed on it have regular firmware updates to enhance their security. However, in most cases, the patched updates are often not required of the user; as a result, users tend to procrastinate on updates. However, patches should be applied as soon as possible to avoid zero-day vulnerability exploits or other type of software-centric attack.

Related Concepts

- Constraints—AD-2.6M
- Hardening—IMP-3.2E

Security+ Objective

1.6: Explain the security concerns associated with various types of vulnerabilities.

Legacy Platforms

Description

Legacy platforms are operating systems or devices that are not provided with security updates from their vendor, as its use has been exhausted and is no longer supported. These systems present a significant vulnerability and should be purged from a system regularly.

Example

An example of a platform that recently became a legacy platform is Windows 7. The Windows 7 OS was launched in 2009 as a successor of Windows Vista. Windows 7 was then succeeded by Windows 8, Windows 8.1, and Windows 10. Microsoft's support for Windows 7 officially ended in January 2015 with extended support terminating in January 2020. Since security updates and patches were not being created or released after 2020, it was important for organizations to switch from Windows 7 in order to remain secure. Similarly, both Windows 8 and Windows 8.1 have seen mainstream support end in recent years.

Related Concepts

- Weak configurations—ATV-1.6C

Security+ Objective

1.6: Explain the security concerns associated with various types of vulnerabilities.

Copyright Goodheart-Willcox Co., Inc.

May not be reproduced or posted to a publicly accessible website.

197

Impacts

Description

Impacts of vulnerabilities should be taken into consideration when implementing control diversity or any security model. A number of impacts can occur due to vulnerabilities, including the following examples.

Examples

- *Data loss* (irretrievable data), *breaches* (data intrusions), and *exfiltration* (data retrieved by an attack) carry significant impact to organizations, as these vulnerabilities have the potential to halt operations. They also open an organization to potential lawsuits depending on the data that was lost or exfiltrated.
- *Identity theft* vulnerabilities are critical, as attackers will obtain customer and client data to commit identity fraud. If a vulnerability is exploited to commit identity theft, an organization's customers may lose faith in their security practices and the organization's reputation could be damaged. Additionally, if an organization is found to be at fault for data loss, they could face financial penalties or lawsuites.
- *Financial attacks* are typical when attackers plan their attacks. These attacks have a negative impact on an organization's financial stability but can also become a security concern, including use of company credit cards or fraudulent access to customer financial information. Furthermore, organizations may be liable for financial damages or fines if data is stolen or compromised.
- *Reputation* of an organization could be impacted as any exploited vulnerabilities may place customers, clients, or shareholders with a mindset that lacks confidence in the organization. Thus, the organization may lose business due to a reputation of relaxed security practices.
- *Availability loss* may occur from DoS or DDoS attacks. If a vulnerability is exploited to implement these attacks, the operations and productions of an organization could be diminished if the attack is not contained, resulting in production and financial hardship.

Related Concepts

- Identity fraud—ATV-1.1N
- Business impact analysis—GRC-5.4E
- Organizational consequences of privacy breaches—GRC-5.5A
- Impact assessment—GRC-5.5G

Security+ Objective

1.6: Explain the security concerns associated with various types of vulnerabilities.

Threat Hunting

Description

Threat hunting is a computer defense practice that entails proactively searching for threats to networks and systems. This search is typically conducted using information that has been researched and implemented regarding attacks.

Examples

The phrase *intelligence fusion* refers to the practice of combining as many intelligence information sources as possible to create comprehensive threat profile. This often includes *threat feeds*, which are websites and forums that provide reports about threats. Implementing these practices allows security professional to perform *maneuvers*, which are methods taken to search for threats on a network rather than waiting for the threat to be detected. The following lists some of the most popular threat intelligence feed providers, advisories, and bulletins:

- Alien Vault: https://cybersecurity.att.com/solutions/threat-intelligence
- SecureWorks: https://www.secureworks.com/about/counter-threat-unit
- Symantec: https://www.broadcom.com/support/security-center/vulnerability-management
- Microsoft: https://www.microsoft.com/en-us/wdsi
- DarkReading: https://www.darkreading.com
- SANS: https://www.sans.org/newsletters

Related Concepts

- Threat intelligence sources—ATV-1.5D
- Research sources—ATV-1.5E

Security+ Objective

1.7: Summarize the techniques used in security assessments.

ATV-1.7B Vulnerability Scans

Description

Vulnerability scans examine an organization's network, systems, and applications, then compare the results to a known list of vulnerabilities. This is usually conducted to assess the efficacy of an organization's existing security measures. There are various types of results and scanners in vulnerability scans, including the following examples.

Examples

- *False positives* are scan results perceived to be a vulnerability when they are actually not.
- *False negatives* are vulnerabilities that are not identified during a scan.
- *Log reviews* are assessments or analyses of logs generated from vulnerability scans or an application such as Windows Event Viewer. In the log, suspect items will be flagged for further review.
- *Credentialed scans* are conducted with a user who has a network account with logon rights to various hosts and resources relevant to the vulnerability scan. One of the more popular credential scan tools is Greenbone OpenVAS for Kali Linux, which can be downloaded from https://www.openvas.org.
- *Noncredentialed scans* require vulnerability scans to be performed without being able to log in to a host on the network. Therefore, the results are only from the host that is used to expose the network and does not scan anything that requires elevated privileges.
- *Intrusive scanning* is an exploitation framework that uses vulnerabilities identified by the scanner to launch scripts and other forms of software. While this is typically performed to test how vulnerable a system is to exploitation, it can also be conducted by a hacker as an entryway to a network.
- *Non-intrusive scanning* is a passive form of searching for and identifying vulnerabilities, often referenced via a CVE entry.
- *Common Vulnerabilities and Exposures (CVE)* is a reference for well-known vulnerabilities and exposures.
- *Configuration reviews* search for and identify weak configurations, outdated patches, and any other miscellaneous vulnerabilities that could be exploited.

Related Concepts

- Penetration testing—ATV-1.8A
- Passive and active reconnaissance—ATV-1.8B
- Exercise types—ATV-1.8C
- Vulnerability scan output—OIR-4.3A

Security+ Objective

1.7: Summarize the techniques used in security assessments.

ATV-1.7C Syslog/Security Information Event Management (SIEM)

Description

System Logging Protocol (syslog) is used to send system log or event messages to platforms such as a (SIEM) system. A *security information event management (SIEM) system* is a software product that supports organizational security through real-time collection, compilation, and reporting of log data generated in a network.

Examples

Examples of assessing security through syslog and SIEM systems include the following.

- *Review reports* are documents that contain findings from log or data analysis. These reports are typically correlated through syslog solutions.
- *Packet capture* is the act of intercepting data packets as they traverse a network. SIEM systems typically have the capability for administrators to review packets in real time or capture and store for later review.
- *Data input* is the collecting and recording of data within syslog files. Often, this data is identified by file, directory, or network inputs.
- *User behavior analysis (UBA)* is a security assessment that monitors user behavior and compares it to established baseline information. This information can be used to record what applications are used by an individual, Internet or network activity, and usage anomalies.
- *Sentiment analysis* is a SIEM feature that analyzes social attitudes and opinions to make predictions about likely outcomes. Often, these programs parse logged data of online social media or social networking activity, e-mails, and instant messages to identify motivations or intentions and provide warning of a potential cyberattack.
- *Security monitoring* is a tool in a SIEM dashboard that summarizes data about security systems.
- *Log aggregation* refers to the collection of SIEM logs from multiple sources such as Windows and Linux-based hosts, switches, routers, firewalls, intrusion-detection system (IDS) sensors, vulnerability scanners, and data loss prevention (DLP) systems.
- *Log collectors* are SIEM software that store and interpret logs from different types of systems, such as firewalls or IDS sensors, and account for the differences among vendor implementations.

Related Concepts

- SIEM dashboards—OIR-4.3B
- Log files—OIR-4.3C
- syslog/rsyslog/syslog-ng—OIR-4.3D
- journalctl—OIR-4.3E
- nxlog—OIR-4.3F

Security+ Objective

1.7: Summarize the techniques used in security assessments.

Security Orchestration, Automation, and Response (SOAR)

Description

Security Orchestration, Automation, and Response (SOAR) is a security solution that employs a variety of software tools and solutions to enable data collection from multiple sources. SOAR also generates automatic responses if needed. The biggest difference between it and SIEM systems is that while SIEMs are platforms for collection and analysis of security data, SOAR is able to integrate security tools that respond to issues.

Examples

SOAR solutions are often used to mitigate the following scenarios.

- *Phishing campaigns.* Information such as headers can be extracted from e-mails using SOAR solutions to determine if messages are authentic or fraudulent.
- *Malicious network traffic.* SOAR systems are designed to discover, alert administrators to, and quarantine malicious network traffic so it does not hinder operation.
- *Vulnerability management.* SOAR solutions can be employed to alert administrators to newly discovered vulnerabilities within a network environment.
- *Case management.* SOAR solutions maintain information from orchestrated and automated activities, meaning the solutions contained highly detailed log data.

Related Concepts

- Secure Orchestration, Automation, and Response—OIR-4.4F

Security+ Objective

1.7: Summarize the techniques used in security assessments.

Penetration Testing

Description

Penetration testing, also referred to as *pen testing* or *ethical hacking*, involves thinking similarly to a hacker to verify threats, bypass security controls, actively test security controls, and exploit vulnerabilities to understand the weaknesses of networks and systems.

Examples

White box pen testing is a form of penetration testing in which an organization provides complete access and information about its network. Since white box pen testers are given complete access and information about an organization's network, reconnaissance is not practiced.

Black box pen testing is a type of pen test in which an organization does *not* give access or information about its network and systems to the pen tester. As a result, the pen tester must conduct reconnaissance to obtain information about the organization and their network. Black box pen testing is useful for organizations to understand how vulnerable they might be from individuals that are not part of the organization and do not have knowledge of their network.

Gray box pen testing occurs when the organization only provides some information about its network. Thus, it requires the pen tester to perform some forms of reconnaissance but not to the level of a black box pen tester. When organizations perform gray box pen tests, they have a better understanding of how vulnerable they are to insider threats.

Rules of engagement refer to the agreements between the organization and the pen tester as to how the pen test will be conducted, along with actions that will take place after the pen test, such as guidelines cleaning up or placing the network back to its initial state.

Pivoting, also termed *privilege escalation*, takes place after the pen tester maintains a persistent foothold in the organization's network and obtains the privileges needed to gain access to and compromise other, elevated portions of the network.

A *bug-bounty program* is an initiative that offers rewards to those who identify flaws and vulnerabilities found in their program. While bug bounties are not technically the same thing as a penetration test, the goals are similar: to identify vulnerabilities that can exploited in a cyberattack.

Cleanup takes place after a penetration test and requires the pen tester to remove any scripts, tools, and created accounts from a system and its network.

Lateral movement occurs when the pen tester is able to compromise a networked device and use that connection to compromise other devices. Often this is performed as a means of searching for opportunities to obtain higher-level privileges within an organization's system and networks.

Persistence refers to actions taken by a pen tester after discovering a successful exploit. The pen tester attempts to maintain their connection by placing tools such as keyloggers to obtain network username and passwords.

Related Concepts

- Vulnerability scans—ATV-1.7B
- Passive and active reconnaissance—ATV-1.8B
- Exercise types—ATV-1.8C
- Vulnerability scan output—OIR-4.3A

Security+ Objective

1.8: Explain the techniques used in penetration testing.

ATV-1.8B Passive and Active Reconnaissance

Description

Passive reconnaissance is a method of discovering and gathering information without alerting the target that reconnaissance is happening. This is usually conducted using publicly available resources, such as Google or various forms of social media. When pen testers utilize passive reconnaissance, they are utilizing "cyber-stalking" techniques to obtain information about an organization and the users of the organization without engaging the organizations network. *Active reconnaissance*, however, engages an organization's network and performs actions such as port scanning to discover open ports on the network or searching for wireless network access. There are a number of reconnaissance methods used by attackers, such as the following.

Examples

- *War flying* is using a flying device with Wi-Fi equipped devices to detect wireless networks. War flying is often accomplished using *drones* or *unmanned aerial vehicles (UAVs)* since they can be used via remote control and record video.
- *War driving* is the use of a vehicle with Wi-Fi–equipped devices to detect wireless networks.
- *Footprinting*, also termed as *topology discovery*, refers to a pen tester identifying the structure of a targeted network.
- *OSINT* collects information from public sources as well as governmental sites and shares findings regarding data and threats to augment security among organizations.

Related Concepts

- Reconnaissance—ATV-1.1Q
- Threat intelligence sources—ATV-1.5D
- Research sources—ATV-1.5E
- Vulnerability scans—ATV-1.7B
- Penetration testing—ATV-1.8A
- Exercise types—ATV-1.8C
- Network reconnaissance and discovery—OIR-4.1A
- Vulnerability scan output—OIR-4.3A

Security+ Objective

1.8: Explain the techniques used in penetration testing.

Exercise Types

Description

Penetration *exercises* are tests that examine the security defenses within an organization. The type of exercise performed dictates simulated hacking attempts and target areas, such as wireless, network intrusion, social engineering, or applications. Examples of exercise types include the following.

Examples

- *Red team exercises* involve a group that attempts to gain access to a system. A red team is an offensive team that typically consists of security professionals who attempt to break into a system.
- *Blue team exercises* involve a group that attempts to defend the red team's access of a system. A blue team is a defensive team of security professionals who respond to threats and are responsible for the security of a network.
- *White team exercises* involve a group refereeing the red team and blue team. White team members do not conduct testing or defensive techniques; they only oversee the exercise.
- *Purple team exercises* involve a group that perform acts of both the red team and blue team. The primary function of this team is to share information between red and blue teams. If effective communication procedures exist between the red and blue teams, a purple team is not necessary.

Related Concepts

- Penetration testing—ATV-1.8A
- Passive and active reconnaissance—ATV-1.8B
- Network reconnaissance and discovery—OIR-4.1A

Security+ Objective

1.8: Explain the techniques used in penetration testing.

Configuration Management

Description

Configuration management is a key concept regarding how a network is built and managed. An important aspect of configuration management is the documentation of changes implemented on a network. Documenting configuration changes will also better enable your organization to understand how a network's design helps to prevent attacks.

Examples

- *Diagrams*, such as the following, are incredibly useful for displaying how systems are connected and serve as the blueprint for your organization's network.

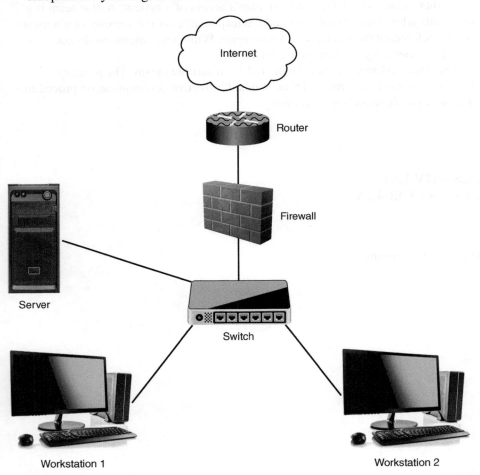

Goodheart-Willcox Publisher; (computer and server) Den Rozhnovsky/Shutterstock.com; (switch) Ulvur/Shutterstock.com; (firewall) beboy/ Shutterstock.com

- A *baseline configuration* is documentation that defines how systems and networks will be built, tested, maintained, and expanded for future growth.
- A *standard naming convention* is a strategy of naming files that identifies the resource and location of devices on a network.
- *Internet protocol (IP) schema* refers to addressing groups assigned to devices on a network to determine the device's function and location.

Related Concepts

- Domain name system (DNS)—ATV-1.4E
- Vulnerability scans—ATV-1.7B
- Network location—IMP-3.7C

Security+ Objective

2.1: Explain the importance of security concepts in an enterprise environment.

AD-2.1B Data Sovereignty

Description

Data sovereignty is a legal concept that states digital data is subject to the jurisdiction and laws of the country in which the data is stored, meaning if you have data stored in another country than your business is located, there can be legal ramifications. Some countries do not allow the storing or backing up of data in foreign servers. Additionally, depending on where the data is stored, the local or national government may have access to the information. As such, it is important to investigate data-related laws in countries where data is to be stored, including data stored in cloud environments.

Examples

- Australia's Privacy Principles (APP) is a collection of regulations that define how private information should be handled and stored.
- Brazil requires companies to obtain consent before collecting data from a user. Additionally, that information must remain on servers in Brazil.
- Canada requires privacy policies to be easily accessible to users, and organizations must follow the Personal Information Protection and Electronic Data Act (PIPEDA).
- The European Union requires the adherence to the General Data Protection Regulation (GDPR).
- The US government has instituted multiple laws to regulate data collection and storage, including HIPPA, COPPA, and CalOPPA.

Related Concepts

- General Data Protection Regulation (GDPR)—GRC-5.2A

Security+ Objective

2.1: Explain the importance of security concepts in an enterprise environment.

AD-2.1C Data Protection

Description

Data protection refers to actions taken to enforce the protection of data within an organization. It is a vital concept that must be included in computer security practices. Therefore, it is important that you understand the concepts mentioned in the following examples.

Examples

- *Data loss prevention (DLP)* products scan content in structural formats, such as e-mails in Microsoft Office 365, to ensure data has not been lost or altered.
- *Masking* obfuscates confidential data such as Social Security numbers.
- *Encryption* of data is a security measure that encodes data in such a way that a key must be used to decode, or decrypt, data so only the intended recipient can view it.
- *At rest* refers to data stored on a device, such as a personal computer, that is not being transmitted.
- *In transit/motion* refers to data being transmitted between devices.
- *In processing* refers to data being processed via the central processing unit (CPU) and memory to output devices.
- *Tokenization* converts data into a random string of characters, known as a *token*, that will not have any value if breached.
- *Rights management* is a security process that ensures sensitive data can only be accessed by those who need it. It also restricts the copying, printing, or distribution of sensitive data.

Related Concepts

- Endpoint protection—IMP-3.2A
- Privacy enhancing techniques—GRC-5.5D
- Full disk encryption (FDE)—IMP–3.2F

Security+ Objective

2.1: Explain the importance of security concepts in an enterprise environment.

Hardware Security Module (HSM)

Description

A *hardware security module (HSM)* is a system or device that performs cryptographic operations and stores or manages keys securely.

Example

Device	Function(s)	Notes
Hardware security module (HSM)	■ Cryptographic device that stores or manages encryption keys and performs cryptographic functions ■ Encrypts communication to prevent it from being intercepted and read	■ Often installed as a plug-in card or external device attached to computer or server

Goodheart-Willcox Publisher

Related Concepts

- Subcriber identity module (SIM)—AD-2.6L

Security+ Objective

2.1: Explain the importance of security concepts in an enterprise environment.

Geographical Considerations

Description

Geographic considerations for recovery sites should be made wisely. The main factors that should be taken into consideration include the chosen location, its distance from the organization's primary location, and the impact the location has on data sovereignty. Often, device limitations can dictate these decisions. In general, there are multiple types of geographic considerations to be made, including the following.

Examples

- *Intrabuilding geography* refers to devices networked within the same building.
- *Interbuilding geography* refers to devices networked in different buildings in the same general location.
- *Distant remote buildings* refer to devices networked with a significant amount of distance between them.

Related Concepts

- Geofencing—IMP-3.7C
- Geotagging—IMP-3.7C
- Geolocation—IMP-3.7C

Security+ Objective

2.1: Explain the importance of security concepts in an enterprise environment.

Cloud Access Security Broker (CASB)

Description

A *cloud access security broker (CASB)* is software that mediates user access to cloud services across all types of devices. A CASB also allows for single-sign on (SSO), scans for malware, and monitors resource activity.

Example

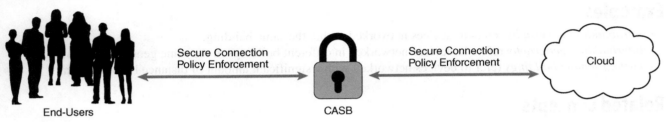

End-Users   Secure Connection Policy Enforcement   CASB   Secure Connection Policy Enforcement   Cloud

Goodheart-Willcox Publisher; (people) Rawpixel.com/Shutterstock.com

Related Concepts

- Authentication—IMP-3.8B

Security+ Objective

2.1: Explain the importance of security concepts in an enterprise environment.

Response and Recovery Controls

Description

Response and recovery controls are controls and strategies in place to continue productivity in the event of an interruption of an organization's normal productivity.

Examples

- *Administrative controls* are those developed and enforced through policies, procedures, and processes in an effort to regulate human interaction with a device or network.
- *Compensating controls* are those that provide alternative or contingency controls in the event a typical control is ineffective or unavailable. A compensating control is an action implemented to act as a backup control.
- *Corrective controls* are controls that work to lessen or repair damage or restore resources after an undesired activity or event. Examples of corrective controls include virus quarantining, process termination, and system reboots.
- *Detective controls* are controls that identify existing problems with company processes.
- *Deterrent controls* are those that attempt to dissuade attacks or violations from occurring. Examples of deterrent controls include laws and organizational policies.
- *Managerial controls* are security controls that use management or administrative processes to implement and measure performance as well as intervene and take corrective actions when needed.
- *Operational controls* are security controls implemented by people who carry out day-to-day operations of a business.
- *Physical controls*, or *physical security controls*, are tangible controls used to protect the physical assets of an organization.
- *Preventive controls* are those that attempt to avoid or prevent an incident from occurring.
- *Security controls* are safeguards to minimize risks to assets of an organization.
- *Technical controls* consist of technology used to automate security functions. These controls are usually software programs or policies that are implemented to protect systems.

Related Concepts

- Incident response process—OIR-4.2B
- Disaster recovery plan—OIR-4.2G
- Business continuity plan—OIR-4.2H
- Continuity of operation planning (COOP)—OIR-4.2I

Security+ Objective

2.1: Explain the importance of security concepts in an enterprise environment.

Secure Sockets Layer (SSL)/Transport Layer Security (TLS) Inspection

Description

Secure Sockets Layer (SSL)/Transport Layer Security (TLS) inspection is performed to ensure that HTTP and TCP application protocols remain secure. In this process, SSL inspectors intercept traffic, decrypt it, and scan it for malicious files. The inspection also creates secure connection between a browser and client so files can transmit securely.

Example

Step 1

I need to send you something encrypted. I will use your public key.

My public key is: **AB872ZQ7**.

Step 2

Sending the encrypted data using the public key **AB872ZQ7**.

Step 3

I will decrypt the data using my private key: **AS995YL8N**.

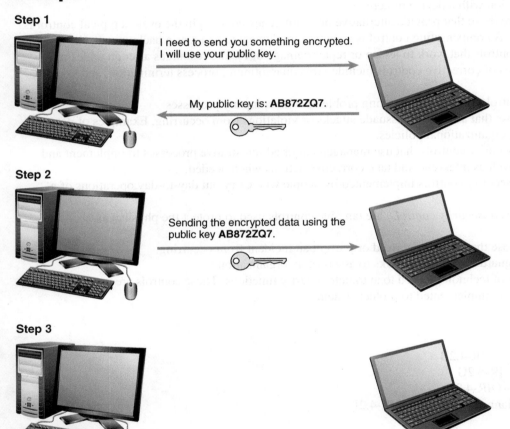

Goodheart-Willcox Publisher; (devices) romvo/Shutterstock.com

Related Concepts

- Hypertext transfer protocol over SSL/TLS (HTTPS)—IMP-3.1A

Security+ Objective

2.1: Explain the importance of security concepts in an enterprise environment.

Description

Hashing algorithms are used in computer programming to generate checksums and create a cryptographic hash to produce a message digest. Although there are multiple hashing algorithms mentioned in other portions of this Reference Guide, the following are two examples that demonstrate how hashing algorithms are conducted.

Examples

- Secure Hash Algorithm (SHA):

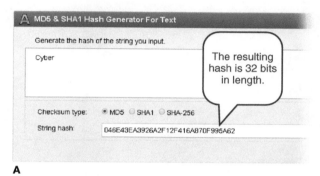

A

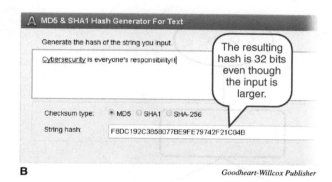

B

Goodheart-Willcox Publisher

- Message Digest Algorithm (MDA/MD5)

Related Concepts

- Pass the hash—ATV-1.3R
- Salting—AD-2.8D
- Hashing—AD-2.8E
- Database—IMP-3.2C
- Integrity—OIR-4.5D

Security+ Objective

2.1: Explain the importance of security concepts in an enterprise environment.

API Considerations

Description

Application Programming Interface (API) considerations refer to the objects and resources used in an API and how they will be used. In other words, software developers need to ensure functions of TCP/IP are implemented for certain aspects of a system. As such, it is important to be sure that data is not exposed and there are no misconfigurations to be exploited.

Example

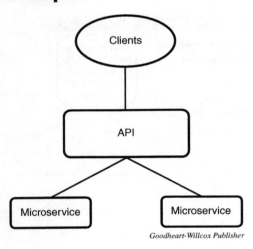

Goodheart-Willcox Publisher

Related Concepts

- Application programming interface (API) attacks—ATV-1.3M
- Micro-services/API—AD-2.2I
- Cloud security controls—IMP-3.6A
- API inspection and integration—IMP-3.6A

Security+ Objective

2.1: Explain the importance of security concepts in an enterprise environment.

Description

The ability to continue limited operations and not suffer a complete failure is known as an organization's system *resilience*. *Site resiliency* is how an organization recovers from an attack or disaster. It also refers to the methods used to continue business operations.

Examples

- *Hot sites* are duplications of functional sites. These are typically used by organizations that cannot afford any downtime, such as banks or airlines. If an organization's primary site were to be hacked or rendered nonfunctional, employees would rely on the hot site to bring their operations back to a restored state immediately.
- *Cold sites* are physical locations that provide office space but require the organization to install and set up their systems to continue their operations. Setup and restoration can often take up to a week. These are the least costly of recovery site solutions.
- *Warm sites* are a middle ground between hot sites and cold sites. They provide minimal equipment for resuming or restoring business operations, such as servers and network connections. However, an organization is responsible for installing additional needed equpment and transferring data.

Related Concepts

- Incident response plans—OIR-4.2A
- Disaster recovery plan—OIR-4.2G
- Business continuity plan—OIR-4.2H
- Continuity of operation planning (COOP)—OIR-4.2I
- Business impact analysis—GRC-5.4E

Security+ Objective

2.1: Explain the importance of security concepts in an enterprise environment.

Deception and Disruption

Description

Deception and *disruption* security concepts involve allowing attackers to access certain portions of a network or system in an effort to study their behaviors and prevent future attacks. The following examples provide deceptive or disruptive opportunities.

Examples

- *Honeypots* are computers that are set up to attract attackers so their attack strategies and tools can be analyzed in an effort to prevent or mitigate a later attack.
- *Honeyfiles* are files placed on a network and disguised as an important file to attract attackers to analyze their attack strategies and tools.
- *Honeynets* are networks that are set up to attract attackers so their attack strategies and tools uses in their attacks can be analyzed and assessed.
- *Fake telemetry* is false information about organizations and their system's statistics. These statistics can be partially or entirely fabricated.
- *DNS sinkholes* are servers designed to trick hackers into believing they are accessing an organization's DNS server.

Related Concepts

- Data protection—AD-2.1C

Security+ Objective

2.1: Explain the importance of security concepts in an enterprise environment.

Cloud Models

Description

A *cloud model* is the organization with which cloud infrastructure is provisioned for use. Cloud models are often named for the online application services and storage that is utilized via cloud computing.

Examples

- *Infrastructure as a service (IaaS)* provides IT resources, such as servers and storage area network (SAN), via an Internet connection. IaaS consists of services rented from the vendor's data center, such as Microsoft Azure Virtual Machines or Amazon Web Services.
- *Platform as a service (PaaS)* provides storage servers, including database platforms such as MySQL.
- *Software as a service (SaaS)* provides customers with the ability to access software and applications via an Internet connection rather than having to install software on local devices. Adobe Cloud and Microsoft Office 365 are examples of commonly encountered SaaS solutions.
- A *public cloud*, also known as a *multi-tenant cloud*, is a collection of cloud-computing services hosted by a third party and shared among users. Since public could computing is shared among multiple individuals, it is important to remember that this shared resource has the potential to be a security risk.
- *Community cloud computing* is a solution in which several organizations share the costs of a cloud, which can be hosted or entirely private. Community cloud computing is normally utilized for collaborative purposes between organizations, such as a partnership or merger between two businesses.
- *Private cloud computing* is a cloud infrastructure that is completely private and owned by an organization. Since the cloud is privately owned, only one organization is dedicated to managing and controlling the cloud-computing services. Additionally, the cloud owner has full control of the cloud's privacy and security.
- *Hybrid cloud computing* is a combination of public, community, or private cloud computing.

Related Concepts

- Cloud access security broker (CASB)—AD-2.1F
- Cloud service providers—AD-2.2B

Security+ Objective

2.2: Summarize virtualization and cloud computing concepts.

Cloud Service Providers

Description

A *cloud service provider (CSP)* is a vendor that provides IT services over the Internet. During the writing of this Reference Guide, popular options for cloud service providers included the following.

Examples

- Amazon Web Services
- DigitalOcean
- Google Cloud
- IBM
- Microsoft Azure
- Oracle Cloud
- Verizon

Related Concepts

- Cloud models—AD-2.2A
- Services integration—AD-2.2L

Security+ Objective

- 2.2: Summarize virtualization and cloud computing concepts.

Managed Service Provider (MSP)/ Managed Security Service Provider (MSSP)

Description

A *managed service provider (MSP)* is a vendor that provides cloud-computing services to customers. A *managed security service provider (MSSP)* is an outsourced third party responsible for information assurance. Only highly trusted or thoroughly vetted vendors should be used as MSSPs.

Examples

Managed service providers:

- Atos
- Bit by Bit Computer Consultants
- HCL
- Infosys
- Tata Consultancy Services (TCS)

Managed security service providers:

- IBM Managed Security Services
- Secureworks
- Trustwave
- Verizon Managed Security Services
- Wipro

Related Concepts

- Vendors—GRC-5.3C

Security+ Objective

2.2: Summarize virtualization and cloud computing concepts.

On-Premises vs. Off-Premises

Description

On-premises cloud computing refers to services that are hosted and monitored in-house by an organization with cloud computing software. However, *off-premises* cloud-computing services are monitored by a vendor where the organization has minimal control or security monitoring. Both on-premises and off-premises cloud-computing methods require monitoring for security purposes.

Examples

- *On-premises:* services hosted and monitored in-house with cloud computing software
- *Off-premises:* monitoring is outsourced to a vendor and organization has minimal security control

Related Concepts

- Cloud models—AD-2.2A
- Cloud service providers—AD-2.2B
- Third-party risk management—GRC-5.3C

Security+ Objective

2.2: Summarize virtualization and cloud computing concepts.

Fog Computing

Description

Fog computing is a decentralized model in which cloud-computing services and storage are implemented or placed in more than one location. Use multiple locations enhances performance and decreases latency.

Example

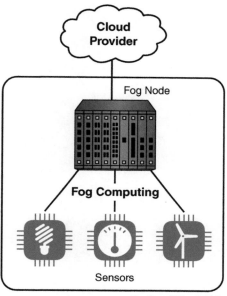

Goodheart-Willcox Publisher

Related Concepts

- Site resiliency—AD-2.1K
- Edge computing—AD-2.2F
- Embedded systems—AD-2.6A
- Internet of Things (IoT)—AD-2.6C

Security+ Objective

2.2: Summarize virtualization and cloud computing concepts.

Edge Computing

Description

Edge computing is a non-cloud model in which information is collected and processed in devices close in proximity. Unlike typical cloud computing, which processes data that is not time-driven, the focus for edge computing is on time-sensitive forms of data, such as media streaming.

Example

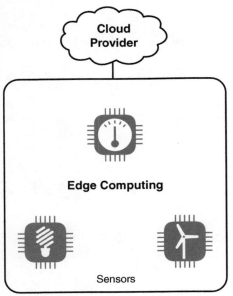

Goodheart-Willcox Publisher

Related Concepts

- Fog computing—AD-2.2E
- Embedded systems—AD-2.6A
- Internet of Things (IoT)—AD-2.6C

Security+ Objective

2.2: Summarize virtualization and cloud computing concepts.

Description

Thin clients are low-power devices that present services from a cloud-computing source via an Internet connection. Often, these devices do not contain internal storage and connect to a network via traditional methods such as Ethernet and Wi-Fi.

Example

Server provides all the software and programs, including an OS, to thin clients

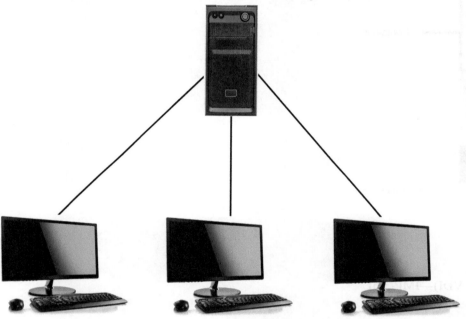

Goodheart-Willcox Publisher; (computers and server) Den Rozhnovsky/Shutterstock.com

Related Concepts

- Cloud models—AD-2.2A

Security+ Objective

2.2: Summarize virtualization and cloud computing concepts.

Containers

Description

A *container*, also called an *application cell*, is executable software that contains applications and the host OS. Containers allow users to run an operating system on a device via an Internet connection. Furthermore, they balance CPU and memory resources to ensure a server is able to distribute the operating system and its applications evenly.

Example

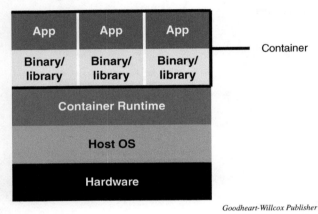

Goodheart-Willcox Publisher

Related Concepts

- Virtualization—AD-2.2O
- Virtual desktop infrastructure (VDI)—IMP-3.5E

Security+ Objective

2.2: Summarize virtualization and cloud computing concepts.

Micro-Services/API

Description

Micro-services are applications composed of reusable components in a cloud-native application. They are essentially segmentations of web services. Recall that *application programming interface (API)* refers to the methods by which a developer is able to interact with web services.

Example

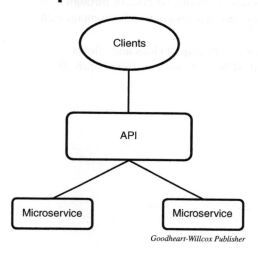

Goodheart-Willcox Publisher

Related Concepts

- Application programming interface (API) attacks—ATV-1.3M
- API considerations—AD-2.1J
- API inspection and integration—IMP-3.6A

Security+ Objective

2.2: Summarize virtualization and cloud computing concepts.

Infrastructure as Code

Description

Infrastructure as code (IaC) is the management of hardware and software through machine-readable files as opposed to physical configuration. IaC helps elevate the complexity with which virtual systems are managed and programmed.

Examples

- *Software-defined networking (SDN)* is used to define and implement policy decisions on control through a network controller. It uses code-based applications to manage a network and enables continuous management regardless of network technology.
- *Software-defined visibility (SDV)* provides platform visibility for ease of connecting devices and allows automation between software programs through a set of open, RESTful APIs. A *Representational State Transfer (RESTful) API* is an API that adheres to the REST architectural style.

Related Concepts

- Network appliances—IMP-3.3H
- Access control list (ACL)—IMP-3.3I

Security+ Objective

2.2: Summarize virtualization and cloud computing concepts.

Serverless Architecture

Description

Serverless architecture is a cloud service that provides on-demand software on an as-needed basis. In these types of environments, applications are able to operate without the need for server management or maintenance.

Example

Function as a service (FaaS) is a good example of serverless architecture. It only uses the cloud resources when needed and treats the resources similarly to an on-demand service for an organization.

Related Concepts

- Cloud models—AD-2.2A
- Cloud service providers—AD-2.2B

Security+ Objective

2.2: Summarize virtualization and cloud computing concepts.

Services Integration

Description

Services integration is a system of cloud tools and technologies that connect systems, applications, data, and IT environments to provide real-time exchange of information between partners, coworkers, or third-party vendors.

Example

Services integration allows organizations to lessen data silos and enables members of an organization to access resources from one cloud location. One of the most popular forms of cloud services integration is SaaS, as it allows members of an organization to access software resources and functionality once they have verified their validity to the organization and its resources.

Related Concepts

- Cloud service providers—AD-2.2B
- Vendors—AD-2.5H

Security+ Objective

2.2: Summarize virtualization and cloud computing concepts.

Resource Policies

Description

Resource policies specify permissions regarding the access and execution of resources. They define how cloud-computing vendors and users will interact with the data and applications via the cloud.

Example

Resource policies can be compared to active directories or group policy objects, as the resource policies determine who has access to resources along with the level of access they have regarding the resources.

Related Concepts

- Cloud security controls—IMP-3.6A

Security+ Objective

2.2: Summarize virtualization and cloud computing concepts.

Transit Gateway

Description

Transit gateways are hubs used to connect an organization's virtual private cloud (VPC) and on-premises network. These gateways function as routers in a cloud environment and simplify the network connection and communication between locations. They also provide encryption and prohibit data from traveling over the Internet.

Example

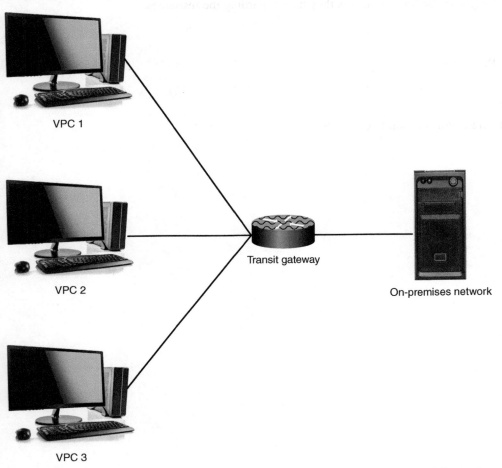

VPC 1

VPC 2

Transit gateway

On-premises network

VPC 3

Goodheart-Willcox Publisher; (computers and server) Den Rozhnovsky/Shutterstock.com

Related Concepts

- Cloud security controls—IMP-3.6A

Security+ Objective

2.2: Summarize virtualization and cloud computing concepts.

Virtualization

Description

Virtualization is a means of managing or presenting computer resources virtually as opposed to physically. It also provides the ability for multiple operating systems to be installed on a computer.

Examples

- *Virtual machines (VM)* are operating systems installed in virtual environments.
- *VM sprawl avoidance* is the practice of securing undocumented access and systems as well as other types of VM sprawl. *Virtual machine (VM) sprawl* is a security concern that occurs when VM deployment is abundant and improperly managed.
- *VM escape protection* is dependent of the virtualization of the vendor that secures vulnerabilities of the hypervisor. *VM escape* is a security concern that occurs when a program breaks out of a virtual environment and interacts directly with a host. This often results in malware or virus infection.

Related Concepts

- Containers—AD-2.2H
- Replication—AD-2.5B

Security+ Objective

2.2: Summarize virtualization and cloud computing concepts.

Environment

Description

In application development, an *environment* is the interface and resources that host an application. Environments are composed of software-based tools that developers use to create applications and software. They enable developers to create code without risking interaction between their computers and in-work code. Many environments are used in the application development process, including the following.

Examples

- *Development:* An application development environment is the hardware, software, and resources used to build software and web applications.
- *Test:* The test environment is a controlled environment in which software components are tested. This environment is also known as a *quality assurance (QA) environment* or *sandbox.*
- *Staging:* Staging environments are preproduction environments used to ensure quality control before an application is deployed.
- *Production:* A production environment is the setting in which the end-users execute the application or program.

Related Concepts

- Sandboxing—IMP-3.2I

Security+ Objective

2.3: Summarize secure application development, deployment, and automation concepts.

Provisioning and Deprovisioning

Description

Provisioning is the process of providing access and resources to network services needed for employees to complete their daily tasks. This often involves making applications and programs available to their target environment, such as enterprise desktops, mobile devices, and cloud infrastructures. *Deprovisioning* is the process of removing the application or program from packages. This is especially important if the software has been reproduced or has exhausted its use.

Example

An organizational example of provisioning is giving employees who work in an organization's payroll department permissions to read, create, and remove payroll-specific files. Deprovisions include removing those rights if the user is transferred to a different department or if they leave the organization.

Related Concepts

- Cloud models—AD-2.2A
- Virtual desktop infrastructure (VDI)—IMP-3.5E

Security+ Objective

2.3: Summarize secure application development, deployment, and automation concepts.

Integrity Measurement

Description

Integrity measurement is measurement and identification of changes made to a system as compared to its baseline. This helps to determine if an application has varied from its original intention or has been tampered with in any way.

Example

Integrity measurement is common among mobile applications and IoT devices. When an application is created, it is tested and measured for functionality and security. However, as time progresses, attackers discover vulnerabilities and may exploit the application. Thus, the inclusion of integrity measurement assures the new version of firmware downloaded to your device adheres to integrity measurement.

Related Concepts

- Baseline configuration—AD-2.1A

Security+ Objective

2.3: Summarize secure application development, deployment, and automation concepts.

Secure Coding Techniques

Description

Secure coding techniques refer to the processes in place to ensure an application's code is safe and secure for end-users. These processes are necessary to ensure an application or program is not vulnerable to threat actors after it is published. Examples of secure coding techniques include the following.

Examples

- *Normalization* is software development techniques in which repairs are made to invalid inputs to remove special encoding that an application cannot process.
- *Stored procedure* is the technique of utilizing saved, prepared SQL statements instead of having to write complex statements for an application.
- *Obfuscation/camouflage* is a technique used to convince attackers into perceiving the code is not worth attacking. The technique is used to confuse the attacker by using code in a context the attacker does not expect or to mask the code in some way. This makes the task of reverse engineering far more complex.
- *Code reuse* is the practice of using existing code in new applications. The use of existing code eliminates the need to write new code, resulting in lower development costs. It also enables developers to work with tested code known to be safe.
- *Dead code* is code that is executed but does not impact the application or program. For example, using integer variables for mathematical calculations can be considered a type of dead code since the results are not stored in variables but rather used for a calculation. Dead code often wastes computational time and memory.
- *Server-side execution and validation* allows for the technology to be more controlled but is also more time-consuming to maintain. *Client-side execution and validation* is more susceptible to forms of malware interfering with validation processes.
- *Memory management* refers to policies created, procedures enforced, and actions taken to allocate, distribute, and remove system memory. It also refers to techniques used to validate inputs, such as strings, to eliminate the possibility of users overwriting the areas of memory in an application.
- Use of *third-party libraries* make the coding of applications and programs less complex and more manageable. These libraries are often available through *software development kits (SDKs)*, which are collections of development tools packaged together.
- *Data exposure* is the release of sensitive, personal, or confidential data. Data exposure typically describes data that was released by accident, but it can also describe data that has been intentionally exposed. For example, if applications or programs only transmit between authenticated hosts, allowing data such as passwords or PII to be read without authorization is relatively safe due to users authenticating prior to use. However, in many cases, this can present a significant vulnerability.

Related Concepts

- Third-party management—ATV-1.6D
- Application security—IMP-3.2D

Security+ Objective

2.3: Summarize secure application development, deployment, and automation concepts.

AD-2.3E Open Web Application Security Project (OWASP)

Description

The *Open Web Application Security Project (OWASP)* is a nonprofit online community for cybersecurity professionals to publish critical cybersecurity risks. Many consider the information in OWASP to be valuable and essential. OWASP can be reviewed at https://owasp.org.

Examples

The OWASP Top 10 web page, seen in the following screen capture, is an important source of information used by developers and security professionals. It lists the most important and critical security risks.

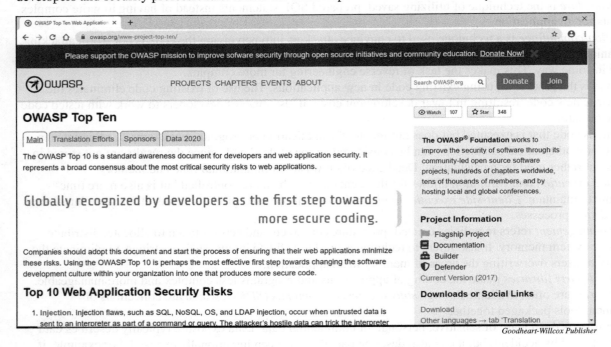

Goodheart-Willcox Publisher

Related Concepts

- Threat intelligence sources—ATV-1.5D
- Research sources—ATV-1.5E
- Key frameworks—GRC-5.2B

Security+ Objective

2.3: Summarize secure application development, deployment, and automation concepts.

Software Diversity

Description

Software diversity is the practice of transforming software into different forms before deployment. The process of diversifying software preserves the original code while ensuring that program implementations vary or perform differently among computer systems. This decreases the likelihood of threat actors finding reliable vulnerabilities within the code.

Examples

- *Compilers* test code to ensure it is correctly written and executes without errors.
- *Binary machine language* is converted from compiled code so it is able to operate on its targeted operating systems.

Related Concepts

- Use of third-party libraries and software development kits (SDKs)—AD-2.3D

Security+ Objective

2.3: Summarize secure application development, deployment, and automation concepts.

Description

Automation/scripting refers to methods and practices used to ensure an organization's infrastructure is resilient. Technologies used for automation and scripting include Software Defined Networking (SDN), virtualization, and DevOps. The following examples allow system provisions via program automation and scripting.

Examples

- *Automated courses of action* comprise a resilience strategy that restores services with little, if any, human interaction.
- *Continuous monitoring* is an automation solution that detects service failures and security breaches while ensuring systems are readily recoverable.
- *Continuous validation* is the process ensuring application performance and, if necessary, recovery solutions at each layer for software operation.
- *Continuous integration* is the practice of developers inserting code into a repository multiple times each day. This can also refer to developers providing updates to their projects.
- *Continuous delivery* is the deployment of continuous integration. This enables an organization to deploy software versions at any time.
- *Continuous deployment* is ongoing testing of software to ensure no changes to the code are necessary.

Related Concepts

- Secure code techniques—AD-2.3D

Security+ Objective

2.3: Summarize secure application development, deployment, and automation concepts.

Elasticity

Description

Elasticity is a system's ability to handle changes in real time. If a system has high elasticity, it will experience less loss of productivity. However, low levels of production elasticity can result in diminished productivity. Incorporating elasticity comes at a financial burden, so low elasticity is often implemented when a technology is not relied on for mass productivity.

Examples

- *Time-based elasticity* is the automatic shutdown of resources no longer used or needed.
- *Volume-based elasticity* is a process in which the scope of a program scales to match its demand.

Related Concepts

- Site resiliency—AD-2.1L
- Scalability—AD-2.3I
- Dynamic resource allocation—IMP-3.6A

Security+ Objective

2.3: Summarize secure application development, deployment, and automation concepts.

AD-2.3I Scalability

Description

Scalability is that ability of a program to cope with increased loads and continue functioning as needed. If a program is not scalable, increased demand can cause it to become dysfunctional or unusable. Scalability helps make programs more resilient and less vulnerable to attacks such as DoS or DDoS campaigns.

Example

A simple example of scalability can be seen in retail stores late in any calendar year. Between the Thanksgiving in Christmas holidays, retail stores often hire a number of temporary employees to accommodate an anticipated increase in demand. These stores are demonstrating the scalability of their staffing needs. This is the same fundamental principle as cloud scalability.

Related Concepts

- Site resiliency—AD-2.1L
- Elasticity—AD-2.3H
- High availability—AD-2.5F
- Dynamic resource allocation—IMP-3.6A

Security+ Objective

2.3: Summarize secure application development, deployment, and automation concepts.

Description

Version control is a method of tracking changes made to a program or file. When implemented correctly, version control can reduce development time and increase deployment rates. When changes are made, a unique identifier should be utilized, such as the date, program ID, or initials of the user who made changes.

Example

Version control monitoring can be accomplished with free options, such as Git, or paid subscriptions, such as Fossil and Vault.

Related Concepts

- Configuration management—AD-2.1A
- Supporting non-repudiation—AD-2.8S
- Metadata—OIR-4.3I
- Non-repudiation—OIR-4.5H

Security+ Objective

2.3: Summarize secure application development, deployment, and automation concepts.

Authentication Methods

Description

Authentication methods are the verification practices that allow users to log on to their devices and accounts. Examples of authentication methods include the following.

Examples

- *Directory services* are software systems that create, store, organize, and allow access to directory information and resources. In essence, these services comprise the means of providing authorization onto a network.
- *Federation* is the notion that a network should be accessible to more than one group, such as an employee group or a group of customers. Federation enables access for trusted accounts managed on networks other than the organization's to authenticate from one source. For example, if Google Apps and Twitter had a shared federation, a user could log in to their Google account and, by virtue of the federation, have access to their Twitter account without having to sign in to Twitter separately.
- *Attestation* declares that something is true and authentic and cannot be denied.
- *HMAC-based one-time password (HTOP)* is a single-use password built from a shared secret and a random value based on the local time stamp generated from the server used to connect a device. An example of a popular, well-known HTOP tool is the Google Authenticator application. For more information, a request for comments (RFC) document on HOTP can be viewed on the IETF website at https://tools.ietf.org/html/rfc4226.
- A *time-based one-time password (TOTP)* is an extension of HTOP. The chief distinction between TOTP and HTOP is that the changing factor in a TOTP is based on time. For more information, a request for comments (RFC) document on TOTP can be viewed on the IETF website at https://tools.ietf.org/html/rfc6238.
- *Short message service (SMS)* is a text-messaging service operated by cellular networks that allows the transmission of text messages and binary files. Organizations may require an SMS be sent to your mobile phone to provide you a temporary passcode for authorization. This is often referred to as *two-step authentication*.
- A *token key* is a physical device s used for authentication, such as an ID badge.
- *Authentication applications* allow users to store their credentials in the application server password cache so they do not have to provide authentication for each application they use. Additionally, third-party applications exist to serve as soft tokens or generate one-time passwords.
- *Push notifications* are services that a mobile app or website can use to display alerts on their customers' mobile device. These notifications can also be used to authenticate users.
- *Phone call authentication* is typically a call to the number that is registered to a user. This phone call serves as a medium for providing a temporary authentication password and confirming a person has the correct device. However, if a phone number is spoofed or a device stolen, this method of authentication can be easily compromised.
- *Smart card authentication* is used via smart card devices that provide authentication for a user.

Related Concepts

- Multifactor authentication (MFA) factors attributes—AD-2.4C
- Authentication, authorization, and accounting (AAA)—AD-2.4D
- Authentication protocols—IMP-3.4B
- Authentication management—IMP-3.8A
- Authentication—IMP-3.8B
- Log files—OIR-4.3C

Security+ Objective

2.4: Summarize authentication and authorization design concepts.

Biometrics

Description

Biometric authentication devices require users to verify "something they are" for authentication.

Examples

- *Fingerprint biometric authentication* requires the user to provide a fingerprint to be authenticated. Since fingerprints are unique and cannot be duplicated, a user's fingerprint must match the fingerprint stored on an origination's database.
- *Retinal biometric authentication* uses eye scans to authenticate users by detecting the unique features of a retina during an eye scan.
- *Iris biometric authentication* utilizes eye scans for authentication. This is different from retinal scans because it utilizes the unique characteristics of a person's iris, not their retina.
- *Facial biometric authentication* scans and verifies the length, width, and texture of a user's face for authentication.
- *Voice biometric authentication* devices analyze the soundwaves of a person's voice for authentication. However, voice-based authentication methods are often time-consuming, and it is possible for an attacker to impersonate another user's voice.
- *Gait analysis authentication* analyzes a user's walk and body movements for authentication.
- A *false acceptance*, also termed as a *false positive*, occurs when access is granted to an unauthorized person via a biometric device.
- A *false rejection* also termed as a *false negative*, occurs when a valid user is denied authentication via a biometric device.
- A *crossover error rate (CER)* is the point where false acceptances and false rejections are equal.

Related Concepts

- Multifactor authentication (MFA) factors and attributes—AD-2.4C
- Locks—AD-2.7J
- Mobile device management (MDM)—IMP-3.5B

Security+ Objective

2.4: Summarize authentication and authorization design concepts.

Multifactor Authentication (MFA) Factors and Attributes

Description

Multifactor authentication (MFA) factors and attributes are methods that augment the security of authentication practices by requiring personal criteria or information about a user. It also requires multiple forms of identity confirmation in order to grant access to authorized users.

Examples

Factors:

- *Something you know* is often a password.
- *Something you have* is typically employed as a physical item, such as a smart card or ID badge.
- *Something you are* can be a user's fingerprint, iris, voice, or retina.

Attributes:

- *Somewhere you are* employs a user's geographical location to provide authentication via geofencing.
- *Something you can do* is a type of behavioral biometric in which a user exhibits measurable patterns such as keystroke speed or providing a matching signature.
- *Something you exhibit* is a measurement of physical or psychological characteristics exhibited by a user, such as common behavior or habits.
- *Someone you know* involves a trusted third party authenticating the user.

Related Concepts

- Authentication methods—AD-2.4A
- Biometrics—AD-2.4B
- Locks—AD-2.7J
- Mobile device management (MDM)—IMP-3.5B
- Account policies—IMP-3.7C
- Authentication management—IMP-3.8A

Security+ Objective

2.4: Summarize authentication and authorization design concepts.

Authentication, Authorization, and Accounting (AAA)

Description

Authentication, authorization, and accounting (AAA) is an access control method that dictates whether users are able to interact with objects and resources and how those same objects and resources may be used.

Examples

- *Authentication* is the process of validating a user. During this step of the AAA process, the user provides evidence of identity, often by entering a password—though other authentication practices can be employed.
- *Authorization* confirms a user is permitted to access a system and its resources. At this step, permission sets are assigned that define actions an authenticated user can or cannot perform when accessing the network. This is often determined through access control lists and the assignment of rights and permissions.
- *Accounting* provides a measurement of resources used by an employee during access of the system. It also allows administrators to track user activity throughout the system.

Related Concepts

- Authentication methods—AD-2.4A
- Authentication protocols—IMP-3.4B
- Authentication—IMP-3.8B

Security+ Objective

2.4: Summarize authentication and authorization design concepts.

Cloud vs. On-Premises Requirements

Description

Authorization requirements vary depending on if an organization utilizes cloud-based or on-premises access. Requirements for *cloud* authorization include a reliable Internet connection and possible a trusted third party to manage and secure data and applications. *On-premises* requirements often entails stringent authentication measures and the ability and resources to host everything needed on the organization's physical premises.

Example

In the following figure, the user is required to enter their username, password, and a code generated via organization-provided token. In this case, the token is the user's phone, and a one-time password has been sent via SMS. Conversely, on-premises resources tend not to require as many forms of authentication since the resources are physically in the organization's premises.

Goodheart-Willcox Publisher

Related Concepts

- Cloud-based vs. on-premises attacks—ATV-1.2F
- Cloud-based vs. on-premises vulnerabilities—ATV-1.6A
- Cloud models—AD-2.2A
- Cloud service providers—AD-2.2B
- On-premises vs. off-premises—AD-2.2D
- On-premises vs. cloud—AD-2.5C
- On-premises vs. cloud—OIR-4.5C

Security+ Objective

2.4: Summarize authentication and authorization design concepts.

Description

Redundancy refers to components that, while not essential for normal functionality of a system, enables a system to continue functioning if a vital component fails.

Examples

Geographic dispersal is the process of distributing redundancy across geographic areas, such as storing backups in an off-site location. It can also refer to the outline and documentation of your organization's network and systems.

Disk:

- *Redundant array of independent disks (RAID)* is a series of hard disks that provide redundancy in the event of disk failure(s). *RAID Level 0* uses striping without parity by writing in blocks across two disks simultaneously to ensure no fault tolerance. *RAID Level 1* uses mirroring to write to two disks simultaneously, so there is a copy of data in the event one disk fails; however, the disk being copied to only has 50 percent storage capacity. *RAID Level 5* uses striping with parity and writes data across three disks. Therefore, if one disk is lost, the volume may still persist and provides better efficiency for storage than RAID 1. *Nested RAID* levels (*0+1, 1+0*, or *5+0*) have better performance and redundancy than other levels of RAID.

Network:

- *Load balancers* allow administrators to spread network connections across multiple NICs.
- *NIC teaming*, also known as *adapter teaming*, provides increased fault tolerance for NICs by using configuring multiple cards to work together. In this scenario, network communication persists even if one NIC fails.
- *Multipath* is the connections among servers to ensure that if one server fails, another server is able to provide a redundant connection.

Power:

- An *uninterruptible power supply (UPS)* provides power to devices immediately after an unexpected loss of electricity. These devices operate via batteries, so power will only be available until the battery drains. Often, these are employed as a safety net, giving administrators enough time to perform a system backup and shut systems down properly.
- A *generator* offers a secondary source of electricity in the event electricity is unexpectedly lost. These often run via gasoline or other type of fuel and last longer than a UPS.

Related Concepts

- Site resiliency—AD-2.1K
- Backup types—AD-2.5D

Security+ Objective

2.5: Given a scenario, implement cybersecurity resilience.

Replication

Description

Replication is the duplication or copying of data between different servers and sites. Replication differs from a backup in the sense that a backup is traditionally stored off-site, and a replication is not.

Examples

- A *storage area network (SAN)* is a computer network that provides access to consolidated storage devices. A SAN consists of components accessed via an Internet link and are rented on an as-needed basis.
- *Virtual machines (VM)* are virtualized computers that allow operating systems and programs to be executed in a sandbox environment and dispersed from one location to multiple locations.

Related Concepts

- Virtualization—AD-2.2O
- SAN—AD-2.5D

Security+ Objective

2.5: Given a scenario, implement cybersecurity resilience.

On-Premises vs. Cloud

Description

In terms of resilience, there are differences between cloud-based and on-premises data storage and access. *Cloud* security controls are processes that enable cloud architecture to protect against vulnerabilities and mitigate malicious attacks. Often, these processes are monitors or carried out by the cloud-hosting vendor, not the data's owner, meaning the organization storing the data have minimal control or security monitoring. *On-premises* data is much easier to secure because everything is stored in-house.

Example

In the following diagram, you can see how on-premises data can still be obtained if the Internet is unavailable. By comparison, data is unavailable in a cloud environment if an Internet connection cannot be established.

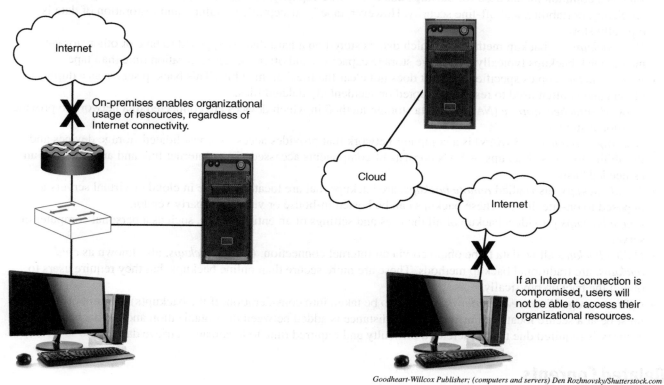

Goodheart-Willcox Publisher; (computers and servers) Den Rozhnovsky/Shutterstock.com

Related Concepts

- Cloud-based vs. on-premises attacks—ATV-1.2F
- Cloud-based vs. on-premises vulnerabilities—ATV-1.6A
- Cloud models—AD-2.2A
- Cloud service providers—AD-2.2B
- On-premises vs. off-premises—AD-2.2D
- Cloud vs. on-premises requirements—AD-2.4E
- On-premises vs. cloud—OIR-4.5C

Security+ Objective

2.5: Given a scenario, implement cybersecurity resilience.

Description

Backup types vary, and each type has benefits along with limitations. Common examples of backup types include the following.

Examples

- *Full backups* save backups of *all* data regardless of when the last backup was performed.
- *Incremental backups* only back up *new* data and data that has been modified since a previous backup.
- *Snapshots* are backups that provide point-in-time copies of data maintained by the file system.
- *Differential backups* create backups of all data that has been modified since the previous full backup.
- *Tape* is a common media used for backups due to its large capacity, low cost, ease of addition, long lifespan, efficiency, portability, and off-line security. However, tape is susceptible to failure, and restoration of data is typically slow.
- *Disk backups* are backup methods in which data is stored on a hard disk as opposed to tape or other storage media. Disk backups typically have large storage capacities and offer a faster restoration time than tape.
- A *copy backup* copies specified files but does not clear the files' archive bits. This backup serves as a duplicate of data and is often used to restore corrupted or accidentally deleted files.
- *Network attached storage (NAS)* is a data storage method in which devices are connected to a network to provide additional storage.
- A *storage area network (SAN)* is a computer network that provides access to consolidated storage devices and the ability to access backups. A SAN consists of components accessed via an Internet link and are rented on an as-needed basis.
- *Cloud backups*, also called *remote backups*, are backups that are located off-site in cloud or virtual servers as opposed to on-site drives. These backups can be hosted in-house or via a third-party vendor.
- *Image backups* provide a backup of all the files and settings of an entire system, such as a personal computer or server.
- *Online backups* allow data to be obtained via an Internet connection. *Offline backups*, also known as *cold backups*, are traditional backup methods. These are more secure than online backups, but they require users to obtain the backup physically.
- *Offsite storage/distance considerations* need to be taken into consideration. If the backup(s) are kept offsite, they must be at a secure location. Furthermore, as distance is added between the organization and the backup, higher security is required due to the increased difficulty and required time to locate and retrieve data.

Related Concepts

- Cloud-based vs. on-premises attacks—ATV-1.2F
- Cloud-based vs. on-premises vulnerabilities—ATV-1.6A
- Site resiliency—AD-2.1K
- Cloud models—AD-2.2A
- Redundancy—AD-2.5A
- Replication—AD-2.5B

Security+ Objective

2.5: Given a scenario, implement cybersecurity resilience.

AD-2.5E Non-Persistence

Description

Non-persistence refers to actions taken to ensure unwanted data is not retained during a recovery event, and instead, clean disk images are used. This also helps to guarantee static functionality of a system after an incident has occurred.

Examples

- *Revert to known state* rolls a system back to its last saved state in which everything was functional. This is similar to rolling a device driver back to a known good driver.
- *Last known good configuration* brings a system back to a baseline configuration. A good example of this is Windows System Restore.
- *Live boot media* uses a boot file from read-only storage to provide functionality to a system.

Related Concepts

- Redundancy—AD-2.5A
- Restoration order—AD-2.5G
- Incident response process—OIR-4.2B
- Disaster recovery plan—OIR-4.2G
- Business continuity plan—OIR-4.2H
- Continuity of operation planning (COOP)—OIR-4.2I
- Data recovery—OIR-4.5G
- Business impact analysis—GRC-5.4E

Security+ Objective

2.5: Given a scenario, implement cybersecurity resilience.

High Availability

Description

High availability (HA) is the ability of a system to remain available with no interruption. This is vital for an organization's productivity. However, it is also important for an organization to monitor costs associated with high availability.

Example

Scalability is the ability of a system to adapt as demand increases. This increases a system resilience by dynamically adapting to system needs. For example, if a network with 10 users suddenly needs to accommodate an additional 10 users temporarily, scalability is vital to ensure data is highly available. However, the costs associated with ensuring scalability should not offset the benefits obtained from doing so.

Related Concepts

- Site resiliency—AD-2.1K
- Elasticity—AD-2.3H
- Scalability—AD-2.3I
- Redundancy—AD-2.5A

Security+ Objective

2.5: Given a scenario, implement cybersecurity resilience.

AD-2.5G **Restoration Order**

Description

Restoration order is the order of priority in which services or applications are restored. Each item is given a priority level based on which services or applications are most essential.

Examples

Although restoration orders usually differ among organizations, the following is one common preferred order to follow:

1. Power units including UPSs and generators
2. Network switches and router
3. Firewalls and IDS
4. Network servers
5. Database(s)
6. Front-end applications
7. End user workstations and devices

Related Concepts

- Cloud service providers—AD-2.2B
- Services integration—AD-2.2L
- Vendors—AD-2.5H
- Business continuity plan—OIR-4.2H
- Continuity of operation planning (COOP)—OIR-4.2I
- Data recovery—OIR-4.5G

Security+ Objective

2.5: Given a scenario, implement cybersecurity resilience.

Diversity

Description

Diversity refers to the use of multiple resources and methods in security. Like software and user training, the use of diverse resources increases the security of a system because it creates more of a challenge for threat actors and provides defense in depth.

Examples

- *Technologies diversity* is the use of various types of technologies to lessen the impact of a cybersecurity incident.
- *Vendor diversity* are security controls that are sourced by multiple suppliers. This eliminates the possibility of a threat actor using one known vendor vulnerability against multiple devices in a system.
- *Crypto diversity* are the multiple forms of cryptographic systems. Diversifying cryptographic methods increases the protection of data in the event one crypto system is compromised.
- *Control diversity* are the layers of controls that combine different types of technical and administrative controls with a range of control functionalities.

Related Concepts

- Software diversity—AD-2.3F
- Diversity of training techniques—GRC-5.3B

Security+ Objective

2.5: Given a scenario, implement cybersecurity resilience.

Embedded Systems

Description

Embedded systems are microprocessor-based devices designed to perform dedicated functions.

Examples

- *Raspberry Pi* devices are small, affordable single-board computers roughly the size of a credit card. Security implications associated with Raspberry Pi devices include the use of default usernames and passwords.
- *Field-programmable gate arrays (FPGAs)* are electronic components used to build digital circuits for carrying out logical operations. Security implications associated with these devices largely involve a criminal stealing a chip and program for personal advantage.
- *Arduino* is an open-source platform that can interact with electronic objects. These devices rely on single-board microcontrollers and associated software applications. Due to its open-source nature, all developers have the ability to manipulate or create programs. As such, programs should be vetted thoroughly before implementation.

Related Concepts

- Internet of Things (IoT)—AD-2.6C
- Specialized—AD-2.6D
- System on a chip (SoC)—AD-2.6K
- Constraints—AD-2.6M

Security+ Objective

2.6: Explain the security implications of embedded and specialized systems.

Supervisory Control and Data Acquisition (SCADA)/Industrial Control System (ICS)

Description

Supervisory control and data acquisition (SCADA) systems are embedded systems used to monitor interfaces with controls for machines and industrial equipment. They are often components of large-scale, multiple-site industrial control systems. An *industrial control system (ICS)* refers to various types of systems, tools, and instruments used to manage and monitor infrastructure, industrial, and facility-based processes. Security implications with these systems include a more complicated process for downloading and applying security patches and the use of customized hardware and software solutions.

Examples

- *Facility* automation is the digital transformation to automatic or electronic control of system monitoring. SCADA systems are typically used to employ this automation.
- *Industrial* automation systems rely on SCADA and ICS systems to perform difficult or unsafe actions.
- *Manufacturing* organizations rely on SCADA systems to collect and analyze tasks such as real-time production data.
- *Energy* companies employ SCADA implementations to monitor power grids, redirect power when necessary, and restore power during outages.
- *Logistics* industries deploy SCADA systems for planning managing the flow of goods, services, and people to destinations.

Related Concepts

- Embedded systems—AD-2.6A
- Constraints—AD-2.6M

Security+ Objective

2.6: Explain the security implications of embedded and specialized systems.

Internet of Things (IoT)

Description

The *Internet of Things (IoT)* refers to devices that are connected to the Internet using embedded operating systems. There numerous examples of IoT devices, including the following.

Examples

- *Sensors* are embedded in many IoT devices and programmed to detect environmental factors such as noise, motion, heat, and network functionalities.
- *Smart devices* are various home appliances, such as TVs, that are integrated with applications, storage, and networking capabilities.
- *Wearables* are embedded devices that are relativity small and can be worn on a person. Wearables are centered on the ecosystem of its user, and they track and provide data about the user's day-to-day activities, such as a Fitbit used as a digital pedometer or heart-rate monitor.
- *Facility automation* is common in embedded devices such as SCADA systems, as they are used to monitor the lighting, surveillance, and energy consumption of an organization.
- *Weak defaults* among IoT consist of default password and configurations that, if unchanged, would enable an attacker to hack the device easily.

Related Concepts

- Embedded systems—AD-2.6A
- Internet of Things (IoT)—AD-2.6C
- System on chip (SoC)—AD-2.6K
- Constraints—AD-2.6M

Security+ Objective

2.6: Explain the security implications of embedded and specialized systems.

Specialized

Description

Specialized embedded systems are created to provide specific functionality for a given profession or use. However, security professionals must be aware of the risk organizations take when utilizing these embedded systems.

Examples

- *Medical systems* are embedded systems that perform, track, and store medical data about a patient. These systems are potentially vulnerable to a wide range of attacks, as attackers often seek data from medical facilities and may hold the data at ransom until the medical facilities meet the attacker's demands.
- *Vehicles* such as automobiles and *unmanned aerial vehicles (UAVs)* often utilize many embedded systems. Although the implementation of specialized provides many features and flexibility in vehicles, users need to be aware that attackers are always seeking vulnerabilities to exploit systems in cars and drones. The risk of these devices being hacked in an automobile or aircraft is very real.
- *Smart meters* are able to send data to a user device or energy provider regarding a building's energy use. However, since smart meters are networked devices, primarily via 802.11 connections, the information can be intercepted if the authentication is weak.

Related Concepts

- Embedded systems—AD-2.6A
- System control and data acquisition (SCADA)/industrial control system (ICS)—AD-2.6B
- Internet of Things (IoT)—AD-2.6C
- Specialized—AD-2.6D
- Drones/AVs—AD-2.6G
- System on a chip (SoC)—AD-2.6K
- Constraints—AD-2.6M

Security+ Objective

2.6: Explain the security implications of embedded and specialized systems.

Voice over IP (VoIP)

Description

Voice over IP (VoIP) is the transmission of data via telephone communications over the Internet. A primary security implication with VoIP is that it is often unencrypted, so attackers can capture and replay VoIP packets to retrieve sensitive information. These systems are also susceptible to DoS/DDoS attacks and malware. As such, it is important for security professionals to use secure protocols, such as SRTP, or configure multiple VLANs to separate voice and data packets.

Example

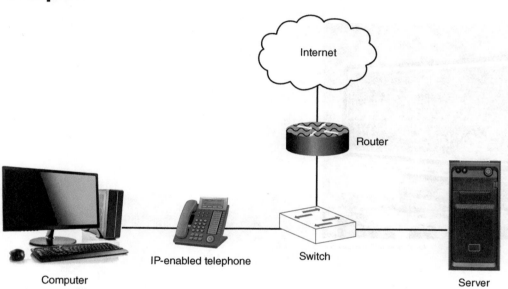

Goodheart-Willcox Publisher; (computer and server) Den Rozhnovsky/Shutterstock.com; (phone) Skalapendra/Shutterstock.com

Related Concepts

- VoIP and call managers—OIR-4.3C

Security+ Objective

2.6: Explain the security implications of embedded and specialized systems.

Heating, Ventilation, Air-Conditioning (HVAC)

Description

Heating, ventilation, air-conditioning (HVAC) systems are used to measure and control the climate of a building to ensure the climate will not cause damage to electrical devices. HVAC controls are frequently included as part of a SCADA system for facility automation. These controls are responsible for maintaining temperature settings for hold and cold aisles in a data center.

Examples

SCADA system:

Leo Pakhomov/Shutterstock.com

Hot and cold aisles:

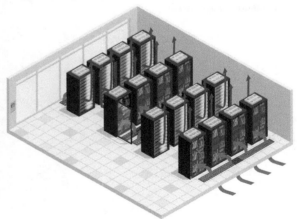

Goodheart-Willcox Publisher; (data center) Macrovector/Shutterstock.com

Related Concepts

• System control and data acquisition (SCADA)/industrial control system (ICS)—AD-2.6B

Security+ Objective

2.6: Explain the security implications of embedded and specialized systems.

Description

Drones, often referred to as *unmanned aerial vehicles* or *uncrewed aerial vehicles*, are remote-controlled aircraft that operate through embedded devices and systems. The main security implications associated with drones include vulnerability to malware, hacking, and injection attacks. Drones can be flown over a building to record audio and video or map wireless signals.

Examples

Commercial drone:

Josh Sorenson/CC-BY-SA 1.0

Military drone:

Lt. Col. Leslie Pratt, US Air Force/Public Domain

Related Concepts

- Passive and active reconnaissance—ATV-1.8B
- Aircraft—AD-2.6D
- Drones/UAV—AD-2.7P

Security+ Objective

2.6: Explain the security implications of embedded and specialized systems.

Multifunction Printer (MFP)

Description

Multifunction printers (MFPs), also known as *multifunction devices (MFDs)*, are output devices that rely on embedded systems to perform printing, faxing, copying, scanning, and e-mailing functionality. These devices are often prone to pivoting as they have normally have AD information stored in them and are connected to entire networks. Disposal of these devices should also be considered carefully; if the internal drives are not wiped, information could be stolen after disposal.

Example

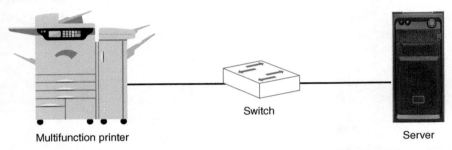

Multifunction printer

Switch

Server

Goodheart-Willcox Publisher; (printer) VectorShow/Shutterstock.com; (server) Den Rozhnovsky/Shutterstock.com

Related Concepts

- Embedded systems—AD-2.6A

Security+ Objective

2.6: Explain the security implications of embedded and specialized systems.

Real-Time Operating System (RTOS)

Description

Real-time operating systems (RTOS) are operating systems designed for use on SoC devices with embedded systems. These operating systems run continuously on systems that have less memory than traditional devices. Security implications include shared memory and vulnerabilities to DoS attacks and code injections.

Examples

- Integrity OS
- Linux Embedded
- QNX
- VxWorks

Related Concepts

- System on chip (SoC)—AD-2.6K

Security+ Objective

2.6: Explain the security implications of embedded and specialized systems.

Surveillance Systems

Description

Surveillance systems utilize embedded systems in cameras and recording equipment. Security professionals need to be aware that these systems can be attacked and are often a primary target for threat actors. Security implications include weak password management and lack of encryption in remote access capabilities. Additionally, security professionals should be made aware that there are environments where traditional security systems might be more effective for the organization.

Example

The following image shows micro aerial vehicle (MAV), which is similar to a drone, that functions as a portable, rapid-response, high-resolution surveillance camera.

MC 3rd Class Kenneth G. Takada, US Navy/Public Domain

Related Concepts

- Specialized—AD-2.6D
- Cameras—AD-2.7F
- Closed-circuit television—AD-2.7G

Security+ Objective

2.6: Explain the security implications of embedded and specialized systems.

System on a Chip (SoC)

Description

System on a chip (SoC) is an integrated circuit that includes fundamental computing components. A CPU, memory, storage, and I/O ports are all included in a single chip, making SoCs incredibly portable and efficient for use in mobile devices. Since everything is stored in a single chip, great care must be taken to secure these systems.

Examples

The following image shows an IoT device known as a smart watch. These devices rely on an SoC to be able to read and present the data.

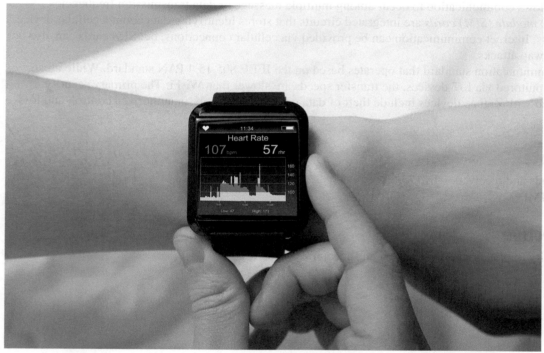

Andrey_Popov/Shutterstock.com

Related Concepts

- Internet of Things (IoT)—AD-2.6C
- Specialized—AD-2.6D
- Real-time operating system (RTOS)—AD-2.6I
- Constraints—AD-2.6M

Security+ Objective

2.6: Explain the security implications of embedded and specialized systems.

Communication Considerations

Description

Communication considerations should be taken by security professionals to determine the appropriate speed(s) and security implementations needed for organizational devices. Examples of considerations include the following.

Examples

- *5G* is the fifth generation of mobile networking communication and offers cellular transmission speeds equal to those of Wi-Fi.
- *Narrow-band* communication does not allow messages or data to exceed its channel's transmission frequency.
- *Baseband radio* allows communication to occur among multiple message or data transmission frequencies.
- *Subscriber identity module (SIM) cards* are integrated circuits that stores identifying data about a cellular device. Through SIM cards, Internet communication can be provided via cellular connections, but SIM cards can also be spoofed via SIM swap attacks.
- *Zigbee* is a telecommunication standard that operates based on the IEEE 805.15.4 PAN standard. While it can be operated and monitored via IoT devices, the transfer speeds are slower than Wi-Fi. The primary security concerns associated with Zigbee devices include theft of data or the device itself, unauthorized control, and loss of service.

Related Concepts

- Connection methods and receivers—IMP-3.5A
- Mobile devices—IMP-3.5C

Security+ Objective

2.6: Explain the security implications of embedded and specialized systems.

Constraints

Description

Due to their unique operation, architectures, usage, and functionality, embedded and specialized systems have a number of *constraints* that must be considered prior to implementation. Examples of constraints include the following.

Examples

- *Power.* These systems often have low-capacity batteries in order to adhere to size and weight requirements. Low-capacity batteries result in less power than traditional computing devices.
- *Computation.* Embedded and specialized systems typically have limited computational abilities, which impedes the ability to run many applications, including encryption and antivirus programs.
- *Network.* These devices are usually incapable of high-speed networking due to their wireless nature. This results in an increased susceptibility to data interception and a decrease in the ability to deliver critical or real-time data.
- *Cryptography.* Since embedded and specialized systems have minimal hardware and processing power, encryption is often not possible. The lack of cryptography typically results in data transmitted as plaintext.
- *Inability to patch.* Often, these devices are incapable of being patched, or the manufacturer simply does not produce security patches, rendering devices more prone to attacks, particularly zero-day attacks.
- *Authentication.* Authentication is often lacking in embedded and specialized system due to limited storage and computational abilities. Additionally, a lack of industry standards for authentication makes it difficult for manufacturers to provide authentication measures. This makes devices generally unsecure and vulnerable to users gaining root access.
- *Range.* Embedded and specialized systems are typically unable to transmit across great distances due to attenuation. As such, they must remain close in proximity or risk becoming inoperable, unreliable, or unsecure.
- *Cost.* While the cost for specialized and embedded devices is usually reasonable, the security often cannot be enhanced while remaining cost effective for an organization.
- *Implied trust.* The trustworthiness of embedded and specialized devices is a significant concern. While the devices or the systems to which they connect may be *secure*, they are not inherently *trustworthy*. In order to be trusted, the device or system must act as expected and be secure.

Related Concepts

- Improper or weak management—AD-1.6E
- Authentication, authorization, and accounting (AAA)—ATV-1.4D
- Internet of Things (IoT)—AD-2.6C
- Specialized—AD-2.6D
- System on a chip (SoC)—AD-2.6K
- Constraints—AD-2.6M

Security+ Objective

2.6: Explain the security implications of embedded and specialized systems.

Bollards/Barricades

Description

Bollards are vertical cylinders permanently installed to prevent access or deny passage. Similarly, *barricades* are objects that prohibit access to a location or entity. Examples of typical barricades include the following.

Examples

- Jersey walls
- Reception desk
- Fencing
- Locks and locked doors
- Mantraps
- Turnstiles
- Security guards

Related Concepts

- Mantraps—AD-2.7B
- Personnel—AD-2.7I
- Locks—AD-2.7J
- Visitor logs—AD-2.7Q
- Secure areas—AD-2.7V

Security+ Objective

2.7: Explain the importance of physical security controls.

AD-2.7B Mantraps

Description

Mantraps are a form of physical access control designed to allow access to only one person at a time.

Examples

- Turnstiles
- Interlocking doors
- Vestibule between a publicly accessible door and a locked, secured door

Related Concepts

- Bollards/Barricades—AD-2.7A
- Locks—AD-2.7J
- Lighting—AD-2.7L
- Fencing—AD-2.7M
- Visitor logs—AD-2.7Q
- Air gap—AD-2.7S

Security+ Objective

2.7: Explain the importance of physical security controls.

Badges

Description

Badges are forms of photographic identification that displays an individual's name, position, and (if applicable) security clearance within an organization.

Example

Goodheart-Willcox Publisher

Related Concepts

- Authentication methods—AD-2.4A
- Personnel—AD-2.7I
- Identity—IMP-3.7A

Security+ Objective

2.7: Explain the importance of physical security controls.

Alarms

Description

Alarms are placed in organizations to alert administrators in the event a secure threshold has been exceeded.

Examples

- Audible alarms provide a deterrent to intruders but allow attackers to test response time.
- Silent alarms quietly notify personnel and authorities to an intruder without alerting the intruder.

Related Concepts

- Internet of Things (IoT)—AD-2.6C
- Sensors—AD-2.7O
- Secure areas—AD-2.7V
- Network appliances—IMP-3.3H
- SIEM dashboards—OIR-4.3B

Security+ Objective

2.7: Explain the importance of physical security controls.

Signage

Description

Signage is a form of control that does not necessarily *prevent* physical access but psychologically discourages a potential threat actor from entering the premises.

Example

Signs labeled *Authorized personnel only* or *Restricted access* can help deter attackers while reminding employees to report suspicious behavior.

Related Concepts

- Personnel—AD-2.7I
- Fencing—AD-2.7M
- Secure areas—AD-2.7V

Security+ Objective

2.7: Explain the importance of physical security controls.

Cameras

Description

Cameras can be used in conjunction with surveillance systems to record a physical premise and its activity.

Examples

- *Motion recognition* cameras record activity when a motion sensor is triggered.
- *Object detection* cameras are able to detect objects in a physical premise, such as individuals and inventory.

Related Concepts

- Specialized—AD-2.6D
- Surveillance systems—AD-2.6J
- Closed-circuit television—AD-2.7G
- Sensors—AD-2.7O
- Secure areas—AD-2.7V

Security+ Objective

2.7: Explain the importance of physical security controls.

Closed-Circuit Television (CCTV)

Description

Closed-circuit television (CCTV) is a cost-effective means of surveillance to monitor physical areas. It is also known as *video surveillance* and utilizes a system of video cameras connected to a centralized monitoring location. It is important to remember that the monitoring location should be locked and accessible only to those who have a need for it. Additionally, the systems should be secured or encrypted to protect against digital attacks.

Example

The following image shows a CCTV camera that records images and broadcasts to a centralized location.

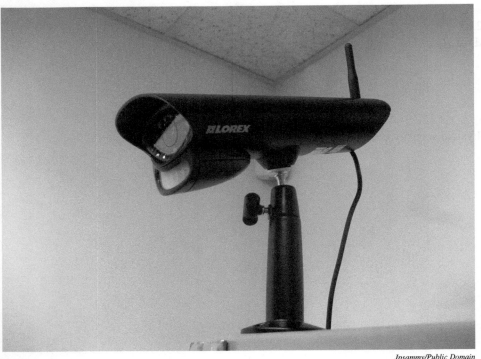

Jpsammy/Public Domain

Related Concepts

- Specialized—AD-2.6D
- Surveillance systems—AD-2.6J
- Cameras—AD-2.7F
- Sensors—AD-2.7O
- Secure areas—AD-2.7V

Security+ Objective

2.7: Explain the importance of physical security controls.

Industrial Camouflage

Description

Industrial camouflage refers to actions taken by an organization to design or configure a facility in such a way to make it unappealing or disguised to attackers.

Examples

- Limited or misleading identification or markings on the outside of the building
- Underground operations
- Remote or mountainous locations to prevent electronic eavesdropping

Related Concepts

- Obfuscation/camouflage—AD-2.3D

Security+ Objective

2.7: Explain the importance of physical security controls.

Personnel

Description

Personnel and *AI* can provide external security means for an organization.

Examples

- *Guards*, whether armed or unarmed, can provide protection around a physical premise and deter would-be intruders.
- *Robot sentries* are forms of AI that are designed to replace human guards. They are autonomous devices that report and monitor for intruders.
- *Reception* and administrative assistants provide an additional layer of security as they greet and log individuals as they enter a premise.
- *Two-person integrity*, also known as *two-person control* or the *two-person rule*, is an access control method in which two people, each with a unique key or fob, are required to unlock a door or computer console.

Related Concepts

- Locks—AD-2.7J
- Drones/UAV—AD-2.7R
- Visitor logs—AD-2.7Q

Security+ Objective

2.7: Explain the importance of physical security controls.

AD-2.7J | Locks

Description

Locks provide physical controls for accessing portions of a building along with securing equipment.

Examples

- *Biometric* locks require an individual provide biometric proof, such as something you are, to gain entry or access.
- *Electronic* locks require a PIN or other form of something you know to gain entry or access.
- *Physical* locks require a key to unlock.
- *Cable* locks are chain-like locks in which a lock is integrated in a cable and used to secure items, much like a chain on a bicycle.

Related Concepts

- Authentication methods—AD-2.4A
- Biometrics—AD-2.4B
- Fencing—AD-2.4M
- Secure areas—AD-2.4V
- Multifactor authentication (MFA) factors and attributes—AD-2.7C
- Mobile device management (MDM)—IMP-3.5B

Security+ Objective

2.7: Explain the importance of physical security controls.

USB Data Blocker

Description

USB data blockers are devices that prevent unauthorized data transfer as well as the installation of malware. It functions by plugging into a computer and gains an electrical charge from the computer. The blocker itself does not transmit to collect data from the computer.

Example

Mi Ga/CC BY-SA 4.0

Related Concepts

- Physical attacks—ATV-1.2C
- Connection methods and receivers—IMP-3.5A
- Enforcement and monitoring of—IMP-3.5D

Security+ Objective

2.7: Explain the importance of physical security controls.

Lighting

Description

Lighting is a security control that allows individuals to feel safe. Moreover, it also serves as an excellent deterrent, as it makes intrusion more complex. Lighting is often activated by motion sensors to prevent people from bypassing other security measures.

Examples

Examples of lighting include the following:

- Timed or motion-activated lights to turn on or off when presence is or is not detected
- Emergency lighting that runs off a UPS or generator and turns on if power is lost
- Security lighting that stays on 24 hours to maintain some visibility and deter potential attackers

Related Concepts

- Signage—AD-2.7E
- Secure areas—AD-2.7V
- Control type—GRC-5.1B

Security+ Objective

2.7: Explain the importance of physical security controls.

AD-2.7M | Fencing

Description

Fencing is placed on the exterior of a building to diminish trespassing. Fencing alone is not secure, as it can be bypassed, but it can help deter potential attackers.

Examples

There are many types of fencing, including

- barbed or razor wire;
- chain-link;
- crowd control;
- perimeter; and
- temporary.

Related Concepts

- Secure areas—AD-2.7V
- Control type—GRC-5.1B

Security+ Objective

2.7: Explain the importance of physical security controls.

Fire Suppression

Description

Fire suppression systems work to prevent fires based on the fire class. There are five classes of fires:

- *Class A* fires are fed by combustibles such as paper, wood, and some plastics. Anything that leaves an ash is considered a Class A fire.
- *Class B* fires are fed by flammable or combustible liquid, such as gasoline or oil.
- *Class C* fires are energized electrical fires. This includes fires caused by outlets, circuit breakers, appliances, and wiring.
- *Class D* fires are fed by combustible metal, such as magnesium or titanium. This type of fire is common in laboratories and industry.
- *Class K* fires are fed by cooking oil, animal fat, and grease.

Examples

Types of Fire			Common Fire Extinguishers			
Class A Ordinary Combustibles		A	Pressurized Water		Use on	Not on
Class B Flammable Liquids		B	Carbon Dioxide		Use on	Not on
Class C Electrical Equipment		C				
Class D Combustible Metals		D	Dry Chemical, Multipurpose		Use on	
Class K Kitchen Fires		K	Class K— Dry and Wet Chemical		Use on	

Goodheart-Willcox Publisher

Related Concepts

- Sensors—ATV-2.7O

Security+ Objective

2.7: Explain the importance of physical security controls.

Description

Sensors are devices that detect, collect, or monitor data and compare it to baseline information. There are various types of sensors used in security computing systems, including the following.

Examples

- *Motion detection sensors* detect movement via microwave radio reflection, which is similar to radar detection. When motion is detected, the sensors can activate additional security controls, such as lighting or alarms.
- *Noise detection sensors* are able to detect when decibel units (dB) are out of the baseline range. For instance, a server room will have a certain amount of dB, and if the dB levels fall too low, it could indicate equipment failure. Conversely, if dB levels are too high, it could indicate the presence of an unauthorized individual.
- *Proximity readers* are electronic sensors that detect the presence of a corresponding card. Often, these are used with secure door locks to allow or prevent access.
- *Moisture detection sensors* measure the amount of moisture in the air and can trigger an alarm if the levels are too high or too low. Moisture levels are vital to server rooms, and if the air becomes too moist or too dry, equipment may fail.
- *Card sensors* function similar to proximity readers. These sensors allow locks to be engaged or disengaged with a smart card. In most deployments, locks are set to a default lock position, and when the sensor detects the smart card for authentication, the lock is disengaged.
- *Temperature sensors* are able to detect a physical location's current temperature along with triggering an alarm if the temperature is either below or above a programmed range.

Related Concepts

- Embedded systems—AD-2.6A
- System control and data acquisition (SCADA)/industrial control system (ICS)—AD-2.6B
- Internet of Things (IoT)—AD-2.6C
- Specialized—AD-2.6D
- Heating, ventilation, air conditioning (HVAC)—AD-2.6F
- Alarms—AD-2.7D
- Cameras—AD-2.7F
- Closed-circuit television (CCTV)—AD-2.7G
- Lighting—AD-2.7L
- Fire suppression—AD-2.7N
- Secure areas—AD-2.7U
- Network appliances—IMP-3.3H
- SIEM dashboard—OIR-4.3B

Security+ Objective

2.7: Explain the importance of physical security controls.

Drones/UAV

Description

Drones and *unmanned/uncrewed aerial vehicles* can be used as security devices, as they are able to record surveillance from the sky and monitor an organization's exterior premise. Additionally, drones can be used as a security control similar to how robot sentries are used as security controls.

Examples

Commercial drone:

Josh Sorenson/CC-BY-SA 1.0

Military drone:

Lt. Col. Leslie Pratt, US Air Force/Public Domain

Surveillance drone:

MC 3rd Class Kenneth G. Takada, US Navy/Public Domain

Related Concepts

- Passive and active reconnaissance—ATV-1.8B
- Drones/AVs—AD-2.6G
- Personnel—AD-2.7I

Security+ Objective

2.7: Explain the importance of physical security controls.

Visitor Logs

Description

Visitor logs are used to record the names of people who have entered and exited an organization's building. This not only provides evidence of who came and went but can also help deter potential social engineering or reconnaissance activities.

Example

Date	Time In	Time Out	Name	Reason for Visit	Signature
11/23/2020	8:00 AM	5:00 PM	Bill Smith	Server maintenance	*Bill Smith*

Goodheart-Willcox Publisher

Related Concepts

- Personnel—AD-2.7I
- Control type—GRC-5.1B

Security+ Objective

2.7: Explain the importance of physical security controls.

Faraday Cages

Description

Faraday cages are used to block electromagnetic signals. Electronic devices are placed inside the Faraday apparatus, which is surrounded with conductive mesh that blocks signals from entering or leaving the confines of the cage. This secures devices against electromagnetic interference (EMI). Some Faraday devices, such as the bag in the following example, provide equivalent EMI protection while also offering portability.

Example

Fullmetalwikial/CC BY-SA 4.0

Related Concepts

- Wireless—ATV-1.4A
- Vectors—ATV-1.5C

Security+ Objective

2.7: Explain the importance of physical security controls.

Description

An *air gap* is an area designed to be completely isolated from secure areas. Air gaps are often used in the following scenarios.

Examples

- *Air-gapped hosts* are devices that are not physically connected to an organization's network.
- *Air-gapped networks* are computer networks designed to be isolated from other networks, including the Internet.

Related Concepts

- Secure areas—AD-2.7V

Security+ Objective

2.7: Explain the importance of physical security controls.

AD-2.7T — Demilitarized Zone (DMZ)

Description

A *demilitarized zone (DMZ)* is a perimeter network that allow some public access but does not allow traffic to pass through to the private portion(s) of the network. A DMZ enables external clients to access data from centralized sources, such as web servers, but has policies in place to ensure security is not compromised.

Example

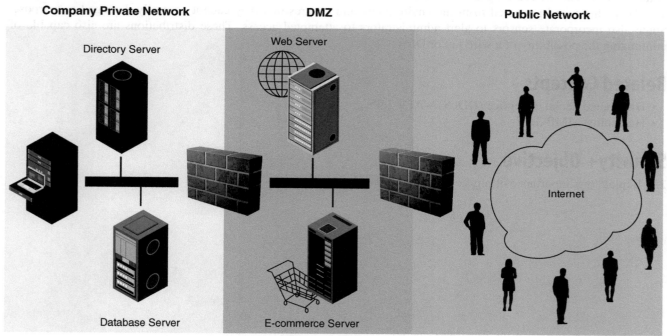

Goodheart-Willcox Publisher; (servers) aShatilov/Shutterstock.com; (wall) beboy/Shutterstock.com; (people) Rawpixel.com/Shutterstock.com

Related Concepts

- Network segmentation—IMP-3.3B

Security+ Objective

2.7: Explain the importance of physical security controls.

Protected Cable Distribution

Description

Protected cable distributions are physical networks that can harden the cabling via thick material to prevent visual representation of the wire.

Example

Often, network cabling is arranged so that it travels through a metal or flexible conduit with locked connection points. This keeps the wired protected from the environment and ensures that they cannot be easily damaged on purpose. Some also incorporate sensors to alert administrators to attempted access. These distributions are also capable of minimizing the possibility of a wire-tap or DoS.

Related Concepts

- Distributed denial of service (DDoS)—ATV-1.4F
- Hardening—IMP-3.2E

Security+ Objective

2.7: Explain the importance of physical security controls.

Secure Areas

Description

Secure areas provide isolation and environmental controls to ensure an organization's equipment is safe.

Examples

- *Air gaps* are areas designed to be completely isolated from secure areas.
- *Vaults* provide augmented physical security for organizational equipment.
- *Safes* provide physical security for authentication devices for an organization's equipment.
- *Hot aisles* are aisles in a server room that are meant to produce a hot airflow.
- *Cold aisle* are aisles in a server room that are meant to produce a cold airflow.

Related Concepts

- Signage—AD-2.7E
- Cameras—AD-2.7F
- Closed-circuit television (CCTV)—AD-2.7G
- Sensors—AD-2.7O
- Air gap—AD-2.7S

Security+ Objective

2.7: Explain the importance of physical security controls.

Secure Data Destruction

Description

Secure data destruction is implemented to ensure attackers are not able to retrieve an organization's equipment or physical forms of data after it has been discarded.

Examples

- *Burning* is the incineration of equipment or data and makes it nearly impossible for hackers to retrieve or use any information. This is especially effective for paper-based information.
- *Shredding* is placing media or paper through a shredder in which the contents are destroyed.
- *Pulping* refers to placing paper-based data into a tray with liquid that strips ink from the paper and dissolves the paper into pulp.
- *Pulverizing* is accomplished by using a machine that shreds devices or drives into tiny pieces. This is the most efficient means of destruction if your organization frequently replaces drives.
- *Degaussing* is exposing disks, such as hard drives, to a power electromagnet current that disrupts the disk's magnetic patterns for data storage.
- *Third-party solutions* include hiring vendors to destroy an organization's equipment and physical data.

Related Concepts

- Data protection—AD-2.1C
- Data sanitization—OIR-4.1H

Security+ Objective

2.7: Explain the importance of physical security controls.

Digital Signatures

Description

Digital signatures are computed values used to validate the sender of a message. They also verify that a message has not been altered.

Example

The following screen capture shows an example of a personal certificate located in the central storage location for a given computer. Notice the numerous folders in the left-side pane that contain various certificate types.

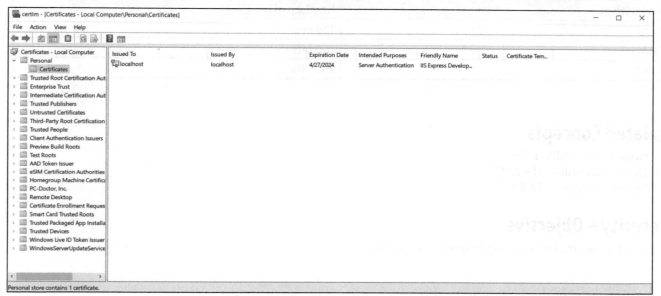

Goodheart-Willcox Publisher

Related Concepts

- Protocols—IMP-3.1A
- Public key infrastructure (PKI)—IMP-3.9A

Security+ Objective

2.8: Summarize the basics of cryptographic concepts.

AD-2.8B   Key Length

Description

Key length refers to the total number of bits in an algorithm's key. The length of a key determines the level of encryption applied to data during transmission. Key length is often referred to as *key size*.

Examples

Algorithm	Key Length
MD5	128 bits
SHA	160 bits
SHA2	256 bits

Related Concepts

- Brute force—ATV-1.2B
- Data protection—AD-2.1C
- Key stretching—AD-2.8C

Security+ Objective

2.8: Summarize the basics of cryptographic concepts.

AD-2.8C Key Stretching

Description

Key stretching is a technique in which a key is generated from a password with extra characters at the end. Additionally, the password is changed often. The combination of lengthening and frequently changing passwords makes it more difficult for threat actors to crack keys.

Examples

Methods such as bcrypt and PBKDF2 are used for key stretching.

- *Bcrypt* is based on the Blowfish cipher but includes a nonce added to the password.
- *Password-Based Key Derivation Function 2 (PBKDF2)* is a technique that employs a pseudorandom function, such as hashing, as well as salting to stretch key lengths.

Related Concepts

- Data protection—AD-2.1C
- Key length—AD-2.8B
- Password crackers—OIR-4.1G

Security+ Objective

2.8: Summarize the basics of cryptographic concepts.

Copyright Goodheart-Willcox Co., Inc.

May not be reproduced or posted to a publicly accessible website.

295

Salting

Description

Salting is a security countermeasure that adds insignificant information to the end of data to create a separate hash value. This process adds random values to plaintext inputs, which helps mitigate rainbow table attacks.

Example

Imagine your login password for your workstation is **4!BlueGuitar**. If your password is unsalted, the hash remains the same. However, through salting, the password hash becomes, for example, **4!BlueGuitar249W**. In this example, **249W** serving as insignificant data for the purpose of creating a new hash.

Related Concepts

- Rainbow tables—ATV-1.2B
- Data protection—AD-2.1C
- Hashing—AD-2.8E
- Database—IMP-3.2C

Security+ Objective

2.8: Summarize the basics of cryptographic concepts.

Hashing

Description

Hashing is a mathematical function that generates values based on data. Hashing algorithms are used in computer programming to generate checksums and create a cryptographic hash to produce a message digest.

Example

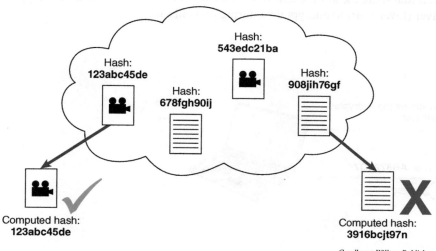

Goodheart-Willcox Publisher

Related Concepts

- Pass the hash—ATV-1.3R
- Data protection—AD-2.1C
- Hashing—AD-2.1I
- Salting—AD-2.8D
- Database—IMP-3.2C
- Integrity—OIR-4.5D

Security+ Objective

2.8: Summarize the basics of cryptographic concepts.

Key Exchange

Description

Key exchanges are cryptographic processes in which keys are transmitted between parties. This exchange is vital in data transmissions, as key exchanges dictate how data is protected and how or if a key will be used to decrypt data once it is received. Asymmetric encryption keys are encrypted by the client and sent to a server, which decrypts the key. The keys are then used to encrypt messages sent between the server and client. However, public keys are not able to decrypt ciphertext, and only the intended individuals that share the key are able to obtain and view the sender's data. Both types of key exchanges rely on the Transport layer (layer four) to encrypt data during transmission.

Example

Step 1

Step 2

Step 3

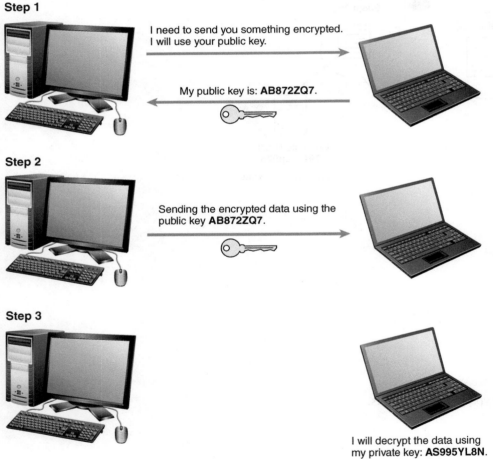

I need to send you something encrypted. I will use your public key.

My public key is: **AB872ZQ7**.

Sending the encrypted data using the public key **AB872ZQ7**.

I will decrypt the data using my private key: **AS995YL8N**.

Goodheart-Willcox Publisher; (devices) romvo/Shutterstock.om

Related Concepts

- Symmetric vs. asymmetric—AD-2.8O

Security+ Objective

2.8: Summarize the basics of cryptographic concepts.

Elliptical-Curve Cryptography (ECC)

Description

Elliptical-curve cryptography (ECC) is an encryption method based on an elliptical curve as opposed to prime numbers. This method is often used to generate public and private key pairs.

Example

An elliptical curve is shown in the following figure. This mathematical curve is the basis for generating public and private key pairs.

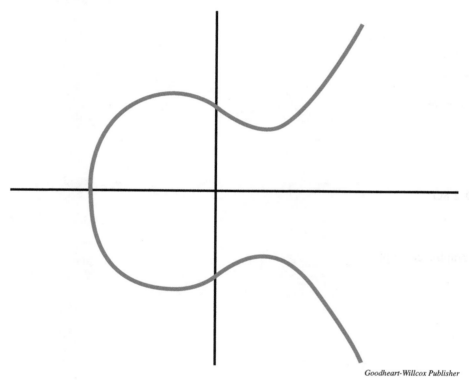

Goodheart-Willcox Publisher

Related Concepts

- Data protection—AD-2.1C
- Symmetric vs. asymmetric—AD-2.8O

Security+ Objective

2.8: Summarize the basics of cryptographic concepts.

AD-2.8H   Perfect Forward Secrecy (PFS)

Description

Perfect forward secrecy (PFS) is a security feature in which keys are changed after each message is sent. It uses the Diffie-Hellman key agreement to generate transactional session keys without using a server's private key.

Example

Goodheart-Willcox Publisher

Related Concepts

- Data protection—AD-2.1C
- Symmetric vs. asymmetric—AD-2.8O

Security+ Objective

2.8: Summarize the basics of cryptographic concepts.

Quantum

Description

Quantum cryptography is a cryptographic method in which quantum mechanics are applied to encrypt data. Until recently, most encryption was based on mathematical solutions, but quantum cryptography relies on *quantum key distribution (QKD)*, which utilizes quantum communications to share a key between the sender and receiver of a message. Quantum cryptography is perceived to be nearly impossible to crack. Since data transfers exist in a quantum state, they are subject to the *no-cloning theorem*, which states that it is impossible to recreate unknown states perfectly. This means that any eavesdropping causes the quantum state to change, which can be easily detected.

Examples

- *Quantum communications* use photons to transmit data over fiber-optic lines.
- *Quantum computing* uses quantum theory to enable computing bits to exist in more than one state. Normally, binary bits must be either off or on (0 or 1, respectively). However, quantum computing allows quantum bits (*QuBits*) to generate any combination of 0 or 1.

Related Concepts

- Data protection—AD-2.1C
- Post-quantum—AD-2.8J

Security+ Objective

2.8: Summarize the basics of cryptographic concepts.

Description

Post-quantum cryptography refers to cryptographic measures used to prevent attacks from a quantum computer. This is often referred to as *quantum-proof*, *quantum-safe*, or *quantum-resistant cryptography*.

Example

- *Quantum communications* use photons to transmit data over fiber-optic lines.

Related Concepts

- Data protection—AD-2.1C
- Quantum—AD-2.8I

Security+ Objective

2.8: Summarize the basics of cryptographic concepts.

Description

Ephemeral keys are keys that use a different secret key for each session, meaning the key is good only for one use. These keys are transactional, meaning if an attacker obtains a key for one session, all other sessions will remain confidential due to a new key having been generated.

Example

An example of when ephemeral keys are used is in *Diffie-Hellman Ephemeral (DHE)* cryptography, which is a specific type of Diffie-Hellman (DH) cryptography. *Diffie-Hellman (DH)* was the first asymmetric cryptographic algorithm developed. It was created to combat the issue of secure encrypted symmetric keys being attacked during transmission.

Related Concepts

- Perfect forward secrecy—AD-2.8H
- Symmetric vs. asymmetric—AD-2.8O

Security+ Objective

2.8: Summarize the basics of cryptographic concepts.

Modes of Operation

Description

Mode of operation is an important concept to modern forms of cryptography. A given operational mode specifies how a corresponding cipher disguises data.

Examples

- *Authenticated* mode of operation verifies to the recipient of an encrypted message that a message is unaltered and coming from a reliable source. Thus, the recipient can trust the sender and understand encryption was generated by forms of identification, authentication, and access control systems.
- *Unauthenticated* mode of operation provides secrecy of encryption but does not verify that the data was not altered during transmission.
- *Counter (CTR)* mode of operation provides both the sender and receiver access to a counter, which generates a new value each time a cipher is exchanged.

Related Concepts

- Data protection—AD-2.1C
- Cipher suites—AD-2.8N
- Symmetric vs. asymmetric—AD-2.8O
- Limitations—AD-2.8T

Security+ Objective

2.8: Summarize the basics of cryptographic concepts.

Blockchain

Description

Blockchain is a list of records—called *blocks*—in which each block contains data, a hash, and a hash from the previous block. The data portion of a block contains data regarding a confidential transaction. For example, a block may contain data relevant to a bitcoin transaction, such as the amount sent, who is to obtain the funds, and who sent the funds. The hash portion of the block includes the encryption of the data. Lastly, the hash of the previous block is attached to the current block to create a chain. Thus, if one block is tampered with, its hash changes, and the subsequent block will not recognize the new hash. *Public ledgers* in blockchain are the cryptocurrency transactions that are available after authentication of users on a network.

Example

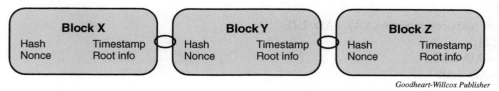

Goodheart-Willcox Publisher

Related Concepts

- Data protection—AD-2.1C
- Authentication, authorization, and accounting (AAA)—AD-2.4E

Security+ Objective

2.8: Summarize the basics of cryptographic concepts.

Cipher Suites

Description

Cipher suites are cryptographic algorithmic methods implemented for data transmissions.

Examples

- *Stream ciphers* transmit data using plaintext that is combined with a key stream. The algorithms are characterized by a variable-sized cipher and based on permutation.
- *Block ciphers* encrypt blocks of data in a fixed size.

Related Concepts

- Data protection—AD-2.1C
- Authentication, authorization, and accounting (AAA)—AD-2.4E
- Modes of operation—AD-2.8L
- Symmetric vs. asymmetric—AD-2.8O
- Homomorphic encryption—AD-2.8R
- Limitations—AD-2.8T

Security+ Objective

2.8: Summarize the basics of cryptographic concepts.

Description

Symmetric encryption ciphers use the same secret key for encryption and decryption of data. Conversely, *asymmetric encryption* ciphers use two related keys, a private key and a public key, to encrypt and decrypt data.

Examples

Symmetric ciphers:

- Data Encryption Standard (DES)
- Advanced Encryption Standard (AES)
- Triple DES (3DES)
- Rivest Cipher
- Blowfish
- Twofish

Asymmetric ciphers:

- Diffie-Hellman
- Elliptical-curve
- Rivest-Shamir-Adleman (RSA)
- Digital Signature Algorithm (DSA)

Related Concepts

- Data protection—AD-2.1C
- Key exchange—AD-2.8F
- Elliptical curve cryptography—AD-2.8G
- Perfect forward secrecy—AD-2.8H
- Ephemeral—AD-2.8K
- Modes of operation—AD-2.8L
- Cipher suites—AD-2.8N
- Homomorphic encryption—AD-2.8R
- Limitations—AD-2.8T
- Public key infrastructure—IMP-3.9A

Security+ Objective

2.8: Summarize the basics of cryptographic concepts.

Lightweight Cryptography

Description

Lightweight cryptography is an encryption method that uses fewer resources to encrypt data so as not to exhaust a device's memory. It is often utilized in devices with low power or computational complexity, such as embedded systems or IoT devices.

Example

Lightweight cryptographic ciphers balance reliable security, efficiency, and cost.

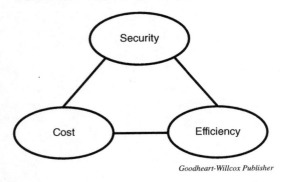

Goodheart-Willcox Publisher

Related Concepts

- Embedded systems—AD-2.6A
- Internet of Things (IoT)—AD-2.6C

Security+ Objective

2.8: Summarize the basics of cryptographic concepts.

Steganography

Description

Steganography is the technique of hiding a message within another message. Often, steganography is performed on audio, video, or image files. The fundamental difference between steganography and other forms of cryptography is that steganography *hides* data, and typical cryptography *masks* it.

Examples

- *Audio steganography* uses forms of encoding that, when played in software, presents a message in text form.
- *Video steganography* is the placement of information within frames of a video file. With the proper software, users can decode the frames.
- *Image steganography*, which is the most common form of steganography, is placing text within an image. Generating image steganography can be performed on many software suites.

Related Concepts

- Summarize the basics of cryptographic concepts—AD-2.8

Security+ Objective

2.8: Summarize the basics of cryptographic concepts.

Homomorphic Encryption

Description

Homomorphic encryption is an encryption method in which data is converted into ciphertext that is able to be analyzed, searched, and modified without decryption.

Example

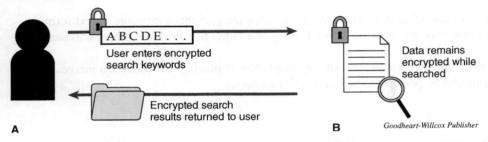

User enters encrypted
search keywords

Encrypted search
results returned to user

A

Data remains
encrypted while
searched

Goodheart-Willcox Publisher

B

Related Concepts

- Cipher suites—AD-2.8N

Security+ Objective

2.8: Summarize the basics of cryptographic concepts.

Common Use Cases

Description

Common use cases are the methods needed to utilize certain cryptographic concepts.

Examples

- *Low-power devices* are devices that require more processing cycles and memory, and as a result makes the devices slower. This can have a negative impact on cryptographic processes, so lightweight cryptography should be used.
- *Low latency* refers to the processing of data with minimal delays and may require minimal cryptographic overhead.
- *High resiliency* in cryptographic systems refers to systems that employ strong encryption keys and processing power.
- *Supporting confidentiality* refers to a cryptographic system maintaining the secrecy or privacy of data. Most ciphers support confidentiality by default.
- *Supporting integrity* guarantees the data encrypted during transmissions will not be modified while traveling to its destination.
- *Supporting obfuscation* is ensuring a message will be difficult to understand, unless you are the originator or intended recipient of the message.
- *Supporting authentication* adds an additional layer of security to cryptography. Suppose a threat actor breaks the encryption of a message. Without an added authentication security layer, the data can be reviewed in plaintext.
- *Supporting non-repudiation* guarantees that data will stay in its original form while transmitting.
- *Resource vs. security constraints* refer to limitations in providing cryptography based on the demands of an algorithm compared to available device power.

Related Concepts

- Data protection—AD-2.1C
- Secure coding techniques—AD-2.3D
- Authentication, authorization, and accounting (AAA)—AD-2.4D
- Embedded systems—AD-2.6A
- Internet of Things (IoT)—AD-2.6C
- Specialized—AD-2.6D
- Constraints—AD-2.6M
- Cipher suites—AD-2.8N
- Symmetric vs. asymmetric—AD-2.8O
- Lightweight cryptography—AD-2.8P
- Limitations—AD-2.8T
- Non-repudiation—OIR-4.5H

Security+ Objective

2.8: Summarize the basics of cryptographic concepts.

Limitations

Description

Limitations are often present when implementing cryptographic methods. Examples of cryptographic limitations include the following.

Examples

- *Speed* is often a limitation in cryptography, and depending on the form of cryptography used, it may take hours to complete.
- *Size* of a key can be a limitation due to short keys being able to be broken. Additionally, the creation of longer, more secure keys often result in more time needed to decrypt or slower encryption speed.
- *Weak keys* are a limitation due to the ease in which they can be decrypted if intercepted.
- *Time* refers to how long a cipher takes to encrypt or decrypt data. Usually, cryptography is not a fast process, often taking hours to complete. If speed is essential, consideration must be made for faster cryptographic processes, such as lightweight or homomorphic encryption.
- *Longevity* refers to the span of time for which a cryptographic key is authorized for use. This is also referred to as a *cryptoperiod*. Keys may be *static*, meaning they have a determined period of time, or *ephemeral*, meaning they are good for a single use only.
- *Predictability* is a limitation due to possibility of the key being guessed easily.
- *Entropy* refers to the degree of randomness with which a key is generated.
- *Computational overhead* refers to the usage of time, memory, and bandwidth of a cryptographic cipher.
- *Resource vs. security constraints* refer to limitations in providing cryptographic algorithms based on the demands of the algorithm compared to a device's power. It can also reflect the comparative strength of one cipher over another, depending on the algorithm used.

Related Concepts

- Weak configurations—ATV-1.6C
- Data protection—AD-2.1C
- Embedded systems—AD-2.6A
- Internet of Things (IoT)—AD-2.6C
- Specialized—AD-2.6D
- Constraints—AD-2.6M
- Ephemeral—AD-2.8K
- Cipher suites—AD-2.8N
- Symmetric vs. asymmetric—AD-2.8O
- Lightweight cryptography—AD-2.8P
- Homomorphic encryption—AD-2.8R

Security+ Objective

2.8: Summarize the basics of cryptographic concepts.

Protocols

Description

Protocols are industry-accepted standardized formats that enable communication between devices. When used in cybersecurity, protocols ensure there is security and integrity when utilizing network connections and transmissions.

Examples

- *Domain Name System (DNS)* is the service that maps domain names, such as the address of a website, to its corresponding IP address. The following demonstrates the ability of a local machine DNS to access Google via its IP address as well as by entering its URL.
- *Domain Name System Security Extension (DNSSEC)* is the protocol that provides authentication of DNS data to validate data integrity.
- *Secure Shell (SSH)* operates on TCP port 22 and is a security protocol for remote administration.
- *Secure/multipurpose Internet mail exchanger (S/MIME)*, also known as *secure/multipurpose Internet mail extension*, is an e-mail encryption protocol that adds digital signatures and public key cryptography to the traditional MIME protocol.
- *Secure real-time protocol (SRTP)* is the extension for the protocol Real-Time Transport Protocol (RTP) that protects Voice over IP (VoIP) communications.
- *Lightweight Directory Access Protocol with SSL (LDAPS)* are directories, typically from domains, that allow users on one platform to access resources from another platform such as Windows OS to MacOS.
- Although *Secure File Transfer Protocol (SFTP)* is now perceived to be an obsolete protocol, SFTP added an extension of SSH to provide security file transfers while using a Secure Shell tunnel to encrypt data that was being transmitted.
- *File Transfer Protocol (FTP)* enables file transmissions among devices that are connected to the Internet.
- *Simple Network Management Protocol (SNMP)* is a framework used for management and monitoring.
- *Hypertext transfer protocol over SSL/TLS (HTTPS)* is a protocol that provides secure communication over a web browser.
- *Internet Protocol Security (IPSec)* is a set of open standards that use the following to secure data as it travels across a network and the Internet:
  - An *authentication header (AH)* performs cryptographic functions on a packet and adds a shared secret key. The AH process then adds the HMAC header as an Integrity Check Value (ICV).
  - *Encapsulated security payload (ESP)* encrypts the packet and attaches the header for the packet's cryptographic function, the trailer, and the ICV.
  - *Tunnel mode* encrypts the entire IP packet to encrypt and adds a new IP header.
  - *Transport mode* does not encrypt each packet for the IP header; rather, it encrypts only the data/payload.
  - *Secure post office protocol (POP)* is used via TCP port 110 and enables a client to obtain e-mail messages stored on a remote server, such as an e-mail exchange server.
  - *Internet message access protocol (IMAP)* is a TCP/IP application protocol that uses TCP port 143 and provides a client access to e-mails that are stored on a mailbox via a remote server.

Related Concepts

- Domain name system—ATV-1.4E
- Virtual private network—IMP-3.4C

Security+ Objective

3.1: Given a scenario, implement secure protocols.

Use Cases

Description

Use cases are the situations and circumstances where a tool or protocol would be best utilized. The following table illustrated various use cases and their appropriate protocols.

Examples

Protocol	Network Service	Usage
Secure Real-Time Transport Protocol (SRTP)	Voice and Video	Provides encryption, authentication, and integrity to VoIP and video conferencing data; secure alternative to Real-Time Transport Protocol (RTP)
Network Time Security (NTS)	Time Synchronization	Provides security and authentication to key exchanges through incorporation of TLS; secure alternative to Network Time Protocol (NTP)
Secure Multi-Internet Mail Extension (S/MIME)	E-mail Services	Enables encryption of e-mails to protect unwanted access and interception
Hypertext Transfer Protocol, Secure (HTTPS)	Web Services	Encrypts information transmitted over the Internet to increase security of data transfers; secure alternative to Hypertext Transfer Protocol (HTTP)
Secure File Transfer Protocol (SFTP) and File Transfer Protocol/SSL (FTPS)	File Transfer	Ensures data is transferred using a private, safe stream of data; secure, encrypted alternatives to File Transfer Protocol (FTP)
Lightweight Directory Access Protocol, Secure (LDAPS)	Directory Services	Provides encryption to directory information data, including usernames and passwords; secure alternative to Lightweight Directory Access Protocol (LDAP)
Secure Shell (SSH)	Remote Access	Provides a secure channel over which applications such as remote login and command-line execution is conducted; secure alternative to Telnet
Domain Name System Security Extension (DNSSEC)	Domain Name Resolution	Provides encryption to information distributed through the Domain Name System; security-enhanced alternative to DNS
Simple Network Management Protocol version 3 (SNMPv3)	Routing and Switching	Provides security, authentication, and privacy to network devices, systems, and applications, particularly routers and switches
IP Security (IPSec)	Subscription Services	Establishes encrypted connections between networked devices and allocates subscription-based updates, such as antivirus signatures and IDS/IPS definitions

Goodheart-Willcox Publisher

Related Concepts

- Domain name service—ATV-1.4E
- Virtual private network (VPN)—IMP-3.3C

Security+ Objective

3.1: Given a scenario, implement secure protocols.

IMP-3.2A Endpoint Protection

Description

Endpoint protection refers procedures and technologies used to protect devices and networks.

Examples

- *Antivirus* protection comes in various forms depending on the operating systems used. In most cases, these programs are installed to block or quarantine malicious software and files that are detected. Similarly, *antimalware* protection prohibits or captures malware on a device.
- *Endpoint detection and response (EDR)* are tools and utilities used to monitor devices to identify possible attacks on endpoint devices.
- *Data Loss Prevention (DLP)* systems execute scans to assure that data has not been lost.
- *Next-generation firewalls* are typically third-party firewalls that run at all levels of the OSI model and actively monitor or filter traffic based on data inside packet headers. Often, next-gen firewalls are managed and monitored by a third-party vendor.
- A *host intrusion-prevention system (HIPS)* is software that can prevent system files from being modified or deleted, services from being stopped, and logging unauthorized users off a network.
- A *host intrusion-detection system (HIDS)* is software that examines and analyzes network activity and notifies administrators of potential threats. Often a HIDS program captures information from a single host and analyzes relevant log files.
- A *host-based firewall* monitors the incoming and outgoing communication of a device generates or prompts the user for approval to allow the program's communications. Host-based firewalls are installed on individual devices as opposed to servicing an entire network.

Related Concepts

- Data protection—ATV-1.1C
- Malware—ATV-1.4A
- Boot integrity—IMP-3.2B
- Hardening—IMP-3.2E
- Network appliances—IMP-3.3H
- Configuration changes—OIR-4.4B

Security+ Objective

3.2: Given a scenario, implement host or application security solutions.

Description

Boot integrity refers to the assurance that a device is booting from a secure drive. Examples of methods to ensure boot integrity include the following.

Examples

- *Unified Extensible Firmware Interface (UEFI)* provides support for 64-bit central processing unit (CPU) operations at boot, utilizes a graphical user interface (GUI), and enables boot security. Furthermore, the UEFI can be modified before rebooting a machine, whereas most Basic Input/Output Systems (BIOS) require modifications to be implemented during the boot process.
- *Measured boot* protects a device from rootkits and malware during the booting process by verifying boot components.
- *Boot attestation* provides validation that a boot device is secure, valid, trustworthy, and true.

Related Concepts

- Improper or weak patch management—ATV-1.6E
- Endpoint protection—IMP-3.2A
- Hardening—IMP-3.2E
- Acquisition—OIR-4.5B

Security+ Objective

3.2: Given a scenario, implement host or application security solutions.

Database

Description

Databases utilize methods of augmenting data security by implementing methods to assure that if data breach occurs, it will not present a useful value or output. Methods for securing databases include the following.

Examples

- *Tokenization* is the process of generating a random string of characters, called a *token*, based on a portion of the information stored in a database, such as a username. Tokens ensure that information cannot be used if a data breach occurs.
- *Salting* is a process that adds a random, insignificant value to passwords. This process results in the creation of a different hash value, which ultimately protects passwords stored in a database from being reverse engineered.
- *Hashing* is a mathematical function that creates a value based on data. When applied to a database, hashing assures data is valid and unaltered and that its integrity is upheld. Lastly, if passwords in a database are hashed, they will not be stored in plaintext, meaning it will be nearly impossible for an attacker to decrypt if the passwords are breached.

Related Concepts

- Data protection—AD-2.1C
- Salting—AD-2.8D
- Hashing—AD-2.8E
- Identity—IMP-3.7A

Security+ Objective

3.2: Given a scenario, implement host or application security solutions.

Application Security

Description

Application security is the preventive measures implemented to diminish or prevent data being compromised in an application. Secure application development practices help ensure web applications and software programs are resistant to threat actors seeking to exploit vulnerabilities within the programming or code.

Examples

- *Input validation* is a programming configuration in which an input field disallows characters that do not match the field's purpose or could result in malfunction. This validation prevents attackers from injecting malicious code or scripts into a program or web application.
- *Secure cookies* are often used as a form of application security, as they can only be sent during encrypted sessions HTTPS.
- *Hypertext Transfer Protocol (HTTP) headers* contain information that is processed by a server and browser. HTTP headers are not always displayed to a user, but applications frequently use portions of the embedded data to encode a user's data or input. Often, one header consists of the action requested by the user, while the other houses custom information inputted by a user.
- *Code signing* is an application security measure that provides a certificate that is issued to a software publisher. The certificate is generated after an identity validation process has been completed via the Certificate Authority (CA). Once a code signing process has occurred, the operating system of a device prompts a user to choose whether they accept the signature of the code signing to run the application or program.
- *Whitelisting* is the process of generating an approved list of applications. Any program not on the list will not be able to operate.
- *Blacklisting* is the opposite of whitelisting. It is the process of generating a list of unapproved applications. Any program not included in the blacklist is permitted to run. Blacklisting is inherently less secure than whitelisting because, while whitelisting will only permit approved applications to run, blacklisting affords an opportunity for a user to choose to run a program not known to be malicious.
- *Secure coding practices* are used to augment the validity and security of applications and programs during the developmental and coding stages of the application's life cycle. One example is *unreachable code*, which is part of an application source code that cannot be executed. In the following screen capture, notice the "If" statement in the Python code. No conditions are present that allow the statement to execute properly; as such, it will result in an error.
- Another secure coding practice to be aware of is *dead code*, which is a vulnerability that enables confidential information such as a password, token, or Personal Identification Information (PII) to be read without the appropriate access controls.
- *Static code analysis* is an application security measure that is performed against the application/program code. This often includes scanning source code with known issues before it is labeled as an executable process. The scanning process is typically based on the Open Web Application Security Process (OWASP) Top Ten Most Critical Web Application Security Risks along with other various injection vulnerabilities that are known by developers. Another valid resource is the National Institute of Standards and Technology (NIST) list of source code analyzers, which can be viewed at https://samate.nist.gov/index.php/Source_Code_Security_Analyzers.html.
- *Manual code review* is the process of reviewing code line by line to locate vulnerabilities. One type of manual review is *manual peer review* which consists of peers that are experienced developers reviewing and examining the original developer's code for any errors. Since the peer reviewer did not generate the code, it provides a non-biased overview when reviewing the developer's code.
- *Dynamic code analysis* is the process of testing an application or program in a real-world environment after it is executed.
- *Fuzzing*, also called *fuzz testing*, is a technique in which an application is tested for bugs and other miscellaneous vulnerabilities through automation.

Related Concepts

- Improper input handling—ATV-1.3I
- Malicious code or script execution—ATV-1.4G
- Secure coding techniques—AD-2.3D
- Open Web Application Security Project (OWASP)—AD-2.3E
- Software diversity—AD-2.3F
- Certificate authority (CA)—IMP-3.9A
- Types of certificates—IMP-3.9B
- Certificate formats—IMP-3.9C

Security+ Objective

3.2: Given a scenario, implement host or application security solutions.

Hardening

Description

Hardening refers to security methods that utilize tools, techniques, and actions to reduce vulnerabilities in an enterprise environment. Various technologies can be used to harden devices. The goal of hardening a device is to augment security by allowing devices to perform only the functions needed of the individual using the device. Thus, while a device might be capable of performing many uses, hardening will limit the device to the capabilities needed for an individual's use.

Examples

- Hardening *open ports and services* may prohibit the uses of Internet and application resources that are irrelevant to an individual's work for an organization. In other words, resources that are not needed for their work, such as social media or gaming websites, should not be accessible.
- *Registry hardening* prohibits users from accessing an operating system's registry. For example, not allowing a user on a Windows operating system to access **regedit.exe**, which is the registry editor for Windows operating systems, is a form of registry hardening.
- *Disk encryption hardening* encrypts data on a disk in such a way so only authorized users with the correct key may obtain or use the disk's data.
- *Operating System (OS) hardening* only enables the services necessary for an individual's work and functionality needed for an organization.
- *Patch management* typically consists of two forms:
  - *Third-party updates* are patches for specific applications and often generated by the application vendor. By hardening third-party updates, only verified patches that solve an issue users are experiencing are installed.
  - *Auto-update hardening* allows patches to be installed that help augment a device's security and protect from flaws in applications.

Related Concepts

- Vectors—ATV-1.5C
- Weak configurations—ATV-1.6C
- Improper or weak patch management—ATV-1.6E
- Data protection—AD-2.1C
- Endpoint protection—IMP-3.2A
- Self-encrypting drive (SED)/full disk encryption (FDE)—IMP-3.2F

Security+ Objective

3.2: Given a scenario, implement host or application security solutions.

Self-Encrypting Drive (SED)/ Full Disk Encryption (FDE)

Description

A *self-encrypting drive (SED)* is a type of drive that has an enabled drive controller to perform cryptographic operations and perform automatic encryption. An SED uses a media encryption key (MEK) to encrypt the data on the device and stores the MEK with a key encryption key (KEK) generated from a user's password. Another option for disk encryption is to utilize full disk encryption (FDE).

Full disk encryption (FDE), also termed as *drive encryption* or *full device encryption*, encrypts the entirety of a drive, including files, folders, and system files. Furthermore, FDE is considered to a simple method for users to encrypt their drives and can be employed using utilities such as BitLocker Drive Encryption. However, since FDE performs cryptographic operations through utilities of an operating system, the performance of a device is usually impacted.

Examples

Opal Storage Specification is a set of SED conditions that are utilized for encrypting and securing drives. These conditions include an authentication process once a device has turned on and the SED is active. As a result, if the authentication results in a failure, the SED is able to deny a user access or delete the contents of the SED. Since SEDs are used for nontraditional hosts that rely on encryption, Opal Storage Specification is the proper disk encryption method for multifunction devices.

Related Concepts

- Data protection—AD-2.1-C
- Hardening—IMP-3.2F

Security+ Objective

3.2: Given a scenario, implement host or application security solutions.

Hardware Root of Trust

Description

Hardware root of trust is the physical starting point in a chain of trust. The chain of trust is the sequence of trusted and validated devices associated with each hardware and software component of a device, such as a UEFI on a Windows operating system computer.

Example

The following is a sample process of a hardware root of trust establishing a chain of trust.

1. Device ensures authorized access

2. Hardware root of trust prevents untrusted boot media from being used

3. Boot to OS further prevents untrusted boot from launching

4. OS transfer to application prevents untrusted applications from launching

5. Execution and attack prevention

Related Concepts

- Boot integrity—IMP-3.2B

Security+ Objective

3.2: Given a scenario, implement host or application security solutions.

Trusted Platform Module (TPM)

Description

A *trusted platform module (TPM)* is a microcontroller that provides the means of authentication to provide a device's boot integrity.

Example

FxJ/Public Domain

Related Concepts

- Boot integrity—IMP-3.2B

Security+ Objective

3.2: Given a scenario, implement host or application security solutions.

Copyright Goodheart-Willcox Co., Inc.

May not be reproduced or posted to a publicly accessible website.

323

Sandboxing

Description

Sandboxing is the act of executing software in an isolated environment. The act of running a program in a sandbox allows developers and security professionals to utilize virtualized environments for testing and observational purposes without effecting a network or connected devices.

Example

The following screen capture shows an Ubuntu OS operating inside as a virtual machine through Oracle VM Virtual Box software.

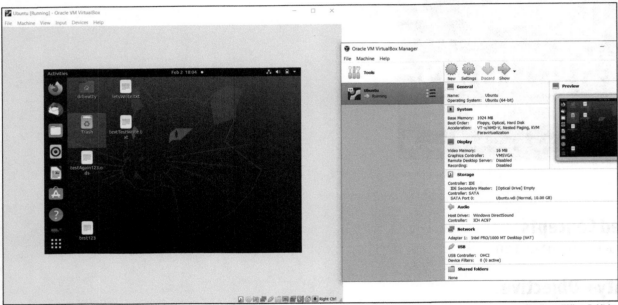

Goodheart-Willcox Publisher

Related Concepts

- Virtualization—AD-2.2O
- Environment—AD-2.3A
- Network reconnaissance and discovery—OIR-4.1A
- Containment—OIR-4.4B

Security+ Objective

3.2: Given a scenario, implement host or application security solutions.

Description

Load balancing is a method of distributing client requests to available server nodes such as web and e-mail servers. Using load balancing provides for higher throughput, supports multiple users connected to a network, and provides fault tolerance. There are a number of configurations possible in load balancing, such as the following.

Examples

- *Active/active (A/A)* load balancing configurations consist of nodes that are processing data simultaneously. Using A/A load balancing allows administrators to use the maximum number of nodes while maintaining functionality. Additionally, if one node experiences failure, another node will immediately take over the workload.
- *Active/passive (A/P)* load balancing configurations uses a redundant array of nodes. The secondary node takes over only if the first node fails.
- *Scheduling* is an algorithm used to determine which node is selected to process each incoming request. This is often accomplished via a round-robin arrangement in which the scheduling algorithm chooses the next node.
- *Virtual IP* load balancing consists of each node having its own virtual IP (VIP) address. The VIP can be generated from various protocols such as ARP, ICMP, NAT, and DNS.
- *Persistence* load balancing maintains user connection to a session by setting a cookie on the node.

Related Concepts

- Redundancy—AD-2.5A
- Network appliances—IMP-3.3H

Security+ Objective

3.3: Given a scenario, implement secure network designs.

Network Segmentation

Description

Network segmentation is a network design model in which a network is divided based on the needs or vulnerabilities of the devices. All hosts connected to a network segment are able to communicate freely with other devices that are also connected to the same network segment. There are multiple methods of establishing network segments, including the following.

Examples

- A *virtual local area network (VLAN)* is a network that is created by switch technology. While the VLANs are connected in the same network, each VLAN has its own data transmissions due to the network segmentation.

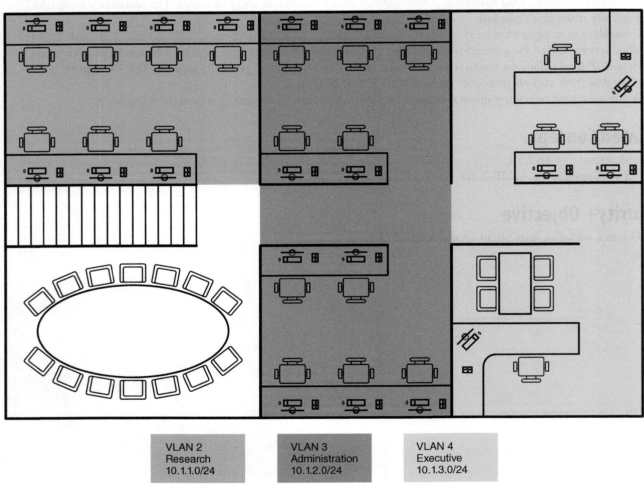

VLAN 2
Research
10.1.1.0/24

VLAN 3
Administration
10.1.2.0/24

VLAN 4
Executive
10.1.3.0/24

Goodheart-Willcox Publisher

- A *demilitarized zone (DMZ)* is a segmented portion of a network that is located either behind one firewall or between two firewalls. A DMZ provides access to the public but only provides certain organizational data to the public.

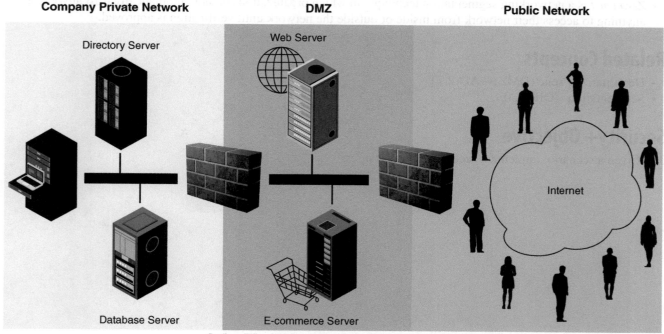

Goodheart-Willcox Publisher; (servers) aShatilov/Shutterstock.com; (wall) beboy/Shutterstock.com; (people) Rawpixel.com/Shutterstock.com

- *East-west traffic* refers to the data transmissions and its flow between servers in a data center. This differs from *north-south traffic*, which is the flow of traffic from an organization's data center to an outside location.

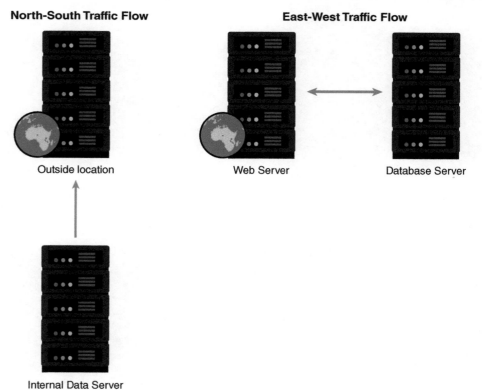

Goodheart-Willcox Publisher; (servers) Sujith RS/Shutterstock.com

- An *extranet* is a private, segmented network that allows limited access to outside affiliates of an organization, such as vendors and customers.
- An *intranet* is a private, segmented network that is only accessible by members of an organization.
- *Zero trust* is a networking segmentation technique in which organizations do not automatically trust anyone or anything to access their network from inside or outside the network until verification is approved.

Related Concepts
- Demilitarized zone (DMZ)—AD-2.7T
- Segmentation—OIR-4.4E

Security+ Objective
3.3: Given a scenario, implement secure network designs.

Description

A *virtual private network (VPN)* is a secure, virtualized connection between two endpoints that are connected via an unsecured network. There are numerous types of VPN connections, such as the following.

Examples

- *Always on VPNs,* initiate connections whenever an Internet connection is established on a trusted network. The network is considered trusted by nature of the user's connection, and the device's cache credentials are authenticated to the VPN.
- *Split tunnel VPNs* require the user to access the Internet directly using their device's native IP and DNS configurations in order to connect to their VPN.
- *Full tunnel VPNs* require the user to connect to the Internet first, and then be mediated by the organization's network. After reaching the organization's network, the user is assigned IP and DNS configurations from the organization, which enables them to connect to the VPN. Therefore, full tunnel VPNs offer users better security, but if there are networking issues in the organization, those same issues will emerge via the user's VPN connection.
- *Remote access VPNs* require users to connect to a VPN gateway, often referred to as a *VPN concentrator*, on the organization's local network. This is commonly used in organizations that enable employees to work remotely.
- *Site-to-site VPNs* use a VPN concentrator to connect two or more local networks. While remote access VPN connections are initiated by the user, site-to-site VPN connections are configured to operate automatically.
- IPSec refers to nonproprietary standards that can be used to secure data as it travels across the Internet and other networks.
- *Secure Shell (SSH)* operates on TCP port 22 and is a security protocol used for remote administration. *Transport Layer Security (TLS)* is a transport protocol that uses port 443. These protocols are often used in VPN connections to transmit encrypted credentials for authorization to connect to servers such as a RADIUS server.
- *HTML5* is the fifth standard of HTML and offers secure remote access.
- *Layer 2 tunneling protocol (L2TP)* is a standard VPN protocol for tunneling Point-to-Point Protocol (PPP) sessions among various network protocols.

Related Concepts

- Protocols—IMP-3.1A
- Use cases—IMP-3.1B

Security+ Objective

3.3: Given a scenario, implement secure network designs.

Description

A *Domain Name System (DNS)* is a hierarchical, decentralized service that maps domain names to their IP address. A DNS enables users to navigate to websites using URLs or domain names in a browser instead of IP addresses.

Examples

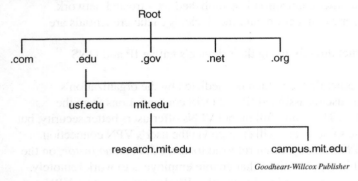

Goodheart-Willcox Publisher

Related Concepts

- Domain name system (DNS)—ATV-1.4E

Security+ Objective

3.3: Given a scenario, implement secure network designs.

IMP-3.3E　Network Access Control (NAC)

Description

Network access control (NAC) is the practice of preventing unauthorized users or devices from accessing an organization's network.

Examples

Agent and *agentless* are two software methods of assessing the health, posture, and endpoints of an organization's network. However, if there are multiple devices to monitor, agentless software is typically used because it monitors an array of devices, such as smartphones and tablets, but only provides minimal information. However, agent software, which can be seen in the following screen capture, gathers information about each device, such as the antivirus software used, applications installed on the device, and other detailed information requested from the software. Nevertheless, since agent software obtains magnitudes of data regarding each device, the number of devices that can be monitored needs to be limited.

Related Concepts

- Endpoint protection—IMP-3.2A
- Hardening—IMP-3.2E
- Network appliances—IMP-3.3H

Security+ Objective

3.3: Given a scenario, implement secure network designs.

Out-of-Band Management

Description

Out-of-band management refers to the management of port interfaces used for managing network equipment. An important note about this management method is that it is not able to block attacks. However, it does provide data loss protection and packet recording. Typically, out-of-band management can be accomplished using modems, terminal servers, or separate management networks.

Example

The following illustrated the difference between in-band and out-of-band management.

Management Method	Connection Type	Attack Blocking	Path of Data Flow	Security Implications
In-Band	Connected directly to network and evaluates original data	Able to block attacks in progress	Routes traffic directly through the device	Used with firewalls, intrusion-prevention systems, honeypots, and threat detection
Out-of-Band	Connected to a port on each device	Unable to block attacks in progress	Receives copy of data	Forensic analysis with data loss protection, intrusion-detection systems, and forensic packet recording

Goodheart-Willcox Publisher

Related Concepts

- Voice over IP (VoIP)—AD-2.6E

Security+ Objective

3.3: Given a scenario, implement secure network designs.

Port Security

Description

Port security is a traffic control feature for preventing unauthorized people or devices from forwarding packets through communication ports. There are a number of ways to implement port security, such as the following.

Examples

- *Broadcast storm prevention* refers to the measures taken to ensure there is not an overload of broadcasts sent to devices on a subnet. One measure for preventing broadcast storms is to identify the source of the broadcast, which can be accomplished via free tools such as Wireshark.
- *Bridge Protocol Data Unit (BPDU) guards* protect against malicious attacks of a BPDU. This is often included as a feature of a network switch and relies on STP/RSTP to accomplish its task.
- *Loop prevention* is the avoidance of broadcast loops by utilizing the Spanning Tree Protocol (STP), which is also defined in IEEE 802.1D and organizes bridges into a hierarchy to avoid loops.
- *Dynamic Host Configuration Protocol (DCHP) snooping* inspects DHCP traffic that arrives on access ports and provides evidence as to whether a host is spoofing its MAC address.
- *Media access control (MAC) filtering* can be implemented on a switch to allow only approved MAC addresses to transmit traffic.

Related Concepts

- Weak configurations—ATV-1.6C
- Network appliances—IMP-3.3H

Security+ Objective

3.3: Given a scenario, implement secure network designs.

Network Appliances

Description

Network appliances are designed to provide network functionality as well as protection and security of its data and data transmissions. Commonly encountered network appliances include the following.

Examples

- *Jump servers* are network appliances that are used to manage devices in separate security zones. Jump servers are typically accessed in less secured zones, and clients are required to utilize Secure Shell (SSH) before accessing the server as a connection to other servers.
- *Proxy servers* direct network communication between a client and other servers to augment network performance. There are two common types of proxies: forward and reverse.
  - *Forward proxy servers* are Internet-facing servers that retrieve data sources from the Internet.
  - *Reverse proxy servers* are internal-facing servers that direct and control access to the proxy server in an organization's private network.
- *Network-Based Intrusion Detection Systems (NIDS)* and *Network-Based Intrusion Prevention Systems (NIPS)* can be inline, meaning they are connected to a network and actively monitor for or stop malicious traffic, or passive, which are systems that connect to a switch through a port that receives a copy of network traffic. NIDS/NIPS provide a variety of monitoring types, such as the following.
  - *Signature-based monitoring* examines network traffic and searches for data patterns that compare against a predefined database signature.
  - *Heuristic-based monitoring*, also known as *behavior-based monitoring*, monitors the processes that occur on systems and networks. It uses artificial intelligence to seek processes that are not in line with baseline behavior and may cause harm to the systems and network of an organization.
  - *Anomaly-based detection* is similar to heuristic-based monitoring as it too searches for irregularities in the use of protocols and data transfers.
- A *hardware security module (HSM)* is a cryptographic device that stores or manages encryption keys. An HSM is also capable of performing cryptographic functions.
- SIEM *sensors* and *collectors* are able to detect, store, and interpret information from various network appliances such as hosts, firewalls, and IDS sensors.
- *Aggregators* are devices or service providers used to provide their own functionalities by transmitting data in an efficient manner.
- *Firewalls* are network appliances used to provide a barrier and offer protection against unwanted in-bound and out-bound traffic of an organization's network. Firewalls come in a variety of types, including the following.
  - A *web application firewall (WAF)* is used to monitor HTTP traffic between web applications and the Internet.
  - A *next-generation firewall* is capable of running at all seven layers of the OSI model to monitor and filter network traffic.
  - *Stateful firewalls* monitor packets for a determined period of time and then only accept packets that were previously tracked.
  - *Stateless firewalls* are designed to inspect packets and to determine if they are permitted to be sent or retrieved to a source or destination address based on the firewall's specified rules.
  - *Unified threat management (UTM)* refers to an all-in-one security device that enables the monitoring of a network to be accomplished with only one device.
  - A *NAT gateway* bridges the connection between a local network and the Internet by translating private IP addresses into public IP addresses or vice versa.
  - A *content filter*, also known as a *URL filter*, monitors Internet traffic to prohibit the access of backlisted websites and web services.
  - *Open-source firewalls* are created by security professionals and allow users to access the source code. While these are often less expensive than proprietary firewalls, they do not provide vendor support, and it

is the organization's responsibility to monitor and fix the functionalities of the open-source firewall. On the contrary, *proprietary firewalls* are more expensive but are also managed, updated, and monitored by the vendor. The decision between open-source or proprietary firewalls is up to the preference of the organization and its administrators.

- *Hardware firewalls* are firewalls that exist between an organization's server and its network, and any data that enters or exits the network must pass through it. However, *software firewalls* are used to protect devices after the firewall is installed onto the device. Organizations are able to use both types, and like open-source vs. proprietary, the decision is based on organizational preference.
- Appliance vs. host-based vs. virtual is another consideration an organization should make regarding firewalls. An *appliance firewall* is a stand-alone hardware firewall that performs only the functions it is configured to perform. *Host-based firewalls* are a form of application firewall, meaning they are software-based, run on, and protect only one device. *Virtual-based firewalls* are considered cloud-based firewalls but act similarly to hardware firewalls while also having the ability to be managed by a remote vendor.

Related Concepts

- Endpoint protection—IMP-3.2A
- Hardening—IMP-3.2E
- Network appliances—IMP-3.3H
- SIEM dashboards—OIR-4.3B

Security+ Objective

3.3: Given a scenario, implement secure network designs.

Access Control List (ACL)

Description

An *access control list (ACL)* determines which users and devices are granted or denied access based on their account type and IP address.

Example

A primary example of an ACL is a VLAN access control list (VACL). The VACL determines which packets are able to travel in and out of a VLAN. It is not uncommon for each VLAN in a network to have individual VACLs configured.

Related Concepts

- Internet protocol (IP) schema—AD-2.1A
- Endpoint protection—IMP-3.2A
- Hardening—IMP-3.2E
- Port security—IMP-3.2G
- Network segmentation—IMP-3.3B
- Route security—IMP-3.3J

Security+ Objective

3.3: Given a scenario, implement secure network designs.

Route Security

Description

Route security is implemented by properly routing traffic via routers (OSI Layer 3 devices) to its appropriate subnet. Since routers are not designed to be security devices, it is vital that security professionals implement precautions such as an ACL to determine which packets are approved or denied access to subnets of an organization's network.

Examples

Route security can be accomplished by taking the following precautions:

- Regularly patch all router firmware and the router's operating system.
- Secure routers with strong passwords that are difficult to guess.
- Only use SSH for remote access.
- Back up all router configuration information.
- Ensure that only traffic that should be on the subnet is allowed.
- Remind users about security access and responsibilities with a router banner.
- Have a plan to check for updates to firmware, and install only patches directly from the manufacturer as third-party patches may not be reliable.

Related Concepts

- Internet protocol (IP) schema—AD-2.1A
- Endpoint protection—IMP-3.2A
- Hardening—IMP-3.2E
- Port security—IMP-3.2G
- Network segmentation—IMP-3.3B
- Access control list (ACL)—IMP-3.3I

Security+ Objective

3.3: Given a scenario, implement secure network designs.

Quality of Service (QoS)

Description

Quality of Service (QoS) refers to the technologies that allow a network to run priority applications and function as expected, regardless of diminished connectivity or limited capacity.

Examples

QoS can be measured quantitatively using the following parameters.

- *Packet loss* occurs when networks become congested. Dropped packets cause jitter and audio/video lag.
- *Jitter* occurs as a byproduct of packet loss. Typically, jitter is caused by network congestion and misconfigured packet routes. Jitter causes QoS to drop significantly, especially in voice or video communication.
- *Latency* is a delay in network-based data transfer. Ideally, a network has zero latency, and increased latency can result in imperfect VoIP sessions, causing users to experience echo or delayed audio.
- *Bandwidth* refers to the capacity of network communication. High QoS results in optimized network performance through proper bandwidth management and assigning priority to applications with higher performance requirements.

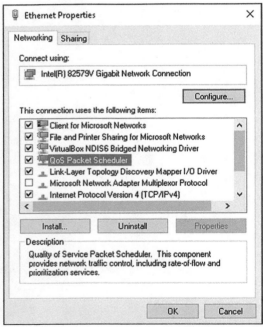

Goodheart-Willcox Publisher

Related Concepts

- Voice over IP—AD-2.6E
- Voice and video—IMP-3.1B

Security+ Objective

3.3: Given a scenario, implement secure network designs.

Implications of IPv6

Description

The implications of *Internet Protocol version 6 (IPv6)* include a vast array of possibilities that IPv4 is not capable of offering. Examples of IPv6-based benefits include, but are not limited to, the following.

Examples

IPv6 offers a virtually inexhaustible number of IP addresses that IPv4 is not able to offer. Since IPv6 offers 128-bit addresses for IP addresses, there are 2^{128}, or approximately 340,282,366,920,938,463,463,374,607,431,768,211,456, possible IP address in IPv6. However, IPv4 is only able to offer 4,294,967,296 IP addresses. Furthermore, IPv6 is able to use hexadecimal for its addressing schema, whereas IPv4 is only able to use octets.

Related Concepts

- Configuration management—AD-2.1A
- Network reconnaissance and discovery—OIR-4.1A

Security+ Objective

3.3: Given a scenario, implement secure network designs.

Port Spanning/Port Mirroring

Description

Port spanning, also referred to as *port mirroring*, is a form of monitoring that occurs when data packets are copied from one switch port to another.

Examples

Port taps, also known as a *network tap (test access port)*, is a networking device installed on a network to monitor traffic. A good example of this is a sensor that monitors traffic among routers to certain IP addresses.

Related Concepts

- Syslog/Security information and event management (SIEM)—ATV-1.7C
- Port security—IMP-3.3G
- Network appliances—IMP-3.3H
- Route security—IMP-3.3J
- Monitoring services—IMP-3.3N

Security+ Objective

3.3: Given a scenario, implement secure network designs.

Monitoring Services

Description

Monitoring services, such as a network tap, are able to monitor data transmissions. Often, these services are software-based utilities that observe the operation of a specific device or network for errors, interruptions, or anomalies. If any errors are detected, an administrator will be notified.

Example

Network security monitoring is an example of a monitoring services that collects, analyzes, and manages warnings and indications for detecting and responding to network breaches. It uses a continuously running system to monitor a network for performance issues or failing devices. These kinds of tools often include

- network-level threat detection;
- monitoring of queries for secure data;
- detection of suspicious behavior;
- threat-feed integration; and
- automated security alerts.

Related Concepts

- Internet of Things (IoT)—AD-2.6C
- Port security—IMP-3.3G
- Network appliances—IMP-3.3H
- Route security—IMP-3.3J
- Port spanning/port mirroring—IMP-3.3M

Security+ Objective

3.3: Given a scenario, implement secure network designs.

File Integrity Monitors

Description

A *file integrity monitor (FIM)* is a software program that audits key system files to verify that they match the authorized versions. An FIM is utilized when it is possible that a file has been compromised, even after manually running file integrity checkers.

Example

Goodheart-Willcox Publisher

Related Concepts

- Data protection—AD-2.1C
- Monitoring services—IMP-3.3N
- Integrity—OIR-4.5D

Security+ Objective

3.3: Given a scenario, implement secure network designs.

IMP-3.4A Cryptographic Protocols

Description

Cryptographic protocols are wireless encryption methods used to ensure that a user accessing a device and network has been authenticated and their data is encrypted during transmission.

Examples

- *Wi-Fi Protected Access II (WPA2)* is a wireless protocol that is compliant with the 802.11i WLAN security standard. It utilizes 128-, 192- or 256-bit Advanced Encryption Standard (AES) for its encryption. WPA2 ensures organizations against attacks such as war driving but not against threats such as evil twins—especially if the network APs have limited coverage. Nevertheless, during the time of the writing of the Reference Guide, WPA2 is the most used and secure wireless protocol for WLANs.
- *Wi-Fi Protected Access III (WPA3)* implements the use and security of WPA2 but also provides two forms of the protocol. WPA3-Personal provides protection to users via robust password-based authentication by utilizing Simultaneous Authentication of Equals (SAE). WPA3-Enterprise offers greater security to enterprise networks than other protocols. However, it should be mentioned that WPA3 is a newer generation of Wi-Fi protocol, and WPA2 is more widely used.
- *Counter-mode/CBC-MAC* is an authenticated block cipher encryption mode that is only defined for 128-bit block ciphers such as AES.
- *Simultaneous Authentication of Equals (SAE)* is the replacement for the password-based security authentication method of a Pre-Shared Key (PSK). A PSK is generated from a passphrase and can utilize group authentication, meaning multiple users share the same secret. However, SAE, also known as the *Dragonfly Key exchange*, requires user interaction to obtain authentication and for authentication keys to be generated.

Related Concepts

- Wireless—ATV-1.4A
- Vectors—ATV-1.5C
- Authentication methods—AD-2.4A
- Modes of operation—AD-2.8L
- Cipher suites—AD-2.8N
- Limitations—AD-2.8T

Security+ Objective

3.4: Given a scenario, install and configure wireless security settings.

Authentication Protocols

Description

Authentication protocols are needed in networks that connect to each other, including wireless networks. The following protocols advise organizations for implementing authentication.

Examples

- *Extensible Authentication Protocol (EAP)* uses various forms of authentication. Many of the forms utilize a digital certificate on either servers or client machines to provide a trust relationship to generate a secure tunnel and transmit authentication credentials.
- *Protected Extensible Application Protocol (PEAP)* provides an encrypted tunnel between a supplicant and authentication server but only requires a server-side public key certificate.
- *Flexible Authentication via Secure Tunneling (EAP-FAST)* is the replacement for Lightweight EAP (LEAP). EAP-FAST uses a protected access credential (PAC) that is generated for all users via the authentication server's master key. Be advised that the concerns of utilizing EAP-FAST stem from the fact it is distributed via out-of-band methods, and many administrators prefer the authentication methods of PEAP to EAP-FAST.
- *EAP-TLS* is currently the most widely supported and strongest form of wireless authentication. The tunnel that is established between the supplicant and authentication server uses Transport Layer Security (TLS) with public key certificates on both the supplicant and authentication server.
- *EAP-Tunneled TLS (EAP-TTLS)* is similar to Protected Extensible Application Protocol (PEAP), as it uses server-side certificates to establish a tunnel through a user's credentials that are transmitted to an authentication server. However, EAP-TTLS is able to use other authentication protocols such as Password Authentication Protocol (PAP) or Challenge Handshake Authentication Protocol (CHAP), whereas PEAP is limited to using either EAP-Generic Token Card (EAP-GTC) or EAP-Microsoft Challenge-Handshake Authentication Protocol (EAP-MSCHAP).
- *IEEE 8021X*, also known as *enterprise authentication*, uses EAP authentication. In this process, the access point sends authentication information to a Remote Authentication Dial-in User Server (RADIUS) on the wired network for validation. The forms of validation may stem from a username, tokens, or smartcards.
- *Remote Authentication Dial-in User Server (RADIUS) Federation* is used when multiple organizations allow access to one another by joining their RADIUS servers. RADIUS servers are used by the majority of EAP implementations.

Related Concepts

- Authentication methods—AD-2.4A
- Authentication, authorization, and accounting (AAA)—AD-2.4D

Security+ Objective

3.4: Given a scenario, install and configure wireless security settings.

Methods

Description

Wireless security *methods* need to be taken into consideration when implementing security for common users and guests of an organization. Examples of wireless security methods include the following.

Examples

- A comparison that needs to be taken into consideration when applying an organization's wireless security needs is that of pre-shared key (PSK) vs. enterprise vs. open.
  - *PSK* implementations should require users to have passphrases of at least twelve characters, use a mixture of uppercase and lowercase letters, and not have any words that could be found in a dictionary or in common names.
  - *Enterprise* authentication methods can include, but are not limited to, username and passwords or tokens to obtain access. Furthermore, enterprise authentication can utilize captive portals to augment its network security.
  - *Open* authentication does not require a user to provide any credentials or information for authentication. This means any user can connect, regardless of authorization.
- *Wi-Fi Protected Setup (WPS)* first requires that a WAP and client device are both capable of using WPS. The WPS method may also require a synchronization process in which the access point and device are joined and collaborated simultaneously to generate a SSID and PSK unique to the access point and device.
- *Captive portals* are used in public locations, such as hotels or airports, that require individuals to agree to wireless terms to obtain authentication to the network. These portals typically appear via a website.

Related Concepts

- Wireless—ATV-1.4A
- Cryptographic protocols—IMP-3.4A

Security+ Objective

3.4: Given a scenario, install and configure wireless security settings.

Description

Installation considerations are decisions that need to be made when implementing and supporting a wireless network. Important considerations include the following.

Example

- *Site surveys* consist of processes and measurements conducted to ensure the best position for wireless access points and antennas. This determination is the result of analysis of an organization's building, environment, and at which sections of an organization's physical premises will have the best and worst wireless signal strength.
- *Heat maps* provide a visual representation of the wireless access and signal strength.

TamoGraph Site Survey by TamoSoft

- *Wi-Fi analyzers* are devices that locate wireless signals and their signal strength in physical locations of an organization.

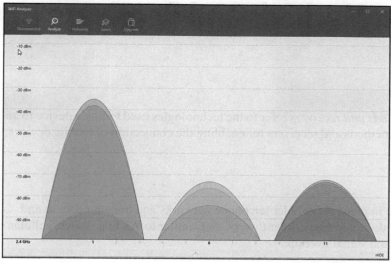

Goodheart-Willcox Publisher

- *Channel overlays* should be documented during a wireless site survey when the observance of possible areas of overlapping wireless channels may emerge. As a result, if one wireless access point fails, it is important to know if or which wireless access points will provide coverage to the resulting dead zones.
- A *wireless access point (WAP)* is a networking device that provides a wireless signal and wireless connections in a wireless or physical network. The placement of WAPs dictates where the wireless network will be accessible. As such, it is important to rely on the information gathered via site surveys and heat maps to determine placement.

mkos83/Shutterstock.com

- *Controller and access point security devices* are typically maintained by devices manufactured from vendors such as Cisco or Ubiquiti. The wireless controller and access point security devices often have default configurations, are simple to configure for an organization's network, and come with vendor support, including security and firmware updates from the vendor.

Related Concepts

- Wireless—ATV-1.4A
- Connection methods and receivers—IMP-3.5A

Security+ Objective

3.4: Given a scenario, install and configure wireless security settings.

Connection Methods and Receivers

Description

In the context of mobile devices, *connection methods and receivers* refer to the technologies used to link a device to an existing network. There are multiple connection methods and receivers for enabling the connection of mobile devices, including the following.

Examples

- *Cellular* connections utilize the infrastructure in place for cellular telephone networks and transmit data to and from mobile devices. Cellular networks provide signal via cellular towers, and similar to Wi-Fi hot sites, cellular towers have maps that outline data coverage and signal overlap.

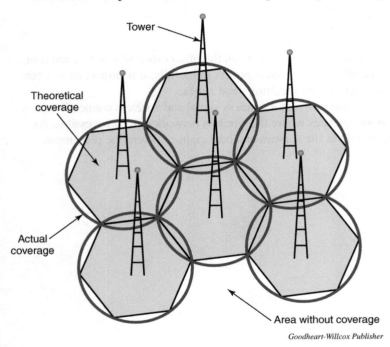

Goodheart-Willcox Publisher

- *Wi-Fi*, often referred to as *wireless*, uses radio waves to transmit data through the air. For devices to receive signals via Wi-Fi, the device must have a wireless NIC with 802.11 capabilities.
- *Bluetooth* is a wireless connection that enables communication via short range, ad hoc sessions. The distance limitation for Bluetooth is approximately ten meters (32 feet), and devices must have Bluetooth enabled in order to maintain the connection. Devices typically have to be paired before they can communicate with one another.
- *Near-field communication (NFC)* is a wireless communication standard in which devices transmit through radio frequency identification (RFID). Devices must be close in proximity to utilize NFC. This connection is frequently used for mobile payment methods, such as Google Pay or Apple Pay.
- *Infrared (IR)* is a wireless communication method that utilizes infrared radiation to transmit data. It functions via a short electromagnetic transmission of infrared radiation and line-of-sight, meaning there can be no blockage between the two devices in order for IR to be effective.
- *Point to point* refers to a connection between two points. *Point to multipoint* refers to connections among multiple devices. Both terms are often used when referring to antenna types and how they transmit wireless signals.

- *Global positioning system (GPS)* refers to communication methods used to enable a GPS receiver on a device in order to obtain to the device's location via global navigation satellite systems (GNSSs).
- *Radio frequency identification (RFID)* is the use of electromagnetic fields to identify objects. Information is encoded into passive tags that are attached to devices. RFID readers then produce an electrometric wave that transmits to the tag to obtain its information.

Related Concepts

- Wireless—ATV-1.4A
- Mobile devices—IMP-3.5C

Security+ Objective

3.5: Given a scenario, implement secure mobile solutions.

Mobile Device Management (MDM)

Description

Mobile device management (MDM) is the software and practices used to secure mobile devices used in an organization. Many MDM strategies enable an organization to control or modify a device remotely. Examples of MDM methods include the following.

Examples

- *Application management*, often referred to as *mobile application management (MAM)*, is the practice used to manage a mobile device's application software. It refers to the download, distribution, and control of apps through centralized tools and services. This solution enables administrators to lock or disable apps and the data stored within them.
- *Content management systems* tag data as confidential or proprietary to prevent the data from being transferred to unauthorized sources, such as e-mail systems and cloud storage services.
- *Remote wipe* is considered a kill switch for a mobile device. When activated, data stored on the device is removed, and the device is resorted to its default state. A remote wipe is typically used when a mobile device is lost or stolen.
- *Geofencing* employs a virtual boundary based on a mobile device's geographical location and has the ability to disable mobile device features, such as its camera. Through geofencing, an organization can also disable a mobile device's applications when the mobile device is in the virtual boundary.
- *Geolocation* is the use of GPS to identify where a mobile device is located.
- *Screen locks* can be used on mobile devices in conjunction with a lockout policy that locks the device for a designated amount of time if an incorrect PIN or password is entered multiple times.
- *Push notifications* are messages or alerts that display on a mobile device without user interaction. Push notifications can be used to alert users to updates, display messages, or notify users of an emergency.
- *Passwords and PINs* function on a mobile device the same way they do on a computer. They authenticate a user based on something the user knows.
- *Biometrics* authenticates users based on something they are, such as a fingerprint, retinal scan, or facial recognition.
- *Context-aware authentication* allows mobiles devices, such as smartphones, to disable screen locks if the device is in a trusted location such as the physical campus of an organization or in the home of a member of an organization.
- *Containerization* refers to the separation of various data types into separate storage pools. Often, employees are limited in what kinds of personal data they can store on mobile devices used for company activity. In other words, both the organization and its members will agree as to whether or not a member may have personal information on their mobile device, how that information will be stored, reasons as to why administrators of an organization may monitor the device, and what applications can or cannot be used while at work and at home.
- *Storage segmentation* is the separation of company or organizational data from a user's personal data on a mobile device. It is often utilized when a member of an organization is in a certain area of an organization's campus and is limited to the applications they may use while they are in that location.
- *Full device encryption (FDE)* is the practice of encrypting all data and contents of a mobile device.

Related Concepts

- Biometrics—ATV-1.4B
- Authentication, authorization, and accounting (AAA)—ATV-1.4D
- Authentication methods—AD-2.4A
- Authentication protocols—IMP-3.4B
- Connection methods and receivers—IMP-3.5A
- Mobile devices—IMP-3.5C
- Enforcement and monitoring of—IMP-3.5D
- Deployment models—IMP-3.5E
- Segmentation—OIR-4.4E

Security+ Objective

3.5: Given a scenario, implement secure mobile solutions.

Mobile Devices

Description

Mobile devices are being used more prominently for business operations. Companies often allow employees to use their own devices, choose devices for employees, or buy equipment for employee use. As such, it is vital to study how mobile devices operate and can be managed to confirm secure usage, operation, and transmission of data.

Examples

- A *microSD HSM* provides cryptographic key management in a microSD card used in a mobile device.
- *Mobile device management (MDM)/unified endpoint management (UEM)* are software tools that allow for the management of mobile devices that are connected to either cellular or wireless networks with an Internet connection.
- *Mobile application management (MAM)* is the practice used to manage and monitor a mobile device's application software.
- *Security Enhancements for Android (SEAndriod)* is a proprietary security tool for Android mobile devices that prohibits apps and processes from obtaining access to private or locked data.

Related Concepts

- Hardware security module (HSM)—ATV-1.1D
- Connection methods and receivers—IMP-3.5A
- Mobile device management (MDM)—IMP-3.5B
- Enforcement and monitoring of—IMP-3.5D
- Deployment models—IMP-3.5E

Security+ Objective

3.5: Given a scenario, implement secure mobile solutions.

Enforcement and Monitoring

Description

Enforcement and monitoring of mobile devices should be implemented on all mobile devices that connect to a company's network. Mobile devices have unique vulnerabilities that require oversight to ensure policies are being following. Often, these vulnerabilities stem from a lack of knowledge or users unintentionally making poor devices. As such, it is vital to develop policies that provide education and awareness to employees. Important mobile aspects to monitor for include the following.

Examples

- *Third-party app stores* are digital marketplaces that only offer third-party apps for mobile devices and are created by a sole developer or outside developers rather than the mobile device company's developers. Amazon App Store, App Sales, and Appland are popular examples of third-party stores. Note, Apple's App Store and the Google Play Store are *not* examples of third-party app stores as these are controlled by mobile device manufacturers and developers.
- *Rooting* (Android) and *jailbreaking* (iOS) refer to the use of privilege escalation tactics on mobile devices to bypass privilege-based restrictions placed by the mobile device provider or organization. While Android does permit users to make modifications to the operating system, it is not recommended—especially on devices used for business purposes—as it can cause the mobile OS to behave unpredictably and potentially create vulnerabilities.
- *Sideloading* occurs when users installing an app onto their mobile device directly rather than purchasing and installing the app from an official app store.
- *Custom firmware* is firmware that is created and modified by developers who are not associated with the mobile device's platform or user's organization. Developers that create and modify custom firmware do so to bypass the device's firmware and its restrictions.
- *Carrier unlocking* is similar to rooting and jailbreaking, but instead of bypassing privilege limitations, a user bypasses cellular restrictions that limit a device to a single carrier.
- *Firmware over-the-air (OTA) updates* refer to the firmware updates that are provided via a cellular or Wi-Fi network. Disabling user ability to install OTA updates provides an organization with greater control over device firmware and versioning.
- *Short message service (SMS)/multimedia message service (MMS)/rich communication services (RCS)* allow the transmission of text messages, media, and binary files. Malware and phishing campaigns can be conducted via messaging services, so these should be limited or monitored to ensure users do not inadvertently activate malicious software.
- *External media* often consists of microSD cards installed into a device. Many devices, such as iPhones and iPads, do not allow for external media, but many Android-based phones do. In general, mobile devices should be configured not to allow for external media since it creates a potential vulnerability.
- *USB on the go (OTG)* refers to mobile devices that are connected to a personal computer via USB connection. USB OTG enables a device to function not only as a mobile computing device but also a storage device. This means that data transfer from one device to another is much simpler and could result in sensitive data being transferred or stolen without much effort or attention.
- *Recording microphones*, *cameras*, and *GPS tagging* may take place via MDM software from a mobile carrier or organization. These features can also be activated via malware, allowing an attacker to see, hear, and locate the user. Microphones, cameras, and GPS capabilities should be limited or, if not needed, disabled via MDM software.
- *Wi-Fi direct/ad hoc* connections are peer-to-peer connections in which one device functions as an access point. Furthermore, ad hoc connections only require WEP security, which is a weak form of security. Wi-Fi direct is able to use WPA2 but should still be prevented due to a lack of control over the connection.

- *Tethering* is the act of turning a mobile device into a Wi-Fi hotspot for Internet connectivity. Since any Wi-Fi device can connect once tethering is activated, it creates a number of vulnerabilities. As such, the ability to tether devices should be prevented on organizational devices.
- *Hotspots* are similar to public wireless access points in that they provide access to the Internet, typically in public locations. However, these connection points are not encrypted and rely on open authentication practices. Since security is generally limited, if present at all, hotspots should be avoided in public settings.
- *Payment methods* enable a device to function as a digital wallet used to make purchased via NFC touchpoints. Using mobile-payment software can be a security risk, especially if the device is company-owned or stores sensitive information. Organizational devices should be restricted in such a way to eliminate this feature.

Related Concepts

- Wireless—ATV-1.4A
- Connection methods and receivers—IMP-3.5A
- Mobile device management (MDM)—IMP-3.5B
- Mobile devices—IMP-3.5C

Security+ Objective

3.5: Given a scenario, implement secure mobile solutions.

Deployment Models

Description

When organizations make the decision to utilize mobile devices, they must determine which deployment model they will utilize. A *deployment model* refers to the responsibility of distributing and managing a device as well as how those devices will be used. In general, there are four common deployment models: BYOD, COPE, CYOD, and VDI.

Examples

- *Bring your own device (BYOD)* is a deployment model in which a member of the organization owns the mobile device. Even though the member of the organization owns the mobile device, they still have to comply with the rules and regulations put in place for the mobile device they own and use for organizational activity. Therefore, the employee is required to install any necessary organizational apps, maintain up-to-date operating systems and versions, and agree upon how the device is used at the organization during work hours.
- *Corporate-owned personally enabled (COPE)* is a deployment model in which an organization purchases and distributes mobile devices to its members. The mobile devices are configured to meet the needs of the organization and will limit or prohibit external uses of the mobile device.
- *Choose your own device (CYOD)* is a deployment model similar to COPE, but instead of distributing a device to employees, the organization creates a list of approved mobile devices from which employees select the one(s) they want.
- *Virtual desktop infrastructure (VDI)* is a deployment model that allows mobile devices to access disk images, similar to desktop operating system images, for organizational use.

Related Concepts

- Mobile device management (MDM)—IMP-3.5B
- Mobile devices—IMP-3.5C

Security+ Objective

3.5: Given a scenario, implement secure mobile solutions.

Cloud Security Controls

Description

Cloud security controls are the implemented practices needed to ensure cybersecurity solutions for could computing technologies. Examples of cloud-based security controls include the following.

Examples

- *High availability across zones* is the assurance that an organization's uptime and connectivity will be available for cloud-computing needs. For the availability rate across zones to be considered high, the zones must have an availability rate of at least 99 percent. The availability rates are typically measured over a year's time—8,760 hours—and can be displayed as the following:

Availability	Annual Downtime (hh:mm:ss)
99.999999 percent	00:00:01
99 percent	87:36:00

Goodheart-Willcox Publisher

- *Resource policies* refer to policies developed by a cloud vendor describing how customers can interact with data and applications in the cloud.
- *Secrets management* refers to the tools, policies, and procedures that ensure confidentiality and available of information as well as the management of cloud-computing authentication.
- *Integration and auditing* cloud security controls were originally implemented by the Cloud Security Alliance (CSA) to ensure of cloud-computing customers were being given the proper installation, service, and performing audits. The audit processes implemented by the CSA are often referred to as the CloudAudit initiative.
- *Storage* cloud security controls include the following.
  - *Permissions* refer to assurances from cloud-computing vendors to their customers that only authorized members of the organization will be able to access specific data.
  - *Encryption* refers to the methods taken by a cloud-computing vendor to prohibit data breaches via cryptographic methods.
  - *Replication* refers to methods taken by a cloud-computing vendor to duplicate data on multiple servers or websites in the event a primary server fails.
  - *High availability* is the assurance that a vendor is able to provide at least 99 percent uptime to their customers.
- *Network* cloud security controls include the following.
  - *Virtual networks* provide organizations with a cloud-based network that performs as though the network were physically hosted at the organization's campus while also providing security for the virtual network.
  - *Public and private subnets* refers to the routing of public subnets to an Internet gateway and private subnet for the IP address of the hosts in an organization.
  - *Segmentation* is the assurance made to an organization from a cloud-computing vendor that the organization's virtual network has its VLANs segmented in the correct subnets.
  - *API inspection and integration* is a security measure cloud-computing vendors take to prevent excessive Address Resolution Protocol (ARP) replies from flooding the virtual network.

- *Computing* cloud security controls include the following.
  - *Security group* is a virtual firewall that filters the traffic in a cloud-computing environment.
  - *Dynamic resource allocation* ensures that the systems integrated with cloud computing will not become overloaded.
  - *Instance awareness* is the implementation and awareness of cloud-computing applications, practices used, and their potential risks and vulnerabilities.
  - A *virtual private cloud (VPC) endpoint* enables users to connect to a VPC via secure channels.
  - *Container security* refers to secure processes and polices employed to ensure containers run as designed and expected.

Related Concepts

- Vectors—ATV-1.5C
- Cloud-based vs. on-premises attacks—ATV-1.5F
- Cloud-based vs. on-premises vulnerabilities—ATV-1.6A
- On-premises vs. off-premises—AD-2.2D
- Virtualization—AD-2.2O
- Cloud vs. on-premises requirements—AD-2.4E
- On-premises vs. cloud—AD-2.5C

Security+ Objective

3.6: Given a scenario, apply cybersecurity solutions to the cloud.

Solutions

Description

Solutions for cloud-computing gaps can be implemented in a variety of ways, including the following examples.

Examples

- A *cloud access security broker (CASB)* is a software platform that manages access to cloud services among all types of devices. A CASB is able to provide single sign-on, malware scans, and user activity monitoring or auditing.
- *Application security* consists of enhancing the security of services and applications used in an organization's cloud-computing solutions. In most cases, application security refers to the act of looking for issues before they emerge.
- A *next-generation secure web gateway (SWG)* prohibits malware from web searches and downloads over an organization's virtual network.
- *Firewall* considerations in a cloud environment include the following.
  - *Costs:* The cost of a cloud-based firewall must considered. If the firewall is managed by the cloud vendor, it will likely increase the amount of money spent on the cloud solution when compared to the cost of managing a firewall in-house.
  - *Need for segmentation:* The virtual network will likely need to be segmented in multiple subnets, just as physical networks are, in order to ensure traffic is transmitted safely and effectively.
  - *Open Systems Interconnection (OSI) layers:* Since there are seven layers of the OSI, vendors and organizations will need to determine at which layer(s) a firewall will operate.

Related Concepts

- Cloud access security broker (CASB)—AD-2.1F
- Cloud service providers—AD-2.2B
- Cloud vs. on-premises requirements—AD-2.4E
- Endpoint protections—IMP-3.2A
- Network appliances—IMP-3.3H
- Single sign-on (SSO)—IMP-3.8B
- Reconfigure endpoint security solutions—OIR-4.4A
- Configuration changes—OIR-4.4B

Security+ Objective

3.6: Given a scenario, apply cybersecurity solutions to the cloud.

Cloud-Native Controls vs. Third-Party Solutions

Description

Cloud-native controls are security controls within the cloud's infrastructure and platform. Often, these controls require more monitoring responsibility from the organization, as well as a determination as to which assets need the most security. *Third-party solutions* are those provided by a vendor that is not part of an organization. These solutions control and monitor cloud services, but may provide limited functionality. Often, third-party solutions are cloud friendly, meaning they will function in the cloud, but if they are not cloud native, they may not function correctly with APIs used in cloud interfaces. The decision between cloud native controls and third-party controls should be carefully considered to ensure the correct solution is chosen based on organizational needs.

Examples

Examples of cloud-native controls are those provided through vendors, such as Amazon Web Services (AWS), IBM. and Microsoft Azure. Examples of third-party solutions are those purchased from a third party and used in a cloud environment.

Related Concepts

- Cloud-based vs. on-premises attacks—ATV-1.2F
- Cloud-based vs. on-premises vulnerabilities—ATV-1.6A
- Third-party risks—ATV-1.6D
- Cloud access security broker (CASB)—AD–2.1F
- Cloud models—AD-2.2A
- Cloud service providers—AD-2.2B
- Cloud vs. on-premises requirements—AD-2.4E
- On-premises vs. cloud—AD-2.5C
- On-premises vs. cloud—OIR-4.5C

Security+ Objective

3.6: Given a scenario, apply cybersecurity solutions to the cloud.

Identity

Description

Implementing *identity authentication* is essential for all organizations. Many methods can be used to verify a person's identity, including the following.

Examples

- *Identity provider (IdP)* is a method in which information regarding a user's identity is authenticated, typically via single sign-on (SSO), and used within a federation system. Use of SSO and federation enables a user access to multiple entities with only one form of identification.
- *Attributes* are the methods of authentication used to confirm a user's identity.
- *Certificates* and public key infrastructure (PKI) can be used to manage a user's identification and authentication across private and public networks.
- *Tokens* are devices that act as keys to gain access to a resource. They fall under the "what you have" attribute in terms of authentication. Similarly, tokens can take the form as randomized data added to information through tokenization processes.
- *SSH keys* are used to authenticate a user's identity when accessing resources remotely.
- *Smart cards* are typically the size of a credit card with an integrated chip that is authenticated via a card reader for a user's identity to be authenticated.

Related Concepts

- Authentication methods—AD-2.4A
- Authentication—IMP-3.8B
- Public key infrastructure—IMP-3.9A

Security+ Objective

3.7: Given a scenario, implement identity and account management controls.

Account Types

Description

Account types vary among users in an organization. Nevertheless, it is vital that users, including guests, are assigned the appropriate account type relevant to their roles in their organization.

Examples

- A *user account* is the account assigned to each user on an organization's active directory or stand-alone machine. The user account, on either an active directory or stand-alone machine, will be assigned permissions as to what they can or cannot do to their machines such as install applications or updates.
- A *shared* and *generic account*, also called a *shared* or *generic credential*, is utilized on the majority of operating systems and active directories. It is typically referred to as a *default user account*. Shared and generic accounts do not have any administrative privileges and allow the user that is logged in to use only limited software and Internet browsing while logged on. These accounts normally require a username and password for authentication.
- A *guest account* is one that exists in an active directory or stand-alone machine that does not require a password to access a system. However, these accounts have limited functionalities when using the machine.
- *Service accounts* are the accounts assigned to users who have service-based roles such as technicians, security personnel, or administrators.

Related Concepts

- Authentication, authorization, and accounting (AAA)—ATV-1.4D

Security+ Objective

3.7: Given a scenario, implement identity and account management controls.

Account Policies

Description

Account policies are the requirements for a member of an organization to obtain a user account, the resources they will be able to access and modify, the extent of limitations to the access they will have to their account, and the authentication methods used for the member to access an organization's system.

Examples

- *Password complexity* enforces passwords rules, such as password not being able to contain the user's name or a minimum requirement of alphanumeric characters.
- *Password history* and *reuse* polices consist of restrictions against using prior passwords associated with a username.
- *Time of day restrictions* refer to limitations that restrict the days and times a user is able to log into their account. For instance, most accounts that utilize this policy will allow users to access their accounts on Monday through Friday from 8:00 AM to 5:00 PM.
- *Network location* policies dictate where a user can logon or access data in certain segments of a network.
- *Geofencing* uses boundaries to implement limitations based on a user's location and has the ability to disable a user's account while the user is inside or outside the boundary.
- *Geotagging* is the ability to gather information about a user's data to determine when and where it was created or modified.
- *Geolocation* is the use of GPS coordinates to identify where a user is located.
- *Time-based logins* consider a user's time of day restrictions and modifies the days and time allowed for access based on where the user is traveling and if it will be in a different time zone than the organization's time zone.
- *Access policies and permissions* dictate the resources and roles a user account has or does not have in regard to its privileges.
- *Account audits* is used to determine if accounts need to have their permissions modified or if the account should be deleted.
- *Impossible travel time/risky login* is a policy that prevents users from accessing a system if a predetermined amount of travel time has not elapsed. For example, assume a user attempts to access a system between two distant locations that are determined to be 20 minutes apart. The user logs out of the system in the first location, travels to the second location, and attempts to log in. If 20 minutes have not elapsed, the user will be denied access.
- *Lockout policies* are placed on user accounts to avoid exploits. For instance, if a user does not match the correct password to a username within a given number of attempts, the account could be locked, and an administrator or certain amount of time will be required for the accounts next login attempt.
- *Disablement policies* are used on user accounts when the user is not to be allowed access to their account but should not be deleted in case there are investigative reasons for the account.

Related Concepts

- Authentication methods—AD-2.4A
- Authentication, authorization, and accounting (AAA)—AD-2.4D
- Authentication protocols—IMP-3.4B
- Account types—IMP-3.7A

Security+ Objective

3.7: Given a scenario, implement identity and account management controls.

Authentication Management

Description

Authentication management is the process of determining how a user will provide their form of authentication to access their accounts or resources in an organization.

Examples

- *Password keys* are the algorithms that generate and suggest passwords for users.
- *Password vaults* are collections of passwords to multiple resources, such as websites, that are kept in a central location and can be accessed once a user provides the password to the vault. These vaults typically need to be installed on each device a user operates.
- A *trusted platform module (TPM)* is a chip placed on a device that generates, stores, and protects keys that provide authentication.
- A *hardware security module (HSM)* is a cryptographic device that stores or manages encryption keys and performs cryptographic functions.
- *Knowledge-based authentication* requires a user to utilize something they know as a form of verification.

Related Concepts

- Hardware security module (HSM)—AD-2.1D
- Authentication methods—AD-2.4A
- Multifactor authentication (MFA) factors and attributes—AD-2.4C
- Authentication, authorization, and accounting (AAA)—AD-2.4D
- Trusted platform module (TPM)—IMP-3.2H
- Network appliances—IMP-3.3G
- Authentication protocols—IMP-3.4B

Security+ Objective

3.8: Given a scenario, implement authentication and authorization solutions.

Authentication

Description

Authentication is typically accomplished through some form of identity and access management (IAM) service and protocol in which users attempt to access various resources and servers.

Examples

- *Extensible Authentication Protocol (EAP)* uses various forms of authentication for 802.1X, many of which utilize a digital certificate on either server or client machines to provide a trust relationship. The resulting trust relationship generates a secure tunnel to transmit authentication credentials.
- *Challenge Handshake Authentication Protocol (CHAP)* is an authentication protocol that sends a challenge to a client after the client has established a connection to a server that has previously identified a shared secret, such as a password, to provide verification. In other words, the CHAP protocol uses a three-way handshake for its encryption challenge for authentication. The three-way handshake functions as follows.

  1. *Challenge:* the server challenges the client with a random challenge message.

  2. *Response:* the client responds with a hash calculated from the server challenge, such as a password.

  3. *Verification:* the server performs its own hash that is stored from the client, in this case a password. If the hashes match, the client is granted access; if not, the client is denied access.

- *Password Authentication Protocol (PAP)* is an outdated authentication protocol that transfers TCP/IP data over serial or dial-up connections. Furthermore, the protocol relies on clear text password exchanges. Since it does not provide secure connections, the protocol is considered obsolete.
- *802.1X*, also known as *enterprise authentication*, uses EAP authentication via the access point sending authentication information to a Remote Authentication Dial-in User Server (RADIUS) for validation. The forms of validation may stem from a username, tokens, or smartcards.
- *Remote Authentication Dial-in User Server (RADIUS) Federation* is used when multiple organizations allow access to one another by joining their RADIUS servers. RADIUS servers are used in the majority of EAP implementations.
- *Single sign-on (SSO)* allows one form of authentication to provide a user with multiple network entities including third-party networks.
- *Security Assertions Markup Language (SAML)* was developed by the Organization for the Advancement of Structured Information Standards (OASIS) to provide federated networks the authentication methods of users. At the time of this writing, the standard is on its second version and operates in the following steps.

  1. A user agent, such as a web browser, requests a resource from the Service Provider (SP).

  2. If the user does not have a valid session, the SP redirects the user to an Identity Provider (IdP).

  3. The user obtains authentication via the IdP with an authorization token.

  4. The user presents the authorization token to the SP.

  5. If the token is valid, it is accepted, and the SP establishes the session.

- *Terminal Access Controller Access Control System Plus (TACACS+)* protocol is similar to RADIUS but is designed to be more reliable. TACACS+ was developed by Cisco and uses TCP port 49 for its connections.
- *OAuth* is an open authentication protocol that supports single sign-on (SSO) but does not provide authentication. Instead, it utilizes a third party to access an authentication server and transfers information or resources between sites.
- *OpenID* is an open authentication protocol that supports single sign-on (SSO) and eliminates the need for a user to share a password with a third-party entity, such as a website.
- *Kerberos* is an authentication protocol that allows a user to authenticate only once to access multiple resources.

Related Concepts

- Hardware security module (HSM)—AD-2.1D
- Authentication methods—AD-2.4A
- Multifactor authentication (MFA) factors and attributes—AD-2.4C
- Authentication, authorization, and accounting (AAA)—AD-2.4D
- Authentication protocols—IMP-3.4B

Security+ Objective

3.8: Given a scenario, implement authentication and authorization solutions.

Access Control Schemes

Description

Access control schemes provide the identification of a user as well as the authentication process that verifies the user is who they say they are. Access control schemes also identify the device being used to obtain authentication.

Examples

- *Attribute-based access control (ABAC)* is considered one of the best forms of access control. The ABAC system makes decisions based on the combination of subject and object attributes along with context-sensitive and system-wide attributes, such as the device's operating system and IP address.
- *Role-based access control (RBAC)* adds more administrative control and flexibility to the discretionary access control (DAC) scheme, as RBAC is able to have a set of roles to users in an organization via the user account. However, only the administrators are able to modify the user accounts and its privileges.
- *Rule-based access control schemes* are access control schemes that are determined via system-enforced rules rather than just the rights and privileges that are provided in a user's account. MAC, ABAC, and RBAC control schemes are examples of non-discretionary and rule-based access control schemes.
- *Mandatory access control (MAC)* are access control schemes based on security clearance levels. This is commonly used in military and governmental organizations.
- *Discretionary access control (DAC)* is an access control scheme that stresses the importance of an owner or creator of an original resource. With DAC, the owner is granted full control over the resource(s), including modifications to an access control list (ACL).
- *Conditional access* is an access control scheme that verifies the users and devices that are allowed to access an organization's data and network.
- *Privilege access management* is the verification of users' privileges to the data and hosts of an organization.
- *File system permissions* refer to an access control scheme that determines if a user is able to read, write, copy, or delete files on an organization's network. These permissions can be assigned in any combination.

Related Concepts

- Authentication methods—AD-2.4A
- Multifactor authentication (MFA) factors and attributes—AD-2.4C
- Authentication, authorization, and accounting (AAA)—AD-2.4D
- Authentication protocols—IMP-3.4B

Security+ Objective

3.8: Given a scenario, implement authentication and authorization solutions.

Public Key Infrastructure (PKI)

Description

Public key infrastructure (PKI) provides proof that the owners of public keys are trustworthy and valid. Many of the PKI methods are mentioned in the following examples.

Examples

- *Key management* refers to the lifecycle and stages of the key's life cycle.
  - *Key generation* refers to the creation of secure keys or key pairs using a given cipher.
  - *Certificate generation* occurs when the identity of a user or a user's device becomes part of a key pair. After becoming part of a key pair, the user or device signs the certificate authority (CA) as a digital certificate.
  - *Storage* refers to the location where a private key is stored—securely—to ensure it is not stolen.
  - *Revocation* occurs when a key is removed from use before it expires. This often occurs if a key has been compromised.
  - *Expiration and renewal* is the assurance that a key that has not been revoked will have an expiration period. Giving the key a designated lifespan before generating new keys enhances the security of key pairs.
- A *certificate authority (CA)* is responsible for validating a digital certificate provided by an owner who issues public keys. The digital certificates contain the public key along with other information regarding the certificate issuer. A CA does not have to be between only an owner of a public key and a user. A CA can be in the form of private CAs that exist internally in an organization as well as a public or for-profit CAs. Regardless of its type, a CA must be trusted by each party.

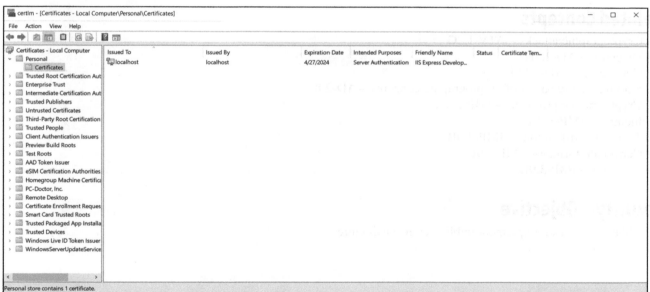

Goodheart-Willcox Publisher

- An *intermediate CA* is based off a hierarchical model, known as a *single/root CA*, in which certificates are issued. Intermediate CAs issue certificates via a *leaf certificate*, also known as an *end-entity certificate*.

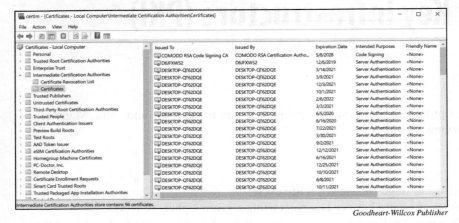

- A *registration authority (RA)* accepts digital certificate requests and authenticates the entities initiating the requests.
- A *certificate revocation list (CRL)* is a list of certificates that have been revoked prior to their expiration date.
- *Certificate attributes* consists of the contents of a public key.
- *Online Certificate Status Protocol (OCSP)* provides the information and status of a requested certificate.
- A *certificate signing request (CSR)* is submitted to a CA when a user or device requests a certificate.
- *Common name (CN)* is an attribute of a certificate relevant to its owner. This is often the fully qualified domain name (FQDN) of the web server that receives a certificate.
- A *subject alternative name (SAN)* provides information regarding the subdomains and extensions as to why a new certificate will need to be issued.

Related Concepts

- Cryptographic attacks—ATV-1.2G
- Diversity—AD-2.5H
- Constraints—AD-2.6M
- Summarize the basics of cryptographic concepts—AD-2.8
- Cryptographic protocols—IMP-3.4A
- Identity—IMP-3.7A
- Types of certifications—IMP-3.9B
- Certificate formats—IMP-3.9C
- Concepts—IMP-3.9D

Security+ Objective

3.9: Given a scenario, implement public key infrastructure.

Types of Certificates

Description

The *types of certificates* issued to users vary based upon the resource, reasoning, and utilization of the certificate. Examples of commonly issued certificates include the following.

Examples

- *Wildcard certificates* are used to verify a domain and its subdomains.
- *Subject alternate name (SAN) certificates* allow multiple hosts to be protected by one certificate.
- *Code-signing certificates* are issued to software publishers after the certificate authority (CA) has performed its identity check and validation process. They are often used by software developers to ensure code is received and has not been compromised.
- *Self-signed certificates* are signed by an organization. These certificates are able to be deployed via devices, web servers, or program code that is marked untrusted by an operating system but trusted by a network or system administrator who obtains the certificate.
- *Machine/computer certificates* are devices, such as computers or mobile devices, that obtain certificates issued via an active directory (AD) of the users of an organization when they log in to the devices. Machine/computer certificates are used for firewall and network trafficking purposes.
- *E-mail certificates* are able to sign and encrypt a user's e-mail messages by using Secure/Multipurpose Internet Mail Extensions (S/MIME) or Pretty Good Privacy (PGP).
- *User certificates* are typically templates used for users in an active directory (AD), based on account type.
- *Root certificates* are the highest point in the chain of trust regarding a certificate authority (CA) and identifies the CA itself.
- *Domain validation (DV) certificates* are issued to entities after an applicant is able to prove they have control of a domain.
- *Extended validation (EV) certificates* provide legal verification of the certificate owner.

Related Concepts

- Replication—AD-2.5B
- Identity—IMP-3.7A
- Public key infrastructure (PKI)—IMP-3.9A
- Types of certifications—IMP-3.9B
- Certificate formats—IMP-3.9C

Security+ Objective

3.9: Given a scenario, implement public key infrastructure.

Certificate Formats

Description

Certificate formats are used for encoding a certificate as a digital file among systems through the schemes mentioned in the following examples.

Examples

- *Distinguished encoding rules (DER)* creates a binary representation of the information regarding the certificate, such as an ASCII file using the Base64 privacy enhanced mail (PEM) format. The file extension **.cer**—short for certificate— is often used when implementing DER.
- *Personal information exchange* (**.pfx**) or *PKCS#12* (**.P12**) allows the export of a certificate and includes its private key. It also makes the file password-protected.
- The *P7B* certificate format bundles multiple certificates within one file.

Related Concepts

- Identity—IMP-3.7A
- Public key infrastructure (PKI)—IMP-3.9A
- Types of certificates—IMP-3.9B
- Configuration changes—OIR-4.4B

Security+ Objective

3.9: Given a scenario, implement public key infrastructure.

Concepts

Description

Concepts of certificate security are the extra precautionary measures and methods used when implementing certificates.

Examples

- An *online CA* is able to accept certificate requests, publish certificate revocation lists (CRLs), and manage the tasks of a certificate. However, security professionals may perceive an offline CA to provide better means of security. *Offline CAs* are root CAs disconnected from a network while being kept in a powered-down state. However, offline CAs require more management, as the CRL must be published manually.
- *Stapling*, also known as *OCSP stapling*, prohibits an OSCP responder from monitoring or recording client browser requests by obtaining a time-stamped OSCP response from a certificate authority (CA) via the SSL/TLS transmissions of a web server.
- *Pinning*, also termed as *certificate pinning*, inspects a certificate by its code-signing application, such as one or more public keys to an HTTP browser through a HTTP header.
- A *trust model* displays the users and different CAs that can be trusted among users and CAs.
- *Key escrow* refers to the practice of an independent vendor or third-party holding keys.
- *Certificate chaining*, also called *chain of trust*, is when each leaf certificate can be traced to its root CA and certification path.

Related Concepts

- Public key infrastructure (PKI)—IMP-3.9A
- Types of certificates—IMP-3.9B
- Certificate formats—IMP-3.9C

Security+ Objective

3.9: Given a scenario, implement public key infrastructure.

Network Reconnaissance and Discovery

Description

Network reconnaissance and discovery refers to actions taken to test a network for potential weaknesses or vulnerabilities and identifying devices connected to a network. These actions are performed in order to determine whether a network has been compromised. Multiple command-line prompts and utilities can be employed to conduct network reconnaissance, including the following.

Examples

- **tracert** (Windows)/**traceroute** (Linux and Mac) are commands used to discover the path between a user's device and a destination, such as a website.

Windows (tracert)

Mac (traceroute)

Linux (traceroute)

Goodheart-Willcox Publisher

- **nslookup** (Windows)/**dig** (Linux and Mac) are commands used to discover an IP address of a source, such as a website.

Windows (nslookup)

Linux (dig)

Mac (dig)

Goodheart-Willcox Publisher

- **ipconfig** (Windows)/**ifconfig** (Linux and Mac) are commands that return information about network adapters and TCP/IP data.

Windows (ipconfig)   **Linux (ifconfig)**   **Mac (ifconfig)**

Goodheart-Willcox Publisher

- **nmap** can be used on Windows, Linux, and Mac operating systems and employs utility tools for host discovery. It also has the ability to bypass security devices such as firewalls and intrusion-detection systems. The following screen captures provide an overview of the utility, but it is highly recommended that you visit the nmap website at https://www.nmap.org to discover the full extent of nmap's abilities. Nevertheless, the nmap utility tool should be used only with an instructor's or administrator's permission.
- **ping** (ICMP availability to a destination) is a command-line prompt for Windows and Linux operating systems that provide information regarding the transmission between a device and its destination.

Windows (ping)   **Linux (ping)**   **Mac (ping)**

Goodheart-Willcox Publisher

- The **pathping** command also returns information regarding a device and the destination of a transmission, but **pathping** also has information about the route taken to a destination. Although Linux and macOS are able to run the **ping** command, they are not able to run the **pathping** command. Instead, they use **traceroute** to retrieve this information.

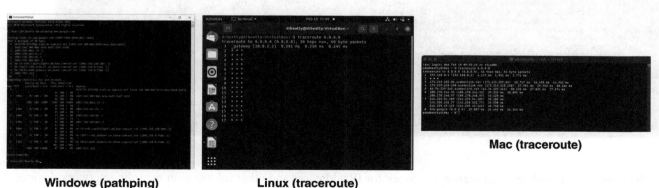

Windows (pathping)   **Linux (traceroute)**

Mac (traceroute)

Goodheart-Willcox Publisher

- **hping** is a command-line prompt used in Kali Linux to scan and analyze ports and test a destination's firewall.

```
root@kali:~# hping3 -c 1 -V -p 80 192.168.133.2
using eth0, addr: 192.168.133.143, MTU: 1500
HPING 192.168.133.2 (eth0 192.168.133.2): NO FLAGS are set, 40 headers + 0 data bytes
len=46 ip=192.168.133.2 ttl=128 id=54155 tos=0 iplen=40
sport=80 flags=RA seq=0 win=32767 rtt=7.3 ms
seq=0 ack=60975573 sum=8a2c urp=0


--- 192.168.133.2 hping statistic ---
1 packets transmitted, 1 packets received, 0% packet loss
round-trip min/avg/max = 7.3/7.3/7.3 ms
root@kali:~#
```

Goodheart-Willcox Publisher

- **netstat** is a command-line prompt for Windows, Linux, and Mac operating systems that allows a user to obtain the status of ports on their device.

Windows (netstat)   **Linux (netstat)**   **Mac (netstat)**

Goodheart-Willcox Publisher

- **netcat** is a command-line prompt for the Windows and Linux operating systems that can be configured as a backdoor to allow an attacker to listen to their victim's traffic. Using this command is a method of implementing a remote access Trojan (RAT). The Mac equivalent of **netcat** is **nc**, as shown in the following.

```
adambeatty — -zsh — 133×24
Last login: Wed Feb 10 10:37:20 on ttys000
[adambeatty@iMac ~ % nc
usage: nc [-46AacCDdEFhklMnOortUuvz] [-K tc] [-b boundif] [-i interval] [-p source_port]
          [--apple-recv-anyif] [--apple-awdl-unres]
          [--apple-boundif ifbound]
          [--apple-no-cellular] [--apple-no-expensive]
          [--apple-no-flowadv] [--apple-tcp-timeout conntimo]
          [--apple-tcp-keepalive keepidle] [--apple-tcp-keepintvl keepintvl]
          [--apple-tcp-keepcnt keepcnt] [--apple-tclass tclass]
          [--tcp-adp-rtimo num_probes] [--apple-initcoproc-allow]
          [--apple-tcp-adp-wtimo num_probes]
          [--setsockopt-later] [--apple-no-connectx]
          [--apple-delegate-pid pid] [--apple-delegate-uuid uuid]
          [--apple-kao] [--apple-ext-bk-idle]
          [--apple-netsvctype svc] [---apple-nowakefromsleep]
          [--apple-notify-ack] [--apple-sockev]
          [--apple-tos tos] [--apple-tos-cmsg]
          [-s source_ip_address] [-w timeout] [-X proxy_version]
          [-x proxy_address[:port]] [hostname] [port[s]]
adambeatty@iMac ~ %
```

Goodheart-Willcox Publisher

- *IP scanners* are tools used to search a network for IP addresses and other information regarding network devices. IP scanning tools are able to operate on Windows, Linux, and Mac operating systems and are primarily used for either reconnaissance or to obtain information that provides an organization for network resources that need augmented security attention.

- **arp** is a command-line prompt for the Windows, Linux, and Mac operating systems that provides data regarding Address Resolution Protocol (ARP).

Windows (arp)   **Linux (arp)**   **Mac (arp -a)**

Goodheart-Willcox Publisher

- **route** is a command-line prompt for the Windows, Linux, and Mac operating systems that allows a user to create manual entries for a network's routing tables.

Windows (route)   **Linux (route)**   **Mac (route)**

Goodheart-Willcox Publisher

- **curl**, which is short for *client URL*, is a command-line prompt that can be used in Windows, Linux, and Mac operating systems to perform network discovery and reconnaissance. This command can also be used to transfer data from a server. It should be noted that curl can only operate on Windows machines with Windows 10 build version 1703 or later.

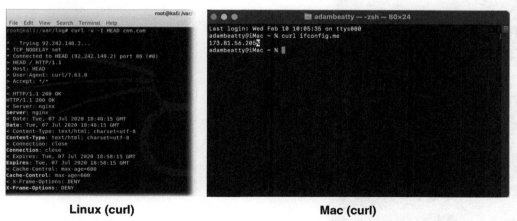

Linux (curl)   **Mac (curl)**

Goodheart-Willcox Publisher

- **theHarvester** is a command-line utility used in the Kali Linux operating system that is able to collect e-mail addresses and names of organizational members as well as subdomains, open ports, and IP addresses of its target network.

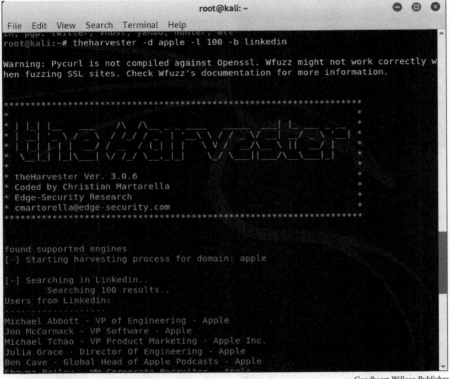

Goodheart-Willcox Publisher

- **sn1per** is a command-line utility used in Linux for network reconnaissance. It is capable of obtaining HTTP headers, TCP and UDP port enumeration, DNS, and WHOIS records of its target.
- **scanless** is a Python-based utility that performs port scanning actions. It is often used as a pen testing tool used to determine a network's vulnerabilities such as open ports.

Goodheart-Willcox Publisher

- **dnsenum** is a command-line tool used in the Kali Linux operating system that retrieves an organization's DNS servers and its entries.

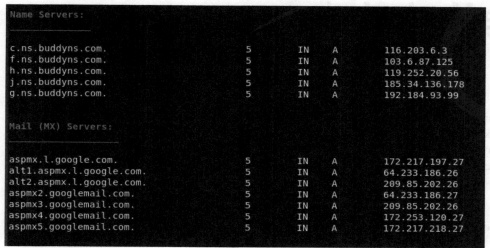

```
Name Servers:
_____

c.ns.buddyns.com.                        5        IN   A     116.203.6.3
f.ns.buddyns.com.                        5        IN   A     103.6.87.125
h.ns.buddyns.com.                        5        IN   A     119.252.20.56
j.ns.buddyns.com.                        5        IN   A     185.34.136.178
g.ns.buddyns.com.                        5        IN   A     192.184.93.99


Mail (MX) Servers:
_____

aspmx.l.google.com.                      5        IN   A     172.217.197.27
alt1.aspmx.l.google.com.                 5        IN   A     64.233.186.26
alt2.aspmx.l.google.com.                 5        IN   A     209.85.202.26
aspmx2.googlemail.com.                   5        IN   A     64.233.186.27
aspmx3.googlemail.com.                   5        IN   A     209.85.202.26
aspmx4.googlemail.com.                   5        IN   A     172.253.120.27
aspmx5.googlemail.com.                   5        IN   A     172.217.218.27
```

Goodheart-Willcox Publisher

- *Nessus* is a vulnerability scanner used by organizations that adhere to regulatory compliances such as Health Insurance Probability and Accountability Act (HIPPA). There are free and commercial options of Nessus available.
- *Cuckoo*, also known as *Cuckoo Sandbox*, is an open-source sandbox environment that can be used in Windows, Linux, and Mac operating systems to test and analyze the capabilities of malware.

Related Concepts

- Reconnaissance—ATV-1.1Q
- Passive and active reconnaissance—ATV-1.8B
- Sandboxing—IMP-3.2I
- Packet capture and replay—OIR-4.1D

Security+ Objective

4.1: Given a scenario, use the appropriate tool to assess organizational security.

File Manipulation

Description

File manipulation can be implemented through various tools, including command-line prompts or utilities. However, the majority of the following examples are used on Linux or Unix platforms as opposed to the Windows command-line interface (**cmd.exe**). Many of these commands can also be used in a Windows PowerShell environment, but discussion of such is outside the scope of the examples provided.

Examples

- **head** is a Linux and Mac command that provides beginning or introductory portions of the files for which the command queries.
- **tail** is a Linux and Mac command that provides the end portions of the files for which the command queries.
- **cat**, short for *concatenate*, is a Linux and Mac command that joins the contents of multiple files.
- **grep** is a command used in Linux and Mac that searches for text patterns or strings in files. The Windows equivalent for this command is **findstr**.
- **chmod** can be used in Linux or Mac to modify file permissions.
- **logger** is a command that can be used in Linux and Mac that allows a user to make entries in a files system log.

Related Concepts

- Integrity—OIR-4.5D
- Non-repudiation—OIR-4.5H

Security+ Objective

4.1: Given a scenario, use the appropriate tool to assess organizational security.

Shell and Script Environments

Description

Shell and script environments allow administrators to perform tasks on an operating system or network that may not be able to be completed with a graphical user interface (GUI) or standard command-line interfaces.

Examples

- *Secure shell (SSH)* is a command-line interface that allows Windows, Linux, and Mac administrators to access resources remotely with a command-line utility.
- *PowerShell* is the Windows replacement of **cmd.exe**. Although **cmd.exe** is still included in Windows, PowerShell enables administrators to perform operative tasks that are not able to be completed via **cmd.exe**.

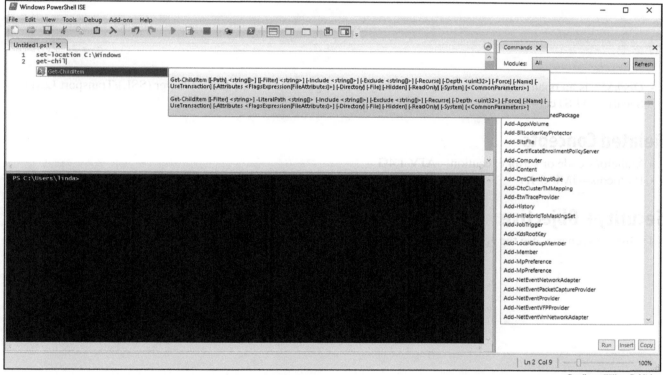

Goodheart-Willcox Publisher

- *Python* is a low-level, yet high-performing, programming language that can be used on Windows, Linux, or Mac operating systems to generate programs or scripts.

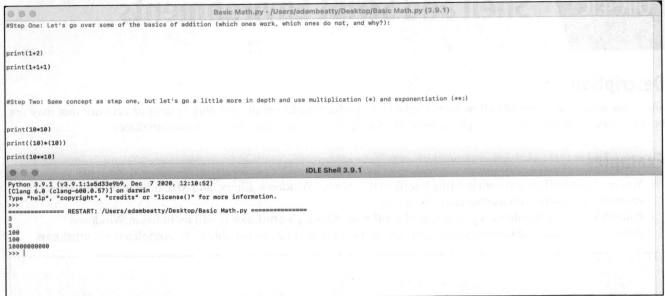

```
Basic Math.py - /Users/adambeatty/Desktop/Basic Math.py (3.9.1)
#Step One: Let's go over some of the basics of addition (which ones work, which ones do not, and why?):


print(1+2)
print(1+1+1)


#Step Two: Same concept as step one, but let's go a little more in depth and use multiplication (*) and exponentiation (**):

print(10*10)
print((10)*(10))
print(10**10)
```

```
IDLE Shell 3.9.1
Python 3.9.1 (v3.9.1:1e5d33e9b9, Dec  7 2020, 12:10:52)
[Clang 6.0 (clang-600.0.57)] on darwin
Type "help", "copyright", "credits" or "license()" for more information.
>>>
============== RESTART: /Users/adambeatty/Desktop/Basic Math.py ==============
3
3
100
100
10000000000
>>> |
```

Goodheart-Willcox Publisher

- *OpenSSL* is an open-source command-line utility used to generate Secure Socket Layer (SSL)/Transport Layer Security (TLS) certificates.

Related Concepts
- Malicious code or script execution—ATV-1.4G
- Protocols—IMP-3.1A

Security+ Objective
4.1: Given a scenario, use the appropriate tool to assess organizational security.

Packet Capture and Replay

Description

Packet capture and replay utilities are able to record and play back network traffic data. Often, packet capture is used to obtain information about a network. In addition to recording and replaying data, some utilities are also able to send malicious or fabricated traffic back to the source.

Examples

- **Tcpreplay** is a utility suite used in the Linux operating system to capture network traffic. It is able to send network traffic to sources such as web servers. However, if used maliciously, attackers can send fabricated network traffic data designed to disrupt services.
- **Tcpdump** is a packet-capturing command-line utility for the Linux operating system. It functions as a packet sniffer and records packets, protocols, and datagrams.

```
09:39:14.123970 ARP, Request who-has kali tell _gateway, length 46
09:39:14.124035 ARP, Reply kali is-at 00:0c:29:ab:01:d5 (oui Unknown), length 28
09:39:14.124320 IP 66.85.78.80.ntp > kali.34927: NTPv4, Server, length 48
09:39:19.173564 ARP, Request who-has _gateway tell kali, length 28
09:39:19.173767 ARP, Reply _gateway is-at 00:50:56:fb:2e:68 (oui Unknown), length 46
09:39:46.326853 IP kali.46244 > 66.85.78.80.ntp: NTPv4, Client, length 48
09:39:46.378131 IP 66.85.78.80.ntp > kali.46244: NTPv4, Server, length 48
```

- Wireshark is an open-source utility for packet capture and analysis. It functions within a GUI and can be used on Windows and Mac operating systems. Wireshark can freely download from https://www.wireshark.org.

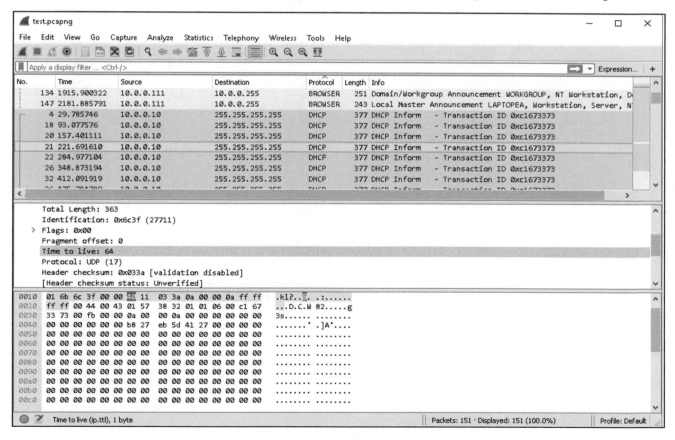

Related Concepts

- Syslog/Security information and event management (SIEM)—ATV-1.7C
- Network reconnaissance and discovery—OIR-4.1A

Security+ Objective

4.1: Given a scenario, use the appropriate tool to assess organizational security.

Forensics

Description

Forensics, also called *digital forensics*, are the proper steps and precautions a security professional follows when collecting data, performing data acquisition, and obtaining evidence regarding a cybersecurity incident.

Examples

- A *dd*, short for *data dump*, is a disk image that replicates a device's hard drive.
- *Memdump*, short for *memory dump*, is a cache that collects the contents of a device's memory, including its random-access memory (RAM), and stores the memdump until it is time to be analyzed.
- *WinHex* is a universal hex editor used to help with data acquisition by enabling an investigator to view or edit any kind of file along with accessing a device's memory.
- *FTK imager* is data forensic software used in the data acquisition process by providing data about a device and determining if further investigation is necessary.
- *Autopsy* is a digital forensics platform that is able to analyze mobile devices and identify key pieces of forensics data.

Related Concepts

- Dump files—OIR-4.3C
- Explain the key aspects of digital forensics—OIR-4.5

Security+ Objective

4.1: Given a scenario, use the appropriate tool to assess organizational security.

Copyright Goodheart-Willcox Co., Inc.

May not be reproduced or posted to a publicly accessible website.

383

OIR-4.1F | Exploitation Frameworks

Description

Exploitation frameworks outline the implementation of intrusive scanning or scripting methods to exploit vulnerabilities. These frameworks can be beneficial or malicious. Security personnel can use them to help identify potential vulnerabilities in a network, and hackers often use them as a playbook of sorts to breach security measures.

Examples

- *Metasploit* is an exploitation framework that contains scripts used to scan and discover services and vulnerabilities. It also includes a number of exploits used to hack targeted devices.
- *Browser Exploitation Framework (BeEF)* is a pen testing utility that targets exploitation of web browsers and web apps. This tool enables a tester to assess an organization's security posture by using client-side attack vectors in the browser.

Related Concepts

- Vulnerability scans—ATV-1.7B

Security+ Objective

4.1: Given a scenario, use the appropriate tool to assess organizational security.

Password Crackers

Description

Password crackers are application programs used to identify miscellaneous or stale passwords of devices and network resources.

Examples

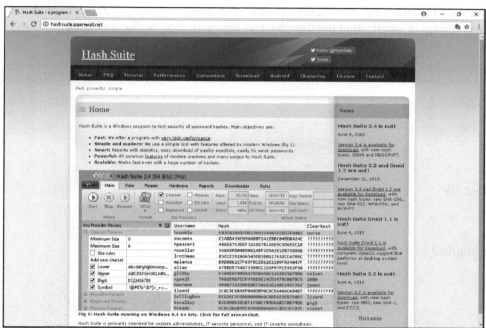

Goodheart-Willcox Publisher

Related Concepts

- Password attacks—ATV-1.2B

Security+ Objective

4.1: Given a scenario, use the appropriate tool to assess organizational security.

Data Sanitization

Description

Data sanitization refers to policies set by an organization for the proper disposal of obsolete data, data storage devices, and other forms of digital equipment.

Examples

The primary example of disk sanitization is performing a low-level reformat of the drive, in which all data is overwritten with binary 0s and 1s. Additional examples of sanitization involve physical destruction of media, including

- breaking;
- burning
- crushing;
- drilling;
- pulverizing; and
- shredding.

Related Concepts

- Secure data destruction—AD-2.7W

Security+ Objective

4.1: Given a scenario, use the appropriate tool to assess organizational security.

Incident Response Plans

Description

An *incident response plan (IRP)* is the frameworks and best practices for creating organizational polices, strategies, and steps that will be taken in response to security incidents.

Example

Incident Response Plan (IRP)

Definition of *Data Breach*

A data breach is defined as the unauthorized access of organizational data that results in compromised confidentiality, integrity, or availability of data. Legitimate access or alteration of data by authorized personnel does not constitute a breach.

Types of Incidents

Events that result in the commencement of the IRP include the following:

- Breach of internal network or data
- Breach of network or data at partner or vendor location
- Breach of website
- Breach of social media account(s)
- Breach of personally identifiable information (PII)
  - Personally identifiable information includes, but is not limited to, the following:
    - Social Security number
    - Driver's license or state identification number
    - Credit card, debit card, and banking account numbers
    - Home or e-mail address
    - Medical or HIPAA-protected data
    - Data governed by regulatory compliance
- Denial of Service (DoS) attack
- Breach of firewall
- Malware outbreak
- Ransomware or phishing attack
- Fire or natural disaster

Goodheart-Willcox Publisher

Related Concepts

- Incident response process—OIR-4.2B
- Exercises—OIR-4.2C
- Incident response team—OIR-4.2J

Security+ Objective

4.2: Summarize the importance of policies, processes, and procedures for incident response.

Incident Response Process

Description

An *incident response process* provides the steps to be taken when an incident occurs. Often, this process is outlined in an organization's incident response plan (IRP). The following examples list the six phases for an incident response process as recommended by the SANS Institute.

Examples

- *Preparation* is the first stage of an incident response process in which organizations conduct a risk assessment to discover any risks or vulnerabilities. Once identified, vulnerabilities are rated based on their severity.
- *Identification* is the stage that determines how and why a cybersecurity breach occurred. This assessment is based on evidence that has been collected and analyzed.
- *Containment* is the stage in which mitigation techniques are implemented to limit further damage from an incident. Affected assets are often segmented or disconnected from the network. Evidence is also isolated to ensure it is not lost, damaged, altered, or destroyed.
- *Eradication* is the stage in which a contained threat is removed. After this stage, evaluation of damages and system repair may begin.
- *Recovery* is the actions involved to return a system back to its normal, stable, and functional state.
- *Lessons learned* is the final stage of the incident response process and includes documentation of the security breach, how it was discovered, measures that were taken to contain the breach, and precautious that still need to be taken to minimize the chances of the breach reoccurring.

Related Concepts

- Incident response plans—OIR-4.2A
- Exercises—OIR-4.2C
- Incident response team—OIR-4.2J

Security+ Objective

4.2: Summarize the importance of policies, processes, and procedures for incident response.

OIR-4.2C   Exercises

Description

Exercises are conducted as part of an organization's incident response plan (IRP) to educate, prepare, and mitigate the possibility of cybersecurity breaches. Examples of IRP exercises include the following.

Examples

- *Tabletop exercises* are discussion-based exercises in which members of an organization are presented with possible security breaches and members of the organization provide recommendations as to how the security breach could be solved.
- *Walkthroughs* are exercises that place members of an organization in situations similar to cybersecurity breaches, such as a *simulation*, while conducting their everyday duties to generate a form of readiness if the cybersecurity breach occurs.

Related Concepts

- Incident response plans—OIR-4.2A
- Incident response process—OIR-4.2B
- Incident response team—OIR-4.2J

Security+ Objective

4.2: Summarize the importance of policies, processes, and procedures for incident response.

Attack Frameworks

Description

Attack frameworks are the policies that have been written, practiced, and implemented among cybersecurity experts from multiple organizations. The following frameworks outline tactics, techniques, and strategies used to augment security against attacks.

Examples

- *MITRE's Adversarial Tactics, Techniques & Common Knowledge (ATT&CK)* outlines the techniques used by red teams and other forms of defenders to better understand and classify an organization's risk. MITRE ATT&CK provides a database regarding topics such as malware and intrusion on their website (https://attack.mitre.org). ATT&CK consists of the following.

MITRE ATT&CK™ Framework

- Initial Access
- Execution
- Persistence
- Privilege Escalation
- Defense Evasion
- Credential Access
- Discovery
- Lateral Movement
- Collection
- Exfiltration
- Command and Control

Goodheart-Willcox Publisher

- The *Diamond Model of Intrusion Analysis* is an approach for conducting intelligence on network intrusion threats. Its name is derived from the four interconnected techniques listed in the following.

Diamond Model of Intrusion Analysis

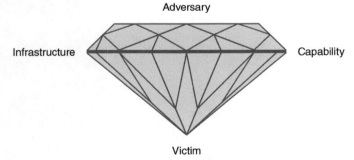

Adversary

Infrastructure

Capability

Victim

Goodheart-Willcox Publisher

- *Cyber Kill Chain* was developed by Lockheed Martin and based off a military model. This framework is comprised of the recommended steps to be taken when a cybersecurity attack is in its early stages in order to identify the attack, prepare to counterattack, engage the threat actor, and mitigate the damage from the attack.

Cyber Kill Chain

1. Reconnaissance
2. Intrusion
3. Exploitation
4. Privilege Escalation
5. Lateral Movement
6. Obfuscation/Anti-forensics
7. Denial of Service
8. Exfiltration

Goodheart-Willcox Publisher

Related Concepts

- Incident response plan—OIR-4.2A
- Incident response process—OIR-4.2B
- Exercises—OIR-4.2C
- Incident response team—OIR-4.2J

Security+ Objective

4.2: Summarize the importance of policies, processes, and procedures for incident response.

OIR-4.2E | Stakeholder Management

Description

Stakeholder management consists of the communication plans to various levels of management, including members outside of organization, as to how cybersecurity attacks may impact their organization.

Examples

The following criteria is crucial for security professionals and their collaboration with stakeholder management:

1. Speak to stakeholders in a transparent way so no miscommunication occurs.

2. Security professionals should understand their stakeholders' expectations.

3. Security professionals will resolve, or at least diminish, disputes and organizational complexity.

Related Concepts

- Communication plan—OIR-4.2F
- Disaster recovery plan—OIR-4.2G
- Business continuity plan—OIR-4.2H
- Continuity of operation planning (COOP)—OIR-4.2I
- Incident response team—OIR-4.2J

Security+ Objective

4.2: Summarize the importance of policies, processes, and procedures for incident response.

OIR-4.2F | Communication Plan

Description

A *communication plan* consists of advising members of an organization of plans for prohibiting or responding to cybersecurity attacks along with the impact of an attack on the organization.

Example

A communication plan may outline how much information can be distributed to news outlets, social media, customers, or users; the preferred order for notification; and how quickly communication should be made to stakeholders.

Related Concepts

- Incident response plans—OIR-4.2A
- Incident response process—OIR-4.2B
- Stakeholder management—OIR-4.2E
- Disaster recovery plan—OIR-4.2G
- Business continuity plan—OIR-4.2H
- Continuity of operation planning (COOP)—OIR-4.2I
- Incident response team—OIR-4.2J

Security+ Objective

4.2: Summarize the importance of policies, processes, and procedures for incident response.

Disaster Recovery Plan

Description

A *disaster recovery plan (DRP)* is part of an organization's continuity of business plan (BCP) and determines how an organization will function after a disaster or cyberattack. A DRP also outlines an organization's ability to adapt with plans through the recovery process.

Example

While DRPs vary among organizations, the following criteria is often considered universal, as they are typically taken into consideration during the development of a DRP:

1. The software, programs, and tools that are approved for use after an attack or incident

2. Continuing organizational functionality after an attack or incident

3. Determining how an attack or incident occurred, amount of time needed to mitigate the incident, and how best to prevent future reoccurrence

Related Concepts

- Business continuity plan—OIR-4.2H
- Continuity of operation planning (COOP)—OIR-4.2I
- Incident response team—OIR-4.2J

Security+ Objective

4.2: Summarize the importance of policies, processes, and procedures for incident response.

Business Continuity Plan

Description

A *business continuity plan (BCP)* is a comprehensive, proactive plan that provides the necessary steps for keeping a business operational before, during, and after a disaster. It outlines process and policies for when systems are created, maintained, and mitigated in the event of a disaster. Often, these plans are put in place that ensure an organization's operations will suffer as little interruption as possible, regardless of state or operation of a system.

Example

A BCP should be implemented in all organizations. Having a BCP allows an organization to understand how they will operate and function during a disruption. A primary example of information found in a BCP includes assurance for customer server and accounting departments to maintain operability during service disruption. In other words, even though an organization may face a disruption, customers will still expect to be able to reach the organization with inquiries, and payments coming from the organization, including both payroll and accounts payable, will remain functional.

Related Concepts

- Continuity of operation planning (COOP)—OIR-4.2I

Security+ Objective

4.2: Summarize the importance of policies, processes, and procedures for incident response.

Continuity of Operation Planning (COOP)

Description

Continuity of operation planning (COOP) is a business continuity plan (BCP) that provides information about the steps taken for an organization to function before, during, and after a disaster occurs.

Example

COOP often focuses on an organization's ability to restore mission-essential functions (MEFs). Assuring MEFs requires organizations to determine how, when, and for the length of time personnel or systems may need to function away from their traditional premises. A recent example of COOP in action was businesses that went remote during the COVID-19 pandemic and ensuing restrictions on attendance and capacity limitations. Since organizations could not have all team members on-site and remain safe, many opted for remote work with minimal, rotating personnel on-site. Additionally, COOP should consider an origination's risk management, essential functions, and how they will train their members when a paradigm shift requires their functionality methods to change.

Related Concepts

- Business continuity plan—OIR-4.2H

Security+ Objective

4.2: Summarize the importance of policies, processes, and procedures for incident response.

Incident Response Team

Description

An *incident response team* is the group of individuals who prepare for disasters and their impact on an organization's functionality. The team's goal is to ensure that as little disturbance as possible is experienced during and after a disaster or cybersecurity incident.

Example

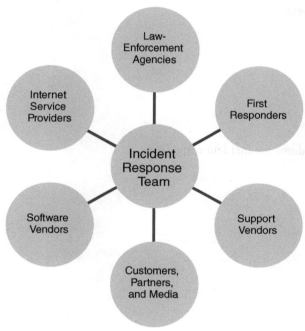

Goodheart-Willcox Publisher

Related Concepts

- Incident response plans—OIR-4.2A
- Incident response process—OIR-4.2B

Security+ Objective

4.2: Summarize the importance of policies, processes, and procedures for incident response.

Retention Policies

Description

Retention policies are guidelines for storing evidence as stipulated by legal and organizational requirements.

Example

Although organizations may have their own policies regarding retention, it is highly advised, and often required, that organizations adhere to frameworks implemented by organizations such as the DoD. The US National Security Agency (NSA) often stores global Internet metadata for up to a year.

Related Concepts

- Incident response process—OIR-4.2B
- Documentation/evidence—OIR-4.5A

Security+ Objective

4.2: Summarize the importance of policies, processes, and procedures for incident response.

OIR-4.3A | Vulnerability Scan Output

Description

A *vulnerability scan output* provides an assessment of an organization's network configuration by displaying a report of their current operations and effectiveness of security controls.

Examples

Scan output identifies missing internal security controls, including outdated patches, lack or firewall, or absence of antivirus software. When reviewing scanner output, be cognizant of the following:

- *False positives* occur when a scanner registers a vulnerability when none is present.
- *False negatives* occur when a scanner is unable to find vulnerabilities when there really are vulnerabilities present.

Related Concepts

- Cloud-based vs. on-premises vulnerabilities—ATV-1.6A
- Vulnerability scans—ATV-1.7B

Security+ Objective

4.3: Given an incident, utilize appropriate data sources to support an investigation.

SIEM Dashboards

Description

Security information and event management (SIEM) dashboards are software programs that provide and assist security professionals with important information regarding a system. Examples of information found in SIEM dashboards include the following.

Examples

- *Sensors*, also known as *intrusion-detection sensors*, are installed on an organization's network to collect data regarding any anomalies in the network's functionality.
- *Sensitivity* is a portion of a SIEM dashboard that provides guidance regarding sensitive data that has entered or exited an organization's network.
- *Trends* are monitored and presented in a SIEM dashboard. This information highlights patterns in network activity, including changes to traffic.
- *Alerts* appear in a SIEM dashboard when a security professional is seeking information, such as messages from logs.
- *Correlations*, also known as *correlation engines*, search through aggregated data and reports on common characteristics. This data is typically stored on a storage area network (SAN) for large organizations.

Related Concepts

- Syslog/Security information and event manager (SIEM)—ATV-1.7C
- Network appliances—IMP-3.3H
- Vulnerability scan output—OIR-4.3B

Security+ Objective

4.3: Given an incident, utilize appropriate data sources to support an investigation.

Log Files

Description

Log files provide insight into events and errors that occur on devices and during network transmissions. Examples of the types of log files than can be utilized in security assessment include the following.

Examples

- *Network* log files present information about a network's functionality and its devices.
- *System logging protocol (syslog)* is the protocol used to send data about a system to a server's event log in one central location.
- *Application logs* present information about events triggered by an application.
- *Web logs* are generated via web servers and include information about websites that have been visited by each user.
- *Domain Name Service (DNS) logs* provide DNS request information to and from DNS servers.
- *Authentication logs* include information regarding authentication login attempts.
- *Dump files* are logs that contain information about services and applications that have crashed. Dump files are generated automatically after a service or application crash.
- *VoIP and call managers* contain logs with information regarding the connection and attempted connections of VoIP transmissions.
- *Session initiation Protocol (SIP) traffic* transmits through end-user devices, such as IP-enabled headsets or client web conferencing software, and each device/session is provided a SIP Uniform Resource Indicator (URI).

Related Concepts

- Syslog/Security information and event management (SIEM)—ATV-1.7C
- Voice over IP (VoIP)—AD-2.6E
- DNS—IMP-3.3D

Security+ Objective

4.3: Given an incident, utilize appropriate data sources to support an investigation.

Copyright Goodheart-Willcox Co., Inc.

May not be reproduced or posted to a publicly accessible website.

401

syslog/rsyslog/syslog-ng

Description

System logging protocol (syslog) is the protocol used to send data about a system to a server's event log in one central location. There are multiple variations of syslog, including *rsyslog*, which is an open-source software utility used with Linux/Unix systems to forward messages, and *syslog-ng*, which is a portable version of rsyslog available on additional platforms.

Example

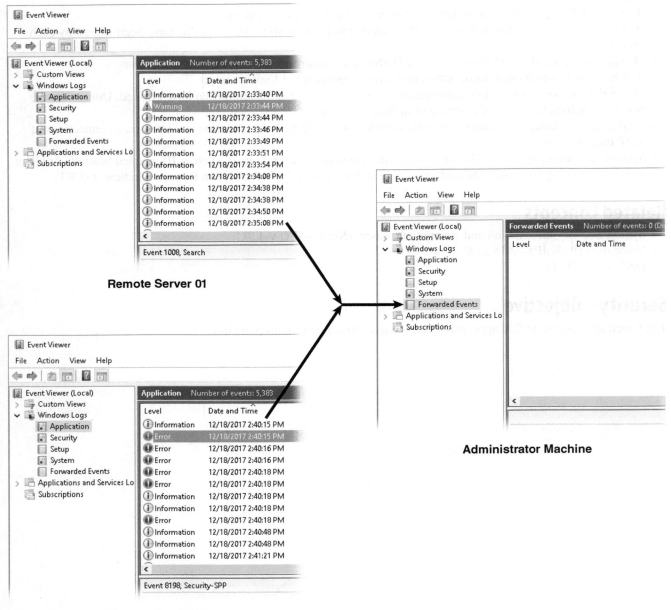

Remote Server 01

Administrator Machine

Remote Server 02

Goodheart-Willcox Publisher

Related Concepts

- Syslog/Security information and event management (SIEM)–ATV-1.7C
- Log files—OIR-4.3E
- journalctl—OIR-4.3D
- nxlog—OIR-4.3F

Security+ Objective

4.3: Given an incident, utilize appropriate data sources to support an investigation.

OIR-4.3E journalctl

Description

Another variation of syslog is journalctl. The *journalctl* is able to query information in the syslog.

Examples

If executed without any parameters, journalctl will display the full contents of the journal, beginning with the oldest collected entry. The inclusion of arguments filters journal output. Acceptable arguments for journalctl include the following:

- journalctl -ef: moves to the end of the journal file and keeps the journal open as new entries are added
- journalctl –b -1: only displays messages from the previous system boot
- journalctl -since "2021-02-12 10:00:00" -until "2021-02-19 10:00:00": displays messages that occurred between the dates and times used in the command, in this case messages occurring between 10:00 A.M. on February 12, 2021 and 10:00 A.M. on February 19, 2021

Related Concepts

- Syslog/Security information and event management (SIEM)—ATV-1.7C
- Log files—OIR-4.3C
- syslog/rsyslog/syslog-ng—OIR-4.3D
- nxlog—OIR-4.3F

Security+ Objective

4.3: Given an incident, utilize appropriate data sources to support an investigation.

OIR-4.3F nxlog

Description

Another variation of syslog is *nxlog*, which is a multiplatform log management tool. The unique feature of nxlog is can identify an organization's policy breaches in its server logs.

Examples

NXLog is similar to syslog-ng and rsyslog, but it is not limited to use on Unix. Examples of = distributions include

- **NXLog Community Edition:** free proprietary log management tool
- **NXLog Enterprise Edition:** includes enhancements to Community Edition, such as low memory footprint and better performance statistics
- **NXLog Manager:** enables remote management of Enterprise Edition

Related Concepts

- Syslog/Security information and event management (SIEM)—ATV-1.7C
- Log files—OIR-4.3C
- syslog/rsyslog/syslog-ng—OIR-4.3D
- journalctl—OIR-4.3E

Security+ Objective

4.3: Given an incident, utilize appropriate data sources to support an investigation.

Retention

Description

Retention is the process of organizing data so it can be controlled and in compliance with organizational policies and laws. Policies for retention serve as guidelines that outline specific details regard what data should be stored and where.

Example

Although organizations may have their own policies regarding retention, it is highly advised, and often required, that organizations adhere to frameworks implemented by organizations such as the DoD. The US National Security Agency (NSA) often stores global Internet metadata for up to a year.

Related Concepts

- Retention policies—OIR-4.2K
- Data—GRC-5.3D

Security+ Objective

4.3: Given an incident, utilize appropriate data sources to support an investigation.

Bandwidth Monitors

Description

Bandwidth monitors are tools used to monitor and analyze inbound and outbound network traffic to determine which device(s) are utilizing the most bandwidth of the organization's network.

Example

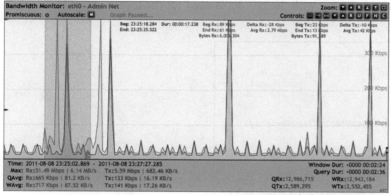

Related Concepts

• Load balancing—IMP-3.3A

Security+ Objective

4.3: Given an incident, utilize appropriate data sources to support an investigation.

Description

Metadata is the information about the creation, modification, and use of data. The information obtained from metadata is a critical component for cybersecurity investigations.

Examples

- *E-mail metadata* consists of a time-stamped history along with the protocols used for the transmission of an e-mail.

```
MIME-Version: 1.0
Date: Sun, 31 Jan 2021 13:49:45 -0500
Bcc:
Message-ID: <                                           @mail.gmail.com>
Subject: IT Leads LLC Payroll Information
From:
To:
Content-Type: multipart/alternative; boundary="00000000000080234a05ba36b393"

--00000000000080234a05ba36b393
Content-Type: text/plain; charset="UTF-8"


Good morning Jordan,

   Due to quarantine, I am not able to access the files in our office nor am
I able to access our files via our online portal.  Furthermore, as luck
would have it, I am not able to reach any of our IT staff to see why I am
not able to access the online portal.  As you are aware, we need to
verify our quarterly reports and payrolls.  Ergo, since you have access to
the content that is needed, please send it to me via email as soon as
possible!

Thank you for all you do for our organization,

Dr. Adam Beatty
C.E.O. IT Leads LLC

--00000000000080234a05ba36b393
Content-Type: text/html; charset="UTF-8"
Content-Transfer-Encoding: quoted-printable

<div dir=3D"ltr">Good morning=C2=A0Jordan,<div><br></div><div>=C2=A0 Due to=
 quarantine, I am not able to access the files in our office nor am I able =
to access our files via our online portal.=C2=A0 Furthermore, as luck would=
 have it, I am not able to reach any of our IT staff to see why I am not ab=
le to access the online portal.=C2=A0 As you are aware, we need to verify=
=C2=A0our quarterly reports and payrolls.=C2=A0 Ergo, since you=C2=A0have a=
ccess to the content that is needed, please send it to me via email as soon=
=C2=A0as possible!</div><div><br></div><div>Thank you for all you do for ou=
r organization,</div><div><br></div><div>Dr. Adam Beatty</div><div>C.E.O. I=
T Leads LLC</div></div>

--00000000000080234a05ba36b393--
```

Goodheart-Willcox Publisher

- *Mobile metadata* is information about a file created on a mobile device, including the file format used. For instance, iPhones use exchangeable image file format (EXIF) to store the metadata of photos and videos, including time and date of recording, resolution, GPS location, and camera setting.

- *Web metadata* consists of information about websites, such as its page title and keywords. Often, this information is used to optimize search engine results.

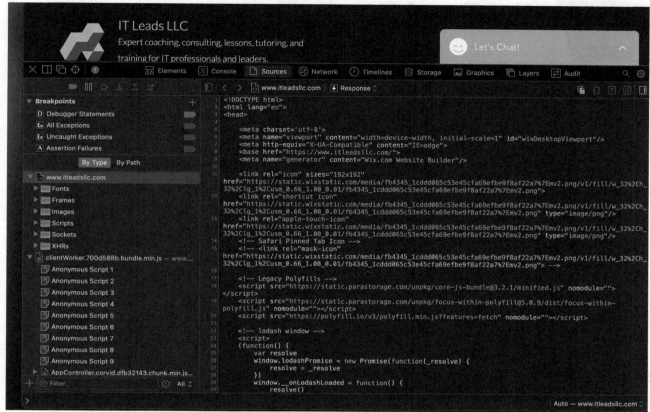

- *File metadata* can provide information such as the author of a file, when it was created, the last time the file was modified, and the amount of time modifications were made to the file.

Related Concepts

- Non-repudiation—OIR-4.5H

Security+ Objective

4.3: Given an incident, utilize appropriate data sources to support an investigation.

Netflow/sflow

Description

Netflow is a network protocol that was created by Cisco to collect IP traffic as it flows in and out of a network interface card. The goal of Netflow is to provide network monitoring in real time. Sampled flow (*sFlow*) is a non-Cisco platform that can capture packet metadata, statistics, and routing information.

Examples

- *Echo* refers to the Internet Control Message Protocol (ICMP) echo requests that send query messages to establish connectivity.
- *IP Flow Information Export (IPfix)* is a framework developed by the Internet Engineering Task Force (IETF) that provides export of information from routers, switches, and firewalls. IPfix was implemented due to NetFlow and sFlow being proprietary protocols.

Related Concepts

- Routing and switching—IMP-3.1B

Security+ Objective

4.3: Given an incident, utilize appropriate data sources to support an investigation.

Protocol Analyzer Output

Description

Protocol analyzer output is collected and saved for reference. The output is compared to baselines and analyzed in and investigation or for troubleshooting purposes. Typically, outputs are organized by time, used protocol(s), or node address.

Example

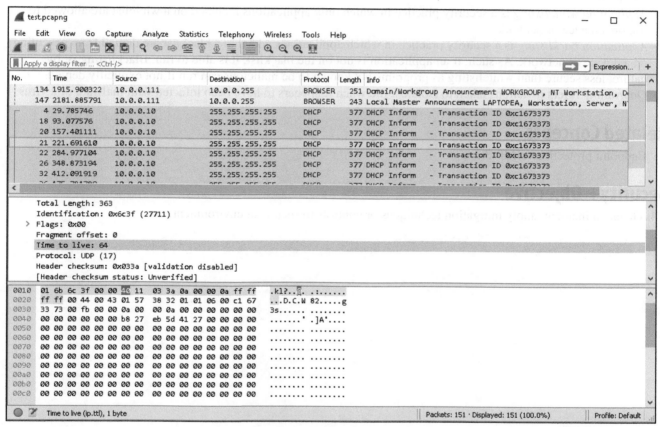

Goodheart-Willcox Publisher

Related Concepts

- Syslog/security information event management (SIEM)—ATV-1.7C
- Protocols—OIR-3.1A
- Packet capture and replay—OIR-4.1C

Security+ Objective

4.3: Given an incident, utilize appropriate data sources to support an investigation.

Reconfigure Endpoint Security Solutions

Description

Reconfiguration of endpoint security solutions is performed when flaws are found in applications and files. During reconfiguration, flawed files are often moved to an inaccessible location to avoid accidental exposure or execution. Examples of actions taken during reconfiguration include the following.

Examples

- *Application whitelisting* is a security practice in which only applications included on a whitelist are allowed to run on a device or network.
- *Application backlisting* is a security practice in which applications added to a blacklist are denied from executing on a device or network. As such, if an application is not on the blacklist, it is able to run. Blacklisting is, by nature, less secure than whitelisting as programs not known to be malicious can run if not explicitly denied.
- *Quarantine* refers to actions taken to isolate a file when it appears to have been infected with malware or a virus.

Related Concepts

- Endpoint protection—IMP-3.2A

Security+ Objective

4.4: Given an incident, apply mitigation techniques or controls to secure an environment.

Configuration Changes

Description

Configuration changes must be implemented in an organization as technologies, users, and organizational methods change. Common changes to configurations include the following.

Examples

- *Firewall rules* require configuration changes since these rules determine what type of traffic is permitted or denied the ability to enter or leave an organization's network. With new services emerging and dated services becoming increasingly vulnerable, firewall rules need to be reconfigured regularly to maintain organizational security and functionality.
- *Mobile device management (MDM)* is the software and practices used to secure mobile devices in an organization. Like firewall rules, MDMs need to be reconfigured regularly to allow or disallow applications to run while also assuring that the proper data transmissions are being utilized for an organization's functionality.
- *Data loss prevention (DLP)* products scan content in structural formats, such as e-mails in Microsoft Office 365, to ensure data has not been lost. As more applications emerge, DLP products and precautions will need to be continually implemented.
- *Content filters*, also known as *URL filters*, monitor Internet traffic to prohibit the access of backlisted websites and web services. As more websites and services are developed daily, filters should be configured and reconfigured to ensure malicious websites and services are not accessible via an organization's network.
- *Updates or revoke certificates* need to be monitored and reconfigured as needed to maintain up-to-date accuracy. This includes updating new certificates from a certificate authority (CA) and revoking certificates that will no longer be used.

Related Concepts

- Data loss protection (DLP)—AD-2.1C
- Firewalls—IMP-3.3
- Mobile device management—IMP-3.5B
- Certificate authority (CA)—IMP-3.9A

Security+ Objective

4.4: Given an incident, apply mitigation techniques or controls to secure an environment.

Description

Isolation is the segmentation of devices so they cannot connect to an organization's network or other devices. Isolation is often performed on devices assumed to be infected with malware to prevent reinfection or spread of infection.

Examples

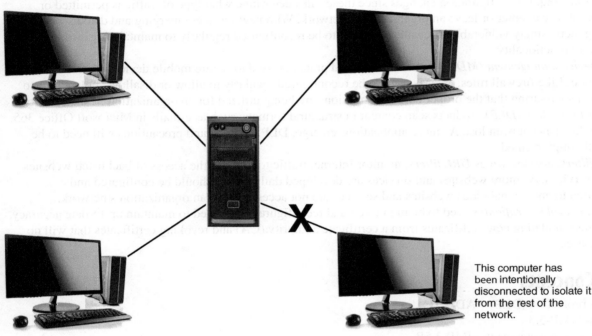

This computer has been intentionally disconnected to isolate it from the rest of the network.

Goodheart-Willcox Publisher; (computers and server) Den Rozhnovksy/Shutterstock.com

Related Concepts

- Network segmentation—IMP-3.3B
- Containment—OIR-4.4D
- Segmentation—OIR-4.4E

Security+ Objective

4.4: Given an incident, apply mitigation techniques or controls to secure an environment.

Containment

Description

Similar to isolation, *containment* is performed on devices that have experienced an attack. The main difference between isolation and containment is that devices *thought* to be infected or compromised are isolated, and devices *confirmed* to be infected or compromised are contained. By containing the device and its infection, it may be able to continue operation, so long as it does not interfere with the functionality of other devices.

Example

Containment is performed largely the same way as isolation: disconnection of network media to avoid additional contamination. For example, in the four-device network illustrated in OIR-4.4C, the isolated computer would remain disconnected once malware is confirmed to be present on the device. Network connectivity is not restored under the incident has been mitigated entirely.

Related Concepts

- Isolation—OIR-4.4C
- Segmentation—OIR-4.4E

Security+ Objective

4.4: Given an incident, apply mitigation techniques or controls to secure an environment.

Segmentation

Description

Segmentation is the act of separating entities. Often, this is performed on a network to divide it into small subnetworks or into virtual LANs (VLANs) to restrict the communication with hosts in other entities.

Example

In the following figure, each VLAN represents a different network segment.

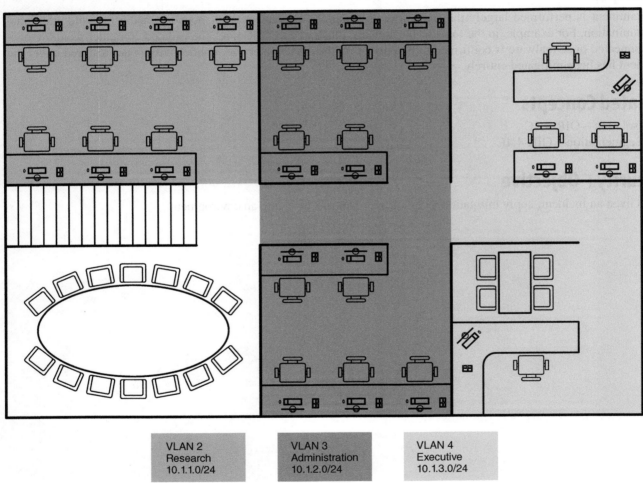

| VLAN 2 Research 10.1.1.0/24 | VLAN 3 Administration 10.1.2.0/24 | VLAN 4 Executive 10.1.3.0/24 |

Goodheart-Willcox Publisher

Related Concepts

- Network segmentation—IMP-3.3B
- Isolation—OIR-4.4C
- Segmentation—OIR-4.4E

Security+ Objective

4.4: Given an incident, apply mitigation techniques or controls to secure an environment.

Secure Orchestration, Automation, and Response (SOAR)

Description

Secure Orchestration, Automation, and Response (SOAR) is an array of software solutions that collect data from various sources and generate an automatic response. For example, these solutions may be configured in a way to automatically notify an administrator or user of incorrect login credentials used while attempting to access a network.

Examples

- *Runbooks* refer to SOAR techniques that provide automatic responses when an error occurs in common recurring situations, such as failed login attempts.
- *Playbooks* refer to SOAR techniques that provide checklists for resolving incidents.

Related Concepts

- Security orchestration, automation, and response (SOAR)—ATV-1.7D
- Response and recovery controls—AD-2.1G

Security+ Objective

4.4: Given an incident, apply mitigation techniques or controls to secure an environment.

Documentation/Evidence

Description

When performing digital forensics activities or investigating an incident, *documentation* and *evidence* can take on many forms, including physical or digital items. The following examples refer to the criteria that could be applicable in an investigation and court of law.

Examples

- A *legal hold* prohibits employees from destroying data or information that could be relevant to a court case.
- *Video* evidence is any footage from surveillance cameras, CCTC, or other recording device(s) that provide visual evidence that could be represented in court.
- *Admissibility* refers to data and information that is permissible as evidence in an investigation and court of law.
- *Chain of custody* refers to forms that record who collected, handled, or stored evidence. The forms also record when and where evidence was collected and stored. Any gap in the chain of custody can create a lack of integrity in the evidence.
- The *timeline* or *sequence of events* leading up to or during an incidence is of high importance in an investigation. The following help piece an accurate timeline together.
  - *Time stamps* are digital records of when an event occurred in a specific time zone. File systems within a given operating system often use their local time zones to provide time stamps. As such, it is important to denote the difference between the files' local time zone and Coordinated Universal Time.
  - *Time offset* is an understanding of how different operating systems and devices may document the time at which an event occurred. Specifically, time offset refers to the difference in hours and minutes when a time stamp is subtracted from the Coordinated Universal Time (UTC) benchmark.
- *Tags*, or stickers, should be placed on evidence while in storage, to avoid or prevent the possibility of evidence being lost or altered.
- *Reports* that detail the investigation process are used to verify that an investigation was conducted correctly. This is of particular importance if subpoenas are issued.
- *Event logs*, such as syslog, should be collected from computers before, during, and after an incident and remain unaltered throughout the investigation and court proceedings.
- *Interviews* should be conducted with witnesses to verify the environment of the scene during the time(s) a crime occurred.

Related Concepts

- Syslog/Security information and event management (SIEM)—ATV-1.7C
- Closed-circuit television (CCTV)—AD-2.7G
- syslog/ryslog/syslog-ng—OIR-4.3D
- Metadata—OIR-4.3I

Security+ Objective

4.5: Explain the key aspects of digital forensics.

Description

Acquisition is the process of collecting data from media identified as evidence. This is an important process because if not following properly, evidence could become unusable or inadmissible in a court of law.

Examples

- *Order of volatility* is the principle of capturing evidence from the most volatile to the least volatility. The following order of volatility is recommended by RFC 3227.

  1. central processing unit and memory cache

  2. routing table, Address Resolution Protocol (ARP) cache, process table, and kernel statistics

  3. random-access memory (RAM)

  4. temporary file systems

  5. disk

  6. remote logging and monitoring data

  7. physical configuration and network topology

  8. archival media

- *Disks*, or *hard* are obtained during the order of volatility process, but duplicate copies should be collected for redundancy.
- *Random-access memory (RAM)* acquisition consists of copying all the programs, files, and other tasks that were running during the order of volatility acquisition process.
- *Swap/pagefile* acquisition consists of copying all of the virtual memory from the extension of the device's RAM.
- *Operating system (OS)* acquisition requires an investigator to record which OS was on a device, its version, and its license and serial numbers.
- *Device acquisition* requires an investigator to record which device was collected, its version, and its license or serial number.
- *Firmware acquisition* requires an investigator to record the firmware version of the device that is being investigated.
- *Snapshot acquisition* requires an investigator to create a snapshot of a device. This generates a point-in-time copy of the data in the device's file system.
- *Cache acquisition* is obtaining a system's cache to determine settings, programs, and web services that were cached for later and faster obtainability.
- *Network acquisition* is the recording of the network topology, including the network settings of the device collected for evidence.
- *Artifacts* are forensic objects that could be considered evidence. This can include computer systems, flash drives, or files created. Additionally, provable user activity on a device and network can also be considered an artifact.

Related Concepts

- Backup types—AD-2.5D
- Enforcement and monitoring of—IMP-3.5D

Security+ Objective

4.5: Explain the key aspects of digital forensics.

Description

On-premises vs. cloud aspects of digital forensics refer to the number of differences in investigating incidents that occur on-sight as compared to those occurring in a cloud environment. These differences are complex. However, the most important topics to remember are referenced in the following examples.

Examples

- *Right to audit clauses* provide assurances that an organization has the right to audit and test cloud security controls on a consistent basis. A right to audit clause can be applied to a third-party cloud computing vendor.
- *Regulatory/jurisdiction* refers to the fact that data is subject to the regulation or jurisdiction of its location. For example, if data is stored in a specific US state, then that data is regulated by the laws of that state and any applicable federal laws. Regulatory and jurisdictional guidance also dictates how data can be managed. When data is managed from one location, such as one state, the laws are relatively straightforward; however, when cloud computing is implemented, the laws can become complex.
- *Data breach notification laws* require organizations to advise their customers when data has been compromised. Notification must occur within three days after the organization is aware of the breach, as mandated by the General Data Protection Regulation (GDPR).

Related Concepts

- Cloud-based vs. on-premises attacks—ATV-1.2F
- Cloud based vs. on-premises vulnerabilities—ATV-1.6A
- Cloud models—AD-2.2A
- Cloud service providers—AD-2.2B
- On-premises vs. cloud—AD2.5C

Security+ Objective

4.5: Explain the key aspects of digital forensics.

Integrity

Description

Integrity, which is one of the portions of the CIA Triad, refers to the storage and transfer of data as intended, and any modifications made are authorized and legal. The following serve as examples as to how data maintains its integrity.

Examples

- *Hashing* uses algorithms that map data into checksums. This ensures that hashed data is only functional via a one-way transmission.
- *Checksums* are values derived from data to ensure no errors occurred during transmission. Often, checksums are placed into a hashing algorithm to help ensure the integrity of the data.
- *Provenance integrity* is a record of data being created or when data was sent into transmission.

Related Concepts

- Hashing—AD-2.1I
- Salting—AD-2.8D
- Hashing—AD-2.8E
- Database—IMP-3.2C

Security+ Objective

4.5: Explain the key aspects of digital forensics.

Preservation

Description

Preservation of evidence and data is the process of protecting evidence from change, corruption, alteration, or damage. It also provides a valid timeline as to how data was collected at a crime scene to assure its integrity.

Example

Preservation is similar to retention in that there are laws and organizational policies that dictate how evidence or relevant incident data is to be preserved. Examples include NSA and DOD regulations as well as custodial chain documentation.

Related Concepts

- Non-repudiation—OIR-4.5H

Security+ Objective

4.5: Explain the key aspects of digital forensics.

OIR-4.5F E-Discovery

Description

Electronic discovery, also known as *e-discovery*, refers to the process of collecting easily accessible digital items, such as e-mails. E-discovery also describes how and when data was sought, discovered, and secured. This is an essential process for an investigation and evidentiary integrity.

Examples

Electronic discovery applies not only to the collection of items but also to

- legal discovery in which each party in legal proceedings is granted access to evidence;
- Freedom of Information Act (FOIA) requests; and
- governmental investigations or commissions.

Related Concepts

- Acquisition—OIR-4.5B

Security+ Objective

4.5: Explain the key aspects of digital forensics.

Data Recovery

Description

Data recovery in cybersecurity forensics refers to obtaining data that was attempted to be destroyed from a suspect before an investigation began.

Examples

Examples of data recovery software include the following:

- BartPE
- CHKDSK
- Finnix
- Foremost
- IsoBuster
- Norton Utilities
- Open Computer Forensics Architecture
- Sleuth Kit
- Windows File Recovery

Related Concepts

- Incident response process—OIR-4.2B
- Documentation/evidence—OIR-4.5A
- Acquisition—OIR-4.5B

Security+ Objective

4.5: Explain the key aspects of digital forensics.

Nonrepudiation

Description

Nonrepudiation is the assurance that the creator of data is not able to deny the generation or modification of their data. This also ensures that data in its original format cannot be altered, even during transmissions.

Examples

Digital signatures and meta data are often used to ensure nonrepudiation. These two types of confirmation are often difficult to duplicate or forge, which is why they are used heavily in incident investigation.

Related Concepts

- Metadata—OIR-4.3I

Security+ Objective

4.5: Explain the key aspects of digital forensics.

Strategic Intelligence/ Counterintelligence

Description

Strategic intelligence is the evaluation, analysis, and dissemination of evidence or data required for creating organizational policy. *Counterintelligence* is the gathering of information about the methods and extent of a cybercriminal's ability to breach systems, obtain data, or infect malware. Both types of intelligence are often derived from analysis of network traffic logs to protect against forms of espionage.

Example

Exploitation frameworks are an excellent type of counterintelligence. Since they often outline how attacks are orchestrated and performed, attack frameworks better enable an organization to harden its systems to prevent an attack before it starts.

Related Concepts

- Exploitation frameworks—OIR-4.1F
- Log files—OIR-4.3C

Security+ Objective

4.5: Explain the key aspects of digital forensics.

GRC-5.1A Category

Description

Security controls are often divided into multiple *categories* that describe the type of control, where it exists in a system, and how it helps to secure data. These categories are essential to understanding governance, risk, and compliance. Examples of control categories include the following.

Examples

- *Managerial* controls use management or administrative processes to implement and measure performance or take corrective action if needed. These types of controls include plans and policies that help manage an organization. Often, these controls are included as an element of an organization's incident response plan (IRP).
- *Operational* security controls are implemented by people who carry out day-to-day operations of a business, such as personnel security, physical security, and data protocols. Examples of controls in this category include user training and system maintenance.
- *Technical* security controls are security controls that require members of an organization to adhere to user and network traffic compliance guidelines. These controls use technology to enhance or automate device management and the access or application of data. Examples of controls in this category include multifactor authentication and firewalls.

Related Concepts

- Response and recovery controls—AD-2.1G
- Diversity—AD-2.5H
- Explain the importance of physical security controls—AD-2.7
- Incident response plans—OIR-4.2A
- Control type—GRC-5.1B

Security+ Objective

5.1: Compare and contrast various types of controls.

Control Type

Description

Various *control types* are used to protect an organization's data and resources from cybersecurity threats and incidents. There are multiple types of security controls. Some prevent or stop attacks, and others attempt to advise or alter an attacker's mindset. Examples of control types include the following.

Examples

- *Preventative* security controls, commonly referred to as *preventive* controls, are those that seek to stop a person from accessing a restricted area. The controls could be physical barriers or policies that make it evident that unauthorized personnel are not to obtain access.
- *Detective* security controls are implemented to identify and record all attempted and successful intrusions. These controls are meant primarily to inform or alert, not prevent or deter access.
- *Corrective* security controls work to lessen or repair damage sustained during an undesirable action of event. For example, malware quarantining is considered a corrective control. Corrective controls can also refer to controls that acknowledge prior security breaches or incidents and place the proper security controls to prevent the known incidents from reoccurring.
- *Deterrent* controls do not prevent access but instead psychological discourage attempted intrusion. Examples of deterrent controls include signage stating only authorized personnel are allowed access and any trespassing can result in legal action.
- *Compensating* security controls provide alternative or contingent strategies in the event a typical control is ineffective or unavailable. While these controls may not prevent access physically or logically, they provide a safety net in the event a security control fails.
- *Physical* security controls are the alarms, gateways, lighting, and locks that deter trespassing of a premises.

Related Concepts

- Response and recovery controls—AD-2.1G
- Diversity—AD-2.5H
- Explain the importance of physical security controls—AD-2.7
- Incident response plans—OIR-4.2A
- Category—GRC-5.1A

Security+ Objective

5.1: Compare and contrast various types of controls.

GRC-5.2A Regulations, Standards, and Legislation

Description

Regulations, standards, and legislation refer to the industry-defined or legal guidelines that must be adhered to regarding data collection, transmission, and storage. Some guidelines or frameworks are optional, but many are legally binding, and failure to comply may result in monetary fines or legal proceedings.

Examples

- *General Data Protection Regulation (GDPR)* is a collection of data breach notification laws that require organizations to advise their customers when data has been compromised within three days after the organization is aware of the breach.
- *National, territory, or state laws* vary, so it is important that security professionals understand the laws as they pertain to their in-house operations along with the laws regulating the locations of third-party vendors.
- *Payment Card Industry Data Security Standard (PCI DSS)* requires organizations that process credit cards or bank card transactions to ensure security of the cards that are stored and transmitted. Furthermore, the PCI DSS is mandated by the majority of credit card and financial companies for transactions. Organizations that do not comply with PCI DSS are not allowed to execute transactions with their brand of card.

Related Concepts

- Card cloning—AD-1.2C
- Cloud-based vs. on-premises attacks—AD-1.2F
- On-premises vs. cloud—OIR-4.5C

Security+ Objective

5.2: Explain the importance of applicable regulations, standards, or frameworks that impact organizational security posture.

Key Frameworks

Description

A *framework* is a document that defines policies and processes for outlining how information is to be managed in an organization. There are many frameworks that augment security and affect that way organizations handle data. Examples of such guidelines include the following.

Examples

- *Center for Internet Security (CIS)* is a nonprofit organization that was founded by The Sysadmin, Audit, Network, and Security (SANS) Institute. The CIS Top 20 Critical Security Controls is a simplified list of recommendations published in an easily understandable format. This list of important controls can be viewed at https://www.cisecurity.org.
- The *National Institute of Standards and Technology (NIST)* is responsible for issuing publications for the Federal Information Processing Standards (FIPS). Two important frameworks published by *NIST include the NIST Cybersecurity Framework (CSF)* and the *NIST Risk Management Framework (RMF)*. The CSF helps organizations manage cybersecurity risks and is organized in three parts: a framework core that serves as a set of cybersecurity activities; framework implementation tires, which include context on how a company views risk; and framework profiles, which represent outcomes based on business needs. The RMF outlines a mandatory six-step process for managing risk and loss associated with it. These publications can be obtained at https://www.nist.gov/federal-information-standards-fips.
- *International Organization for Standardization (ISO) 27001/27002/27701/31000* are cybersecurity frameworks that are in collaboration with the International Electrotechnical Commission (IEC). Unlike NIST frameworks, ISO frameworks may need to be purchased.
  - *ISO 27007* provides guidance for managing risk within information security management systems.
  - *ISO 27002* defines establishing and continuing improvement for information security management systems.
  - *ISO 27701* defines establishing and continuing improvement of privacy information management systems.
  - *ISO 31000* contains standards related to risk management.
- *Statement on Standards for Attestation Engagements (SSAE)* is an auditing standard that governs how companies report compliance. Through the SSAE audit, *Service Organization Control (SOC) reports* are created that detail a company's reporting controls based on the Trust Services Criteria (TCS). *Type II* reports are only obtainable via certain members or collaborators of an organization, but *Type III* reports are freely attainable and distributed.
- The *Cloud Security Alliance (CSA)* is a nonprofit organization that offers frameworks for best practices in cloud security. Two important CSA frameworks include the Cloud Control Matrix (CCM) and CSA Reference Architecture.
  - The *Cloud Control Matrix (CCM)* is a framework for cloud computing that covers 133 control objectives distributed among 16 domains. Information regarding CCM can be obtained at https://cloudsecurityalliance.org/.
  - The *CSA Cloud Reference Architecture* framework provides documentation of known individuals, professions, or technologies that provide an organization with a common set of solutions to help manage security needs between an IT department and cloud provider.

Related Concepts

- Cloud service providers—AD-2.2B
- Incident response process—OIR-4.2B

Security+ Objective

5.2: Explain the importance of applicable regulations, standards, or frameworks that impact organizational security posture.

Benchmark/Secure Configuration Guides

Description

Benchmarks and *secure configuration guides* provide a high-level perception as to how an organization should plan their IT services. However, since they are typically presented in a template format, they are not easily understood by novice administrators. The templates are provided through vendors, and it is up to the organization to build upon its template. Guides and templates exist for a variety of devices, including the following examples.

Examples

- Web server
- Operating system (OS)
- Application server
- Network infrastructure devices

Related Concepts

- Configuration management—AD-2.1A

Security+ Objective

5.2: Explain the importance of applicable regulations, standards, or frameworks that impact organizational security posture.

Personnel

Description

Personnel management policies should be implemented in organizations so employees are aware of proper device usage. Additionally, these policies help hold members of the organization accountable in the event a breach, misconfiguration, or user error occurs. Examples of commonly encountered personnel policies include the following.

Examples

- An *acceptable use policy (AUP)* is the organizational and third-party vendor policies that outline how certain personnel is to utilize equipment and resources.
- *Job rotation*, also called *rotation of duties*, is the act of transferring personnel to different departments within an organization. The use of job rotation provides different perspectives and avoids forms of boredom, burnout, or apathy among members of an organization.
- *Mandatory vacation* is a policy in which personnel are required to use their vacation days and time. During mandatory vacations, audits can be conducted on the vacationing employee's account or device by security professionals.
- *Separation of duties* is the practice of requiring multiple people to complete a job or task. This is widely used in financial departments or other organizational areas that handle confidential or sensitive data.
- *Least privilege* is used to grant a member of an organization the rights to access the data and resources needed only for their job. Therefore, if a user attempts to access or execute data, applications, or resources not related to their work, they will be denied access.
- A *clean desk policy* mandates that members of an organization should not leave documents or other forms of information on their desk or workspace.
- *Background checks* verify an individual is who they claim to be. Included in the report is information regarding criminal records and, in some cases, financial information such as bankruptcy claims or credit data.
- A *nondisclosure agreement (NDA)* is a bonding document that states a member of an organization will not provide confidential information with individuals who are not affiliated with the organization.
- *Social media analysis* is the collection of data from social media outlets. Organizations utilize social media analysis to verify their members are not disclosing confidential information about the organization and its productivity methods.
- *Onboarding* is the welcoming of a new member to an organization. The first step of onboarding is typically a meeting with an organization's HR department. During the onboarding process, new members of an organization should be advised of the polices regarding its data and network policies.
- *Offboarding* is the process of withdrawing a member's account and access privileges when they either stop performing their duties, leave a group project, or resign from their position.
- Various methods of *user training* are often employed to ensure users understand security policies. Examples of user training include the following.
  - *Gamification* is user training that places personnel into a game-like scenario. These activities are often team- and score-based to augment and engage learning processes.
  - *Capture the flag (CTF)* is a computer security-based competition in which members of an organization learn about cybersecurity tactics and methods as a team. CTF formats can be in the form of a trivia-style game or an attack-defend style.
  - Mock *phishing campaigns* are often used to test employee knowledge regarding phishing. Organizations use the following to test employee susceptibility to phishing.
    - *Phishing simulations* are training techniques for teaching members of an organization about fraudulent e-mails that can, and often do, lead to other forms of cybersecurity attacks.
    - *Computer-based training (CBT)* provides members of an organization the ability to be trained by a computer or device via e-learning.
    - *Role-based training* places members of an organization in hypothetical roles of an attacker and security professional so they may better understand the roles of processes of both parties.

Related Concepts

- Phishing—ATV-1.1A
- Reconnaissance—ATV-1.1Q
- Influence campaigns—ATV-1.1V
- Principles (reasons for effectiveness)—ATV-1.1W
- Exercises—OIR-4.2C

Security+ Objective

5.3: Explain the importance of policies to organizational security.

GRC-5.3B   Diversity of Training Techniques

Description

Diversity of training techniques is needed to provide different forms of cybersecurity training to members of an organization. If an organization completes the same cybersecurity training on a consistent basis, the members being trained might not be stimulated, as the content and methods are perceived as stagnate trainings. Moreover, since each employee processes and retains knowledge differently, varying the methods used to instruct employees increases the likelihood of employee retention.

Examples

- *Gamification* places members of an organization into a setting where trainings are presented into a form of game play to augment the engagement of everyone's learning.
- *Capture the flag (CTF)* places members of an organization into a security competition to either protect or intercept another team's data (flag). This type of training enables personnel from departments outside of an IT department to better understand how security and hacking tactics are utilized.

Related Concepts

- Exercise—OIR-4.2C
- Personnel—GRC-5.3A

Security+ Objective

5.3: Explain the importance of policies to organizational security.

Third-Party Risk Management

Description

Third-party risk management is the process of identifying and controlling risks that occur from conducting business with third parties or vendors. These risks can often be mitigated via the following examples.

Examples

- *Vendors* are third parties that provide products or services to an organization.
- The *supply chain* is the end-to-end methods that culminate in a customer obtaining goods or services from a vendor.
- *Business partners* will typically have a business partner agreement (BPA) in which an organization is provided with resellers and solution-providers regarding third-party products and services.
- A *service level agreement (SLA)* is a contractual agreement that details the products or services will be provided by a third-party vendor.
- A *memorandum of understanding (MOU)* is a preliminary agreement to advise how work will be completed before it actually begins. MOUs are frequently used in conjunction with nondisclosure agreements (NDAs) during pen testing exercises.
- *Measurement systems analysis (MSA)* is an agreement the outlines timeframes in which products, services, or projects will be completed through a third-party vendor.
- *End of life (EOL)*, also known as *end of service (EOS)* and *end of service life (EOSL)*, refers to a product or service that has reached the end of its life cycle and no longer provides or supported by a third party or vendor.
- A *nondisclosure agreement (NDA)* is a bonding document that states an inside or outside member of an organization will not provide confidential information with individuals that are not affiliated with the organization.

Related Concepts

- Third-party risks—ATV-1.6D
- Summarize risk management processes and concepts—GRC-5.4

Security+ Objective

5.3: Explain the importance of policies to organizational security.

Description

Policies regarding *data* are often implemented into organizations to confirm employees handle and treat data appropriately. The following examples are policies and roles typically implemented to ensure data integrity.

Examples

- *Classification* of data restricts who is able to see a file's contents.
- *Governance* of data is a policy that details roles regarding data. The following roles identify user responsibilities.
  - *Data owner* is a role typically assigned to a senior executive. This role is responsible for determining who will or will not have access to certain data sets.
  - *Data steward* is a role responsible for data quality and ensuring data is identified with the appropriate metadata.
  - *Data custodian* is a role that is responsible for managing where the data is stored.
- *Retention* of data assures that an organization is able to comply with data storage laws and regulations.

Related Concepts

- Non-repudiation—OIR-4.5H
- Regulations, standards, and legislation—GRC-5.2A

Security+ Objective

5.3: Explain the importance of policies to organizational security.

Credential Policies

Description

Credential policies are established to provide forms of authentication and outline the credentials that will be accepted for authentication. Credentials and policies governing them vary depending on the account type and the user's access and capabilities. Each of the following examples follow a form of password authentication, even if a default account does not need a password inserted.

Examples

- *Personnel* credentialing is based on the members of an organization, their roles in the organization, the permissions they have for their devices, and the data they are accessing or modifying.
- *Third-party* credentialing consists of allowing users and third-party members to utilize single sign-on to access various resources.
- *Devices* typically have default forms of credentials for authentication. It is highly recommended that default accounts be removed and authentic accounts be created on the device instead.
- *Service accounts* are accounts used by a scheduled process for situations such as maintenance tasks or system access. For instance, the following are Windows service accounts that allow users to run processes and background services. These accounts do *not* accept user interactive logons.
  - *System service accounts* provide the most privileges of any Windows account. They have administrative control of the device and create the host process for Windows before the user logs on.
  - *Local service accounts* provide the same account privileges as a standard user account in a Windows environment, but they access network resources anonymously.
  - *Network service accounts* provide the same account privileges as a standard account in a Windows environment and are able to provide a device's account credentials while accessing network resources.
- *Administrator* (Windows operating system) and *root* (Linux operating system) accounts are most utilized to install an operating system. To avoid forms of duplicated account credentialing or misuse, it is recommended that administrative accounts are disabled once they have exhausted their need.

Related Concepts

- Authentication, authorization, and accounting (AAA)—AD-2.4E
- Account types—IMP-3.7B

Security+ Objective

5.3: Explain the importance of policies to organizational security.

Organizational Policies

Description

Organizational policies, particularly security policies, are used to advise and protect members of an organization from attacks and maintain an organization's security posture. Examples of organizational policies include the following.

Examples

- A *change management policy* is the process or plan that outlines the actions taken by an organization to prepare, equip, and support personnel during the incorporation or adaptation of IT changes.
- *Change control policies* ensure that changes made to an organization's functionalities, including its IT infrastructure, are documented, needed, and integrated with minimal interruption.
- *Asset management* is a policy in which all assets purchased will be tracked to determine their locations and uses.

Related Concepts

- Secure orchestration, automation, and response (SOAR)—ATV-1.7D
- Account policies—IMP-3.7C
- Configuration changes—OIR-4.4B
- Secure orchestration, automation, and response (SOAR)—OIR-4.4F
- On-premises vs. cloud—OIR-4.5C

Security+ Objective

5.3: Explain the importance of policies to organizational security.

Risk Types

Description

Within an organization, various *risk types* should be identified in order to manage them effectively. Examples of risk types include the following.

Examples

- *External* risks are threats that exist from outside an organization. Examples of external risks include attackers, hackers, or natural disasters that prohibit an organization's functionality.
- *Internal* risks of an organization are members within an organization that do not adhere to the organizational policies or pose a threat, such as espionage.
- *Legacy systems* pose a risk as they are typically outdated systems with weak security.
- *Multiparty* environments pose risks as multiple individuals or vendors providing products or services increases the likelihood of mistakes, oversights, or vulnerabilities. The increase in vulnerabilities could potentially result in incomplete or incorrect implementation of products, services, and projects.
- *Intellectual property (IP) theft* occurs when an organization's ideas or methods are provided to external sources for ill gain.
- *Software compliance and licensing* can pose a risk to an organization if a license is being used illegally or does not adhere to the *Terms of Use (TOU)* or *Terms of Service (TOS)* of the software.

Related Concepts

- Actors and threats—ATV-1.5A
- Attributes of actors—ATV-1.5B
- Third-party risks—ATV-1.6D
- Third-party management— GRC-5.3C
- Risk management strategies—GRC-5.4B
- Risk analysis—GRC-5.4C

Security+ Objective

5.4: Summarize risk management processes and concepts.

Risk Management Strategies

Description

Risk management strategies refer to the processes and concepts regarding potential risks to an organization and its networks or data.

Examples

- *Acceptance* is a risk management strategy in which an organization assumes that risk will occur. This strategy also determines how best to prepare for losses that occur as a result.
- *Avoidance* is a risk management strategy in which an organization eliminates a risk by avoiding agents that may cause the risk.
- *Transference* is a management strategy in which responsibility of risk-based loss is assigned to another party through insurance or a contract. A primary example of risk transference is insurance. *Cybersecurity insurance* is a risk management strategy in which the responsibility of a loss regarding a risk is handled via a third party.
- *Mitigation* strategies involve taking the proper steps and methods to lessen a risk and its effects on an organization.

Related Concepts

- Risk types—GRC-5.4A
- Risk analysis—GRC-5.4C

Security+ Objective

5.4: Summarize risk management processes and concepts.

Risk Analysis

Description

Risk analysis provides a review of how an organization is able to monitor, accommodate, or mitigate risks and the resulting impacts. Examples of strategies and techniques for analyzing risk include the following.

Examples

- A *risk register* is an analysis tool that provides a list of identified risks in an organization and the instructions for managing them. Also included in a risk register is a severity or priority level
- A *risk matrix/heat map* is a display of levels regarding the impact a risk may have on an organization. Do not confuse a risk matrix with a heat map that displays wireless coverage.

Impact Level	Description	Example
Catastrophic	Refers to events that stop or severely hinder an organization's functionality	Office is destroyed due to severe weather or fire
Major	Refers to events that have a major negative impact on an organization and its revenue	System is hacked and customer data is stolen
Significant	Refers to events that cause a loss of employee productivity or significant financial burden	Malware outbreak on a network
Minimal	Refers to events that create minor inconveniences for employees and may result in a change of process or procedure	Hardware failure such as a defective hard drive or fan
None	Refers to events that have no impact on an organization	Failure of a peripheral device, such as a wireless mouse or keyboard

Goodheart-Willcox Publisher

- *Risk control assessment* is a risk analysis that is used to determine how an organization can safeguard its assets if or when a risk is presented.
- *Risk control self-assessment* is an organizational analysis that examines the degree to which controls are effective in the occurrence of a risk.
- *Risk awareness* allows security personnel to understand which intrusive threats an organization could experience.
- *Inherent risk* is a risk that occurs if controls are not utilized properly to mitigate risk.
- *Residual risk* is risk that is still capable of occurring, even when mitigation controls are utilized.
- *Control risk* is a risk analysis that determines which controls may not detect or protect against potential risks.
- *Risk appetite* is the analysis that determines the amount of risk an organization is able to tolerate before any actions need to be taken to mitigate or eliminate the risk.
- *Regulations that affect risk posture* include keeping a valid inventory of an organization's assets, along with understanding the cybersecurity risks associated with the organization's assets.
- In general, there are two types of risk assessment:
  - *Qualitative assessments* provide numeric data to demonstrate a loss, such as funds, from an attack.
  - *Quantitative assessments* provide perceptions of how the members of an organization perceive the impact the organization has experienced due to an attack.

- *Likelihood of occurrence* is an analysis that determines the severity of a risk and how detrimental it will be to an organization, should it occur.
- *Impact risk analysis* is the estimated losses that may emerge due to a risk.
- *Asset value* is the risk analysis that results in values assigned to tangible assets, such as computers and devices; intangible assets, such as intellectual property (IP); and members of an organization.
- *Single loss expectancy (SLE)* is the financial loss that results from an asset suffering an attack or damage.
- *Annualized loss expectancy (ALE)* is a financial amount that is expected to be lost within a year and is determined by the formula SLE × ARO = ALE.
- *Annualized rate of occurrence (ARO)* is the number of times an organization predicts an incident will occur during a year.

Related Concepts

- Risk management strategies—GRC-5.4B
- Business impact analysis—GRC-5.4E

Security+ Objective

5.4: Summarize risk management processes and concepts.

Disasters

Description

Disasters are events that could possibly cause damage to the functionality of an organization and, more importantly, humans. Disasters are often divided into three different categories: environmental, man-made, and internal/external.

Examples

- *Environmental* disasters are events caused by humans that damage the environment, such as forest fires. Environmental disasters should not be confused with natural disasters, such as tornadoes or hurricanes.
- *Man-made* disasters are accidental or deliberate actions that cause an organization's functionality to diminish, such as intentional actions, errors, or negligence.
- *Internal vs. external* disasters refer to whether a disaster impacting an organization is occurring internally or externally along with whether or not members of the organization can control or mitigate the disaster.

Related Concepts

- Disaster recovery plan—OIR-4.2G
- Business impact analysis—GRC-5.4E

Security+ Objective

5.4: Summarize risk management processes and concepts.

Business Impact Analysis

Description

A *business impact analysis (BIA)* is a detailed process that determines potential consequences of business disruptions. A BIA takes into consideration the amount of loss experienced by an organization's functionality and how to preemptively mitigate an event that could lead to that loss.

Examples

- *Recovery time objective (RTO)* determines the amount of time a system will remain offline after a disaster occurs.
- *Recovery point objective (RPO)* is a measure of the amount of data loss and interruption an organization can withstand in regard to time.
- *Mean time to repair (MTTR)* is the amount of time needed to restore a system back to its fully operational state after a disaster or attack.
- *Mean time between failures (MTBF)* is a calculation that determines an approximate time of failure for a device. It is calculated by dividing one or more device's total operational time by the number of its failures. For example, if three devices operate at ten hours and two of them fail, the formula would be $(3 \times 10) \div 2$. Thus, the MTBF would be 15 hours.
- *Functional recovery plans* are analyses about how functionality can be restored, and to what level, after a disaster or attack occurs.
- A *single point of failure* is a vulnerability that occurs when a single part fails and causes an entire system to stop working. Assessing a system for a single point of failure enables administrators to determine where, if any, "pinch points" exist on a server or other device that controls the organization's network and resources.
- A *disaster recovery plan (DRP)* is a part of an organization's continuity of business plan (BCP) and determines how an organization will function after a disaster or cyberattack. A DRP also details the organization's ability to adapt with plans through the DRP recovery process.
- *Mission essential functions (MEF)* is an impact analysis that determines how other methods, such as RTO and RPO, will be implemented if a disaster or attack occurs.
- *Identification of critical systems* compiles information regarding an organization's tangible assets such as equipment, intangible assets such as intellectual property (IP), and its members.
- *Site risk assessments* are analyses regarding the environments of specific sites, including their conditions and potential hazards that could emerge.

Related Concepts

- Business continuity plan—OIR-4.2H
- Continuity of operation planning—OIR-4.2I
- Risk analysis—GRC-5.4C

Security+ Objective

5.4: Summarize risk management processes and concepts.

Organizational Consequences of Privacy Breaches

Description

Organizational consequences of privacy breaches are the negative results on an organization as a result of employees not complying with policies or regulations or suffering a breach and data loss. Examples of these ramifications include the following.

Examples

- *Reputation damage* could result from an organization's system being compromised and private information being leaked. As a result, customers may lose confidence in the organization's security platform.
- *Identity theft* occurs when private information about a person's identity is stolen and used to purchase items or fund lines of credit with the stolen identity. If identity theft persists due to a privacy breach of an organization, customers will fear that their personal information could be stolen and used for ill gain.
- *Fines* may occur if an organization experiences a data breach. Furthermore, an organization may also face lawsuits from customers if the organization experiences a privacy breach that exposes a customer's personal information.
- *Intellectual property (IP) theft* occurs when an organization's ideas or methods are provided to external sources for ill gain. As a result, an organization could face losses in revenue.

Related Concepts

- Impacts—ATV-1.6FG
- Regulations, standards, and legislation—GRC-5.2A

Security+ Objective

5.5: Explain privacy and sensitive data concepts in relation to security.

GRC-5.5B | Notifications of Breaches

Description

Notifications of breaches must be provided to customers of an organization if their privacy has been breached. Also, depending on the severity of the privacy breach, higher-level security personnel may be needed to tend to the resulting issue(s).

Examples

- *Escalation* is a process in which senior-level staff become involved in the management of a privacy breach.
- *Public notifications and disclosures* are typically required if a breach includes data an organization assured their customers that will remain safe. Standards such as the General Data Protection Regulation (GDPR) require organizations to alert their customers that data has been breached within 72 hours (three days) of a breach being discovered.

Related Concepts

- Regulations, standards, and legislation—GRC-5.2A

Security+ Objective

5.5: Explain privacy and sensitive data concepts in relation to security.

Data Types

Description

A *data type* is a classification in which data is organized by a given quality or characteristic. Often, data is categorized by sensitivity. Examples of data classification types include the following.

Examples

- Common *classifications* for data include public, private, sensitive, confidential, critical, and proprietary.
  - *Public* data does not have restrictions and may be obtained by anyone.
  - *Private* data is to be viewed only by the owner of the data, such as an organization, along with any third parties that are partnered via a nondisclosure agreement (NDA).
  - *Sensitive* data should only be accessible by approved personnel, as it likely includes health or financial information.
  - *Confidential* data contains information that is highly sensitive and should only be viewed by members of an organization or any third parties that are partnered via a nondisclosure agreement (NDA).
  - *Critical* data includes information that is important to an organization's functionality and success.
  - *Proprietary* data is created by an organization and should be accessible only to members of the organization.
- *Personally identifiable information (PII)* is a data type that consists of an individual's identity such as their Social Security number (SSN), address, phone number(s), and date of birth.
- *Health information*, such as *protected health information (PHI)*, consists of an individual's medical records, insurance records, and even lab results recorded from hospital visits and stays.
- *Financial information* consists of information that pertains to an individual's income, taxes, and other forms of financial data.
- *Governmental data* contains information that is owned by a government and is typically classified.
- *Customer data* has information regarding a customer and may include the customer's address, phone number(s), and even stored credit or banking card information.

Related Concepts

- Regulations, standards, and legislation—GRC-5.2A

Security+ Objective

5.5: Explain privacy and sensitive data concepts in relation to security.

Privacy Enhancing Technologies

Description

Privacy enhancing technologies are used to diminish the possibility of data breaches along with withholding or masking data in case it is intercepted. Examples of privacy enhancing technologies include the following.

Examples

- *Data minimization* refers to measures taken in an organization to limit the amount of data collected from individuals by only processing the information that is relevant to the task that needs to be accomplished.
- *Data masking* is the obfuscation of sensitive data when it is copied.
- *Tokenization* protects data by replacing data with tokens.
- *Anonymization* is a form of data sanitization with the intent of removing private information.
- *Pseudo-anonymization* replaces personal information fields in a data record with one or more fake identifiers.

Related Concepts

- Data protection—AD-2.1C
- Secure coding techniques—AD-2.3D
- Summarize the basics of cryptographic concepts—AD-2.8
- Database—IMP-3.2C

Security+ Objective

5.5: Explain privacy and sensitive data concepts in relation to security.

Roles and Responsibilities

Description

The *roles and responsibilities* for data management define who is responsible for a given aspect of data, such as how it is managed or handled. Examples of data roles include the following.

Examples

- *Data owners* are responsible for data compliance; policy management, and privilege use.
- *Data controller* is responsible for overall data privacy by establishing policies and procedures for an organization's data.
- *Data processor* is responsible for the processing of personal data via a data controller.
- *Data custodian/steward* determines the rights to data and implements necessary controls.
- *Data privacy officer (DPO)* is responsible for data's privacy by setting the policies and procedures that will guarantee that the data remains secure.

Related Concepts

- Data—GRC-5.3D
- Data types—GRC-5.5C

Security+ Objective

5.5: Explain privacy and sensitive data concepts in relation to security.

Information Life Cycle

Description

The *information life cycle* determines how data is created, acquired, captures, and entered into a system. It tracks the stages data goes through from its initial creation to its eventual archival or deletion.

Example

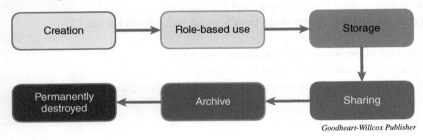

Goodheart-Willcox Publisher

Related Concepts

- Metadata—OIR-4.3I
- Acquisition—OIR-4.5B

Security+ Objective

5.5: Explain privacy and sensitive data concepts in relation to security.

Impact Assessment

Description

An *impact assessment* consists of organizational outcomes that may emerge if sensitive data is breached. A *Data Protection Impact Assessment (DPIA)* is an important part of an organization's accountability obligations as outlined in the General Data Protection Regulation (GDPR). A DPIA is a process used to analyze data to minimize risks of individuals when moving personal data. For example, consent must be given before an organization can collect data from a person. Companies must comply with this law.

Examples

Impact Level	Description	Example
Catastrophic	Refers to events that stop or severely hinder an organization's functionality	Office is destroyed due to severe weather or fire
Major	Refers to events that have a major negative impact on an organization and its revenue	System is hacked and customer data is stolen
Significant	Refers to events that cause a loss of employee productivity or significant financial burden	Malware outbreak on a network
Minimal	Refers to events that create minor inconveniences for employees and may result in a change of process or procedure	Hardware failure such as a defective hard drive or fan
None	Refers to events that have no impact on an organization	Failure of a peripheral device, such as a wireless mouse or keyboard

Goodheart-Willcox Publisher

Related Concepts

- Regulations, standards, and legislation—GRC-5.2A
- Business impact analysis—GRC-5.4E
- Organizational consequences of privacy breaches—GRC-5.5A

Security+ Objective

5.5: Explain privacy and sensitive data concepts in relation to security.

Description

Terms of agreement advise customers to how an organization will use their personal data. A data use agreement (DUA) is often created before there is any data collected. This allows customers to review the policy so they can be sure to understand how their data will be used before they agree to its collection.

Example

The following screen capture shows the terms of agreement that govern the use of the XYZ Corp. website and its digital products.

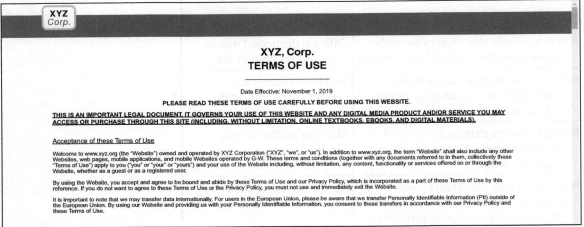

Goodheart-Willcox Publisher

Related Concepts

- Personnel—GRC-5.3A
- Data types—GRC-5.5C

Security+ Objective

5.5: Explain privacy and sensitive data concepts in relation to security.

Privacy Notice

Description

Privacy notices are statements to individuals outside of an organization that advise how an organization's data is used and from whom information is obtained.

Examples

The following are examples of notices that may be seen depending on an organization and its data usage.

- **Corporate data:** Data is owned by the issuing corporation and subject to proprietary and intellectual property laws.
- **Governmental data:** Data is owned by the local, state, or federal government. As such, it is made freely available to citizens for research and usage.
- **Customer data:** Data about customers, including personally identifiable information, is collected for research and marketing purposes. This data is for organizational use only and will not be sold to third parties.

Related Concepts

- Data types—GRC-5.5C
- Terms of agreement—GRC-5.5H

Security+ Objective

5.5: Explain privacy and sensitive data concepts in relation to security.